PHYSICAL EDUCATION

A PRACTICAL GUIDE

PHYSICAL EDUCATION

A PRACTICAL GUIDE

Key Stage 2

Elizabeth Robertson

JOHN MURRAY

Other titles in the **Key Strategies** series:

Planning Primary Science by Roy Richardson, Phillip Coote and Alan Wood
Primary Science A Complete Reference Guide by Michael Evans

Illustrations by Bob Currier and Chartwell Illustrators
Cover illustration by Clive Spong/Linden Artists
Playing at Circuses by EJM Woodland published in *Poems for Movements* reprinted by kind permission of HarperCollins Publishers Limited

First published in 1994
by John Murray (Publishers) Ltd
50 Albemarle Street, London W1X 4BD

Designed by Amanda Hawkes

Record-keeping documents devised by Elizabeth Robertson

Typeset by Litho Link Ltd, Welshpool, Powys, Wales in 10.5pt Rockwell

Printed in Great Britain by St Edmunsbury Press, Bury St Edmunds, Suffolk

A CIP catalogue record for this book is available from the British Library

ISBN 0-7195-5294-X

Acknowledgements

The ideas and information presented within this book are the result of many experiences and conversations shared with physical education colleagues, primary school teachers and children over a number of years. I wish to acknowledge their expertise, enthusiasm and professionalism and to thank them for their generosity. Some of the ideas have been developed from work initiated while I was a member of the Advisory Service with Calderdale Education Authority and I would like to extend special thanks to Linda Dempsey and Jenny Dickson for their contributions, support and friendship over the years.

I am also grateful for the support of colleagues in the Department of Physical Education at the University of Warwick.

The advice and help given by Grant Jarvie when the ideas for the book were being formulated has been invaluable.

I am indebted to Paula Parker for her enthusiastic contribution towards the chapter on Dance.

Sincere thanks are extended to friends who have provided practical advice and moral support.

Elizabeth A. Robertson

Contents

Introduction

Physical Education is an absolutely fundamental and essential part of a balanced education for young people. It provides a contrast to the relative inactivity of the classroom setting, and is both physically and psychologically beneficial to health. No other single subject in the curriculum provides the stimulation for mind and body to work together in harmony.

Physical Education should be concerned with educating children about the benefits and enjoyment of participation in physical activities, sports and leisure pursuits. It should aim to provide them with the skills, knowledge and understanding to prepare them to make informed decisions about their level of participation throughout adult life. A balanced physical education is the right of every child and should be an integral part of every primary school curriculum, irrespective of the existence of the National Curriculum.

This book provides guidance, advice, and ideas to assist teachers with the planning and delivery of a balanced Physical Education curriculum in the light of the 1988 Education Reform Act. Information about the content of the National Curriculum, and suggested strategies for organisation and planning to facilitate implementation of the statutory requirements for Physical Education, are provided. Individual chapters are devoted to each of the six areas of activity that must be taught at Key Stage 2. Except in the case of Swimming, each chapter presents an example of a Scheme of Work and a Sample Forward Plan and Lesson Plan which schools and teachers will find useful, and may adapt for their own planning and preparations towards curriculum delivery and use as official school policy documents. Ideas are presented in the form of suggestions; however, individual schools may decide to be more prescriptive in the writing of their own documents. (The chapter on Swimming provides only a suggested Scheme of Work, since any teacher who takes responsibility for teaching swimming will be specifically qualified and already have knowledge relating to planning units of work and lessons.)

Practical ideas for teaching content are presented in an easy to follow and accessible form. Guidance towards manageable and effective record-keeping and assessment procedures and practices is provided in a separate chapter. Other current issues relating to teaching Physical Education are highlighted in the final chapter.

The planning model presented in Chapter 2 will not be totally appropriate for every school, but it is one which can be adapted by schools, taking into consideration their own particular needs and circumstances. Similarly the content of the Schemes of Work in each area of activity may be used as guidance towards the planning of teaching content and progression to meet an individual school's needs.

Finally, the Schemes of Work, Sample Forward Plans, Lesson Plans and assessment documents in this text were originally produced using an Acorn A5000 computer and *Impression II* software (Computer Concepts, 1992) and schools are strongly recommended, where possible, to produce their planning documents using a computer. Adaptation of planning documents and record-keeping for future cohorts of children is then much less time-consuming.

Why teach Physical Education?

It is not the intention of this chapter to attempt to offer a new and unique justification for the inclusion of Physical Education in the curriculum. Nor does it set out new and original philosophical or reasoned arguments that extol the virtues of the subject in order to persuade teachers of the benefits of teaching it. (Arguably, this is no longer necessary, since the inclusion of Physical Education as a foundation subject in the National Curriculum under the 1988 Education Reform Act requires that it be taught in schools.) However, it is important that teachers have an understanding of the value and benefits of Physical Education within the school curriculum. To help towards this understanding this chapter provides extracts from recent DFE and NCC publications that have contained justifications for the inclusion of Physical Education in the school curriculum and explanations of the contribution the subject can and should make to the all-round development of every child.

The Education Reform Act (1988) states that the curriculum should:

> *'promote the spiritual, moral, cultural, mental and physical development of pupils at the school and of society'* and *'prepare pupils for the opportunities, responsibilities and experiences of adult life.'*
>
> (DES 1989, page 2)

The Secretary of State's Proposals for Physical Education 5–16 (DES 1991) present a rationale for Physical Education that states the following:

> *'**Physical Education** educates young people in and through the use and knowledge of the body and its movement. It:*
>
> - *develops physical competence and enables pupils to engage in worthwhile physical activities;*
> - *promotes physical development and teaches pupils to value the benefits of participation in physical activity while at school and throughout life;*
> - *develops artistic and aesthetic understanding within and through movement; and*
> - *helps to establish self-esteem through the development of physical confidence and helps pupils to cope with both success and failure in competitive and co-operative physical activities.*
>
> ***Physical Education** also contributes to:*
>
> - *the development of problem-solving skills;*
> - *the development of inter-personal skills; and*
> - *the forging of links between the school and the community, and across cultures.'*
>
> (DES 1991, page 5)

This extract provides an indication of the contribution that Physical Education can make to achieving the aims of the curriculum as described in the 1988 Education Reform Act and as quoted above.

The Statutory Order for Physical Education includes six areas of activity that should be taught at Key Stages 1 and 2. The Proposals of the Secretary of State (DES 1992) offer a rationale for the inclusion of each of these areas as follows.

Athletic Activities

'Athletic Activities concern the pursuit of the fulfilment of individual potential . . .' and *'build on children's natural capacities to run, jump and throw. They promote all-round physical development – speed, strength, stamina and flexibility.'*

(DES 1992, page 75)

Dance

'It is an art form and as such is an essential part of a balanced physical education programme. As well as the development of the artistic and aesthetic elements, Dance is also concerned with acquiring control, co-ordination and versatility in the use of the body, and helps to maintain flexibility and develop strength.'

(DES 1992, page 75)

Games

'Competitive games, both individual and team, are an essential part of any programme of Physical Education. They are part of our national heritage and offer a range of educational opportunities. To explore to the full these opportunities . . . means learning about the full range of games, their interrelationship with each other and the skills, tactics and principles of play involved.'

(DES 1992, pages 75-76)

Gymnastic Activities

'Like dance, gymnastic activities focus on the body. They are concerned with acquiring control, co-ordination and versatility in the use of the body in increasingly challenging situations and with developing strength, especially of the upper body, and maintaining flexibility. These activities are based on natural actions such as leaping, balancing, inverting, rolling and swinging.'

(DES 1992, page 76)

Outdoor and Adventurous Activities

'Outdoor and Adventurous Activities involve physical activity in different contexts which require the application of basic physical skills in such a way that they enhance motor skill development. There are long-term benefits in terms of the development of endurance and physiological training which are complemented by mental challenges where the focus can be competitive or non-competitive. The activities enable pupils to experience a degree of challenge and risk which can develop the confidence to travel and manage the body in potentially hazardous environments where pupils can choose their own level of participation and adventure threshold.'

(DES 1992, page 77)

Swimming

'Swimming is a crucial survival skill and an essential prerequisite for participation in a whole range of activities in and around water. Swimming is also the activity with the most consistent participation across age groups for both women and men, and which provides the best all-round exercise in terms of enhanced flexibility, strength, speed and stamina.'

(DES 1992, page 77)

Together, these extracts provide one very simplistic answer to the question 'Why teach Physical Education?' posed at the beginning of this chapter, and explain the contribution which the subject can make to a balanced school curriculum and to the education and development of every child.

In order that Physical Education can make this contribution it is essential that the curriculum is structured, planned and well organised, and that the aims are clearly defined and set out so that teachers know what and how they are going to teach.

Structure and planning of the Physical Education curriculum

2.1 The structure of the Physical Education National Curriculum

It is appropriate at this point to present a descriptive summary of the structure of the National Curriculum for Physical Education. In so doing the aims of the subject, together with the inherent processes, can be understood in context.

The Attainment Target

The Statutory Order presents a single untitled attainment target, the sum total of all the end-of-Key-Stage statements, which should be met through a demonstration of knowledge, skills and understanding in six **areas of activity.** The six areas are Athletic Activities, Dance, Games, Gymnastic Activities, Outdoor and Adventurous Activities, and Swimming.

End-of-Key-Stage statements

The Physical Education National Curriculum does not include ten levels of attainment across four Key Stages. Instead, there are a number of end-of-Key-Stage statements which are presented in relation to each of the general Programmes of Study. These statements describe the expected level of attainment that children should have reached by the end of each Key Stage. The statements, together with the Programme of Study requirements, reflect the age-range specific aims of the Physical Education curriculum. The end-of-Key-Stage statements and their corresponding general Programme of Study requirements for Key Stage 2 are shown in table 2.1.

The Programmes of Study

The Programmes of Study are concerned with providing schools and teachers with a description of what must be taught in order to give pupils a balanced physical education and to enable them to achieve the end-of-Key-Stage statements. The Programmes of Study list a number of requirements that indicate the experiences and opportunities that pupils should be exposed to, and the guidance they should receive, through the presentation of the curriculum content.

There are three levels of Programme of Study:

- the cross-phase, cross-activity Programme of Study
- four Key-Stage general Programmes of Study, one for each Key Stage
- activity-specific Programmes of Study at each Key Stage.

The cross-phase, cross-activity Programme of Study requirements are primarily concerned with encouraging good practice and safety, and presenting the fundamental aims of a balanced curriculum. The requirements as stated in *Physical Education in the National Curriculum* (DES 1992) are as follows.

'In physical education lessons pupils should be taught to:

- *be physically active;*
- *demonstrate knowledge and understanding mainly through physical actions rather than verbal explanations;*
- *be aware at the same time of terminology relevant to activities undertaken; and*
- *engage in activities that involve the whole body, maintain flexibility and develop strength and endurance.*

In order to become independent learners pupils should be enabled to:

- *solve for themselves the problems that they will encounter in the course of their physical activities;*
- *evaluate initial attempts and decide how to modify subsequent attempt; and*
- *consolidate particular skills through practice and repetition.*

In order to develop positive attitudes pupils should be encouraged to:

- *observe the conventions of fair play, honest competition and good sporting behaviour;*
- *understand and cope with a variety of outcomes, including both success and failure;*
- *be aware of the effects and consequences of their actions on others and on the environment; and*
- *appreciate the strengths and be aware of the weaknesses of both themselves and others in relation to different activities.*

To ensure safe practice pupils should be taught to:

- *be concerned with their own and others' safety in all activities undertaken;*
- *understand the importance of warming up for, and recovery from, exercise, thus preventing injury;*
- *adopt good posture and the correct use of the body at all times;*
- *lift, carry and place equipment safely;*
- *observe the rules of good hygiene;*
- *understand why particular clothing, footwear and protection are worn for different activities;*
- *understand the safety risks of wearing inappropriate clothing, footwear and jewellery; and*
- *respond readily to instructions and signals within established routines, and follow the relevant rules and codes.'*

(DES 1992, page 3)

The Key Stage general Programmes of Study present the guidance, experiences and opportunities that all pupils should be exposed to through all the areas of activity that are taught at the relevant Key Stage. These are presented with direct reference to the end-of-Key-Stage statements. Those relevant to Key Stage 2 are shown in table 2.1 (see page 5).

Each activity-specific Programme of Study at any one Key Stage presents the guidance experiences and opportunities that all pupils should be exposed to through the teaching of that specific activity. These are given consideration in later chapters where the Programme of Study is presented in relation to the teaching content of each activity.

END-OF-KEY-STAGE STATEMENTS Pupils should be able to:	GENERAL PROGRAMME OF STUDY Pupils should:
■ plan, practise, improve and remember more complex sequences of movements	■ be assisted to plan, refine and adapt performances when working with others ■ be encouraged to develop, consolidate and combine physical skills through practice and rehearsal ■ be enabled to remember, select and repeat a range of movements and perform more complex sequences alone and with others
■ perform effectively in activities requiring quick decision making	■ be encouraged to plan and use simple tactics and judge their success ■ be enabled to respond quickly to changing environments or adjust to other people's actions
■ respond safely, alone and with others, to challenging tasks, taking account of levels of skill and understanding	■ be helped to explore and present different responses to a variety of tasks and stimuli ■ be given opportunities to work alone to ensure the development of their own personal skills ■ be encouraged to adopt good sporting behaviour and recognise and reject anti-social responses including unfair play
■ swim unaided at least 25 metres and demonstrate an understanding of water safety	see PoS for Swimming for Key Stage 2
■ evaluate how well they and others perform and behave against criteria suggested by the teacher, and suggest ways of improving performance	■ be taught to help themselves to improve by making simple comments and judgements on their own and others' performance ■ be helped to understand their roles as members of teams/groups and take into account others' ideas
■ sustain energetic activity over appropriate periods of time in a range of physical activities and understand the effects of exercise on the body.	■ be taught to understand the value of and demonstrate sustained activity over appropriate periods of time ■ be taught to understand the immediate and short-term effects of exercise on the body ■ be taught to understand and demonstrate how to prepare for particular activities and to recover afterwards.

Table 2.1
Key Stage 2 end-of-Key-Stage statements and associated Programme of Study requirements

The aims of the Physical Education curriculum

In order for the requirements of all the Programmes of Study, and in particular the cross-phase, cross-activity Programme of Study to be met, it is essential that the aims of the Physical Education curriculum are identified. The Programmes of Study described above are presented in a way designed to encapsulate the underlying fundamental **processes** (strands) involved in teaching and learning in Physical Education. These fundamental processes are:

- planning and composing
- participating and performing
- appreciating and evaluating.

A diagrammatic representation of these processes and their inter-relationship is presented in figure 2.1. This model was first presented by the Working Party for Physical Education in the National Curriculum Interim

Report (DES 1991), to represent what it felt at the time should be three attainment targets for inclusion in the National Curriculum. In effect, they represent the processes that are fundamental to teaching and learning at all levels of attainment within Physical Education.

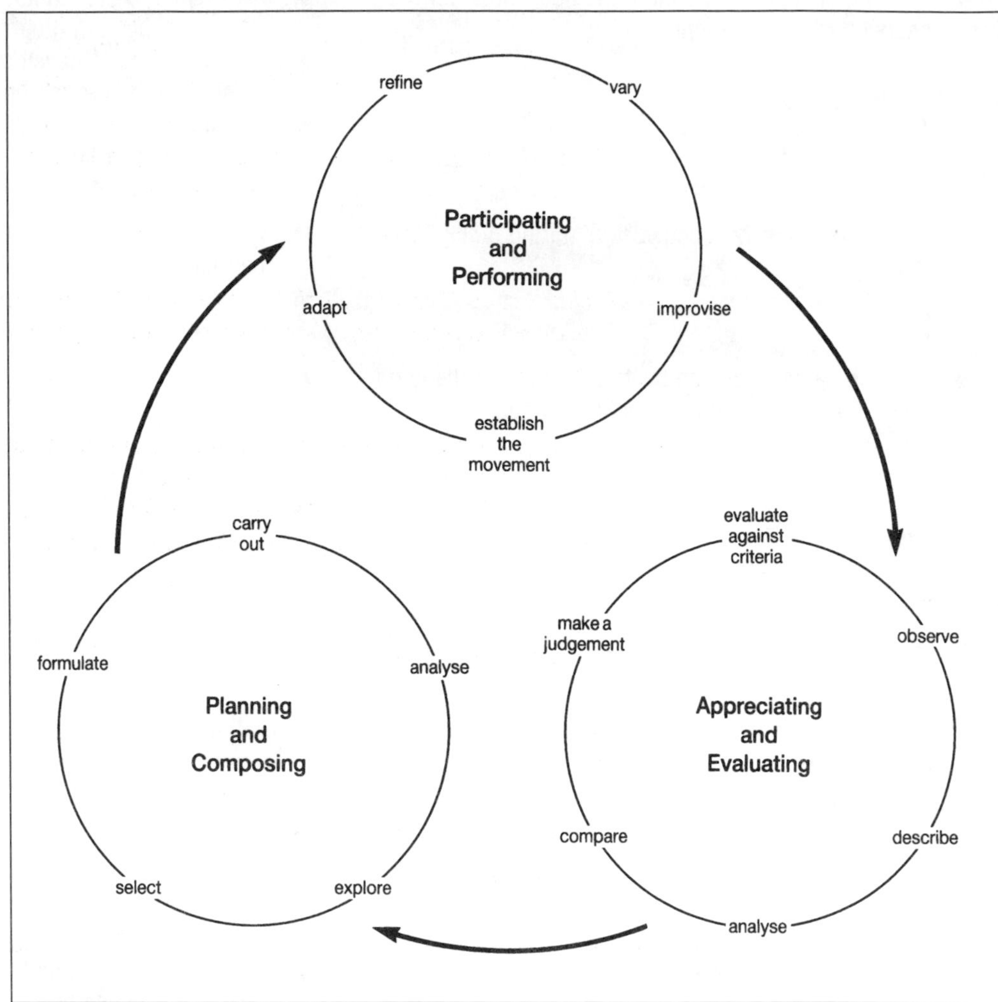

Figure 2.1
Attainment target processes

These three strands are reflected in the Programme of Study requirements that form the basis of the National Curriculum Statutory Orders and all good practice in Physical Education should give due consideration to these processes. It is stressed, however, that teaching should concentrate primarily on performance, and the emphasis in lessons should be on the active nature of the subject.

It is suggested that aims specific to each of the six areas of activity should be identified. They should reflect the processes involved in teaching and learning, the Programme of Study requirements and the end-of-Key-Stage statements that the children are working towards, and they should always fit in with the ethos and curriculum philosophy of the school concerned. **Process aims** in each area of activity are suggested as part of the sample Schemes of Work presented in later chapters.

2.2 Planning a balanced Physical Education curriculum

In order that the requirements of the Statutory Order are fulfilled it is essential that a balanced Physical Education curriculum is planned and presented to all children. There is no specific stipulated time requirement in the Order but it does state that at Key Stage 2 'pupils should pursue the Programmes of Study for six areas of activity' (DES 1992). The NCC Consultation Report (1991) also contains the following recommendations:

> *'at Key Stages 1 and 2 all pupils should experience the five areas of Athletic Activities, Dance, Games, Gymnastic Activities and Outdoor and Adventurous Activities. Council also supports the Working Group's recommendations that at these key stages emphasis should be on dance, games and gymnastics'*
>
> (NCC 1992, page 13, paragraph 3.17)

> *'Council also supports in principle the proposal that by the end of Key Stage 2 all pupils should be able to swim at least 25 metres and demonstrate an understanding of water safety.'*
>
> (NCC 1992, page 13, paragraph 3.18)

> *'All six areas (Athletic Activities, Dance, Games, Gymnastic Activities, Outdoor and Adventurous Activities, and Swimming) should be experienced as recommended by the Working Group.'*
>
> (NCC 1992, page 14, paragraph 3.24)

In effect, the above extracts constitute a requirement that all six areas of activity should be taught during at least part of Key Stage 2 and that Dance, Games and Gymnastic Activities should form a major part of the Physical Education curriculum throughout all four years.

In order for the above requirements to be fulfilled, it is strongly suggested that a **whole school policy** for planning is implemented, and that planning of teaching content and timing for each activity must occur at least over an entire Key Stage. Recommemded stages of planning are:

- whole curriculum planning
- planning Schemes of Work
- forward planning of Units of Work
- lesson planning.

Whole curriculum planning

Whole curriculum planning considers the Physical Education curriculum across an entire Key Stage with reference to the teaching time required, the areas of activity that must be taught and the requirements of the general and specific Programmes of Study. One model that would ensure that all the Programmes of Study requirements at Key Stage 2 can be fully met is shown in table 2.2. The model is based on three forty-minute lessons of Physical Education per week and each term is split into half term **units.** Three areas of activity, Dance, Games and Gymnastic Activities, form the core and are taught for a major part of the curriculum throughout all four years. The Programmes of Study for Athletic Activities, Outdoor and Adventurous Activities and Swimming at Key Stage 2 require less time for the Programme of Study requirements to be met and consequently the number of units allocated to the teaching of these activities reflects this. Individual schools may need to adapt this model to cater for their own individual situations, such as timetable constraints, available facilities and perhaps staff expertise. Nevertheless, it is strongly recommended that children should have a minimum of three lessons of Physical Education per week throughout Key Stage 2. The Appendix (page 169) contains a blank Whole Curriculum Planning document which allows schools to plan their own programme with up to three lessons of Physical Education a week.

Year (age)	Term		Lesson 1	Lesson 2	Lesson 3
Y3	Autumn	1st half	Out.&Adv.	Dance	Gymnastics
(7/8)		2nd half	Games	Dance	Gymnastics
	Spring	1st half	Games	Dance	Gymnastics
		2nd half	Games	Dance	Gymnastics
	Summer	1st half	Games	Athletics	Swimming
		2nd half	Games	Athletics	Swimming
Y4	Autumn	1st half	Out.&Adv.	Dance	Swimming
(8/9)		2nd half	Games	Dance	Gymnastics
	Spring	1st half	Games	Dance	Gymnastics
		2nd half	Games	Dance	Gymnastics
	Summer	1st half	Games	Athletics	Swimming
		2nd half	Games	Athletics	Swimming
Y5	Autumn	1st half	Games	Swimming	Gymnastics
(9/10)		2nd half	Games	Swimming	Gymnastics
	Spring	1st half	Games	Dance	Gymnastics
		2nd half	Games	Dance	Gymnastics
	Summer	1st half	Games	Athletics	Out.&Adv.
		2nd half	Games	Athletics	Out.&Adv.
Y6	Autumn	1st half	Games	Dance	Gymnastics
(10/11)		2nd half	Games	Dance	Gymnastics
	Spring	1st half	Games	Dance	Gymnastics
		2nd half	Games	Dance	Gymnastics
	Summer	1st half	Games	Swimming	Out.&Adv.
		2nd half	Games	Athletics	Out.&Adv.

Table 2.2
Physical Education whole curriculum planning at Key Stage 2

Note: the Autumn term is divided into half terms of seven and eight weeks, the Spring term into half terms of seven and six weeks, and the Summer term into two half terms of six weeks.

Planning Schemes of Work

Once whole curriculum planning has taken place, a Scheme of Work can be planned for each of the six areas of activity across the Key Stage. To assist with this it is useful to use a Scheme of Work document which summarises all the essential information necessary for planning at this stage. Each document should include:

- the number, timing and length of units of teaching
- the process aims
- the activity-specific Programme of Study
- a summary of teaching content for each unit of learning
- organisational strategies
- staff, facilities and equipment
- safety precautions
- special needs provision
- record-keeping and assessment procedures
- end-of-Key-Stage statements towards which the scheme will contribute.

In planning a Scheme of Work, the aims of the curriculum should first be determined. The aims must take into consideration the content of the three relevant Programmes of Study, the general requirements, the Key Stage 2 general requirements and the activity-specific requirements. They should also reflect the processes of planning and composing, participating and performing, and appreciating and evaluating, which are fundamental to teaching and learning in Physical Education. Once the aims of the scheme have been determined, the curriculum content of each of the allocated units should be planned and a brief description recorded, showing progression from one unit to the next. This is probably the most difficult aspect of planning since to do this well requires a clear understanding and knowledge of the skills and progression in each area of activity for pupils aged seven to eleven years. It also requires an ability to translate the Programme of Study requirements in the Statutory Order into lesson content that must be taught to the children from Y3 to Y6.

A suggested Key Stage 2 Scheme of Work for each area of activity is provided in Chapters 4 to 9. Each scheme shows when the units of teaching take place, how many lessons are in each unit and their length. The aims are clearly stated and they reflect the learning processes that the children will be involved in. The Teaching Content Outline describes the curriculum content of each unit, showing progressive development through the four years. The organisational strategies and the staff, facilities and equipment required to teach the content of the scheme are described. It is considered advisable and appropriate to record the safety precautions that will be taken throughout the teaching of the scheme, and a section is included for noting any special needs requirements of individual pupils within the cohort. Record-keeping and assessment procedures and relevant end-of-Key-Stage statements are indicated. Finally, a section allowing on-going evaluation and a summary of the scheme with recommendations for future planning is provided.

The Scheme of Work document is recommended as a model for planning areas of activity in the Physical Education National Curriculum. As with whole curriculum planning, individual schools may wish to adapt this suggested format and content to cater for their own individual needs. Nevertheless, it is strongly recommended that the planning of areas of activity across Key Stages within the National Curriculum is thorough and clearly recorded.

Forward planning of Units of Work

Once a Scheme of Work has been formulated by a school staff (or a group of teachers), forward planning can be undertaken by individual class teachers to determine the detail of teaching content for each unit within the scheme. A sample model format suitable for this purpose is used in each chapter to show the content of a selected Unit of Work in each area of activity.

Each Unit of Work Forward Plan should indicate the title of the unit and should show all the necessary information about dates, times, venue, teachers and pupils. Since it is vital that learning is progressive, a description of the previous knowledge and experience of the class should be included, based on the known content and evaluation of previous Units of Work. Using this information, and the content outline for the unit within the Scheme of Work, the aims of the unit can be determined and recorded. The detailed content of each lesson within the scheme can then be planned in order that these aims are met. Each lesson outline should specifically indicate the skills and activities that will be taught during each developmental phase of the lesson, and give an indication of the teaching styles that will be used. The amount of detail that is recorded at this stage will vary from teacher to teacher. However, it is suggested that sufficient information should be provided to allow a fellow professional to follow the plan should this be required. A description of the organisational strategies that will be used, together with the facilities and equipment needed, should then follow. Activity-specific safety precautions should also be recorded at this stage of planning. Provision for individual pupil's special needs should be given careful consideration. Finally, individual lesson evaluations should be recorded as teaching progresses.

Lesson planning

If the above stages of planning are followed by school staff and class teachers, individual lesson planning should not be time consuming and will be relatively simple. It is likely that experienced and knowledgeable teachers will not need to record formally individual lesson plan details beyond those included in the Unit of Work Forward Plan. Inexperienced teachers, or those with less confidence and knowledge of areas of activity in Physical Education, are well advised to plan individual lessons in more detail. The amount of detail should be left to individual teacher's needs and discretion, but for those wishing guidance a suggested Lesson Plan format is shown in the Appendix, pages 178–179.

For all children, a structured approach is required for maximum value to be gained from each lesson. The lesson structure for each area of activity is shown in the relevant chapter, but a standard format for consideration for a forty-minute lesson could be as follows.

OPENING ACTIVITY AND WARM-UP

This section takes the form of a simple introductory task that is part of the 'main theme'. In many cases the task can be set in the classroom and the children begin practising as soon as they arrive in the hall. It is useful to make the task a development of or direct extract from the previous week's lesson. It should also have the function of providing a warm-up activity which will stimulate cardio-vascular circulation and develop flexibility. This section will normally last for five to ten minutes.

SKILL LEARNING AND DEVELOPMENT

Skill learning This is the core of the lesson, during which the tasks set will be related to the current skill theme. Development of these tasks will occur through practice, exploration, selection, consolidation and refinement, and should include development through the sub-themes. This is more likely to be achieved through a question-and-answer technique providing problem-solving opportunities with direction and encouragement from the teacher. This section should last for ten to fifteen minutes.

Skill practice This is a direct extension of the work covered during the skill learning phase and should be relevant to the current theme. It should allow practice, development and/or application of the skills that have been learned earlier. This section should normally last for ten to fifteen minutes.

CLOSING ACTIVITY

This part of the lesson should include activity designed to maintain and develop body strength and should end with a useful settling down activity to prepare the children to return to the classroom. It should normally last for not more than five minutes.

Evaluation of individual lessons is essential and, at the least, a record of the taught content should be made, together with appropriate information about the achievement of lesson objectives. Children need a variety of differentiated and challenging opportunities to work individually to improve their own skill level. They should also have the experience of working with a variety of partners, in small groups and as a whole class, developing their individual skills in co-operation with others and learning to work in teams. The use of appropriate teaching styles, with a balance between 'direct teaching' methods and 'task exploration' by the children, will result in success and improvement. By setting differentiated, appropriate and stimulating tasks, children can be presented with opportunities to be creative and active participants at their own level of skill learning. It is therefore vitally important that teachers evaluate the effectiveness of their own teaching.

Chapter 3 Organisation

There are a number of cross-activity organisational factors that should be taken into consideration when planning to implement the Physical Education curriculum. These are:

- staff
- the class
- facilities
- equipment
- dress
- safety.

3.1 Staff

It is envisaged that the Physical Education National Curriculum will be implemented by schools using class teachers to deliver the majority of the teaching content. Nevertheless, a subject leader or consultant, with expertise in Physical Education, is invaluable to provide advice about the planning and presentation of the curriculum. This individual should work closely with staff in the formulation, development and implementation of a school policy for Physical Education. Their knowledge, expertise and interest should allow them to develop their role as curriculum consultant in Physical Education, which should include:

- advising and assisting the head teacher with whole curriculum planning, planning of Schemes of Work, and continuous assessment of the Physical Education curriculum based on the needs and development of the children in the school and the requirements of the National Curriculum
- designing and co-ordinating a curriculum development plan according to the changing needs of the school, to provide a model for continuity and progression throughout the school
- advising the head teacher and colleagues about the planning and organisation of Units of Work and lessons and the provision, use and care of facilities, apparatus, equipment and resources
- supporting and advising teaching colleagues as required on teaching methods and specific curriculum content based on sound subject knowledge and understanding
- where necessary and appropriate being inspiring, approachable, accessible, available and empathetic
- being prepared to be observed as a model of good practice, and to provide sensitive, analytical, constructive and positive feedback following observation and evaluation of colleagues
- promoting and encouraging continuous school based in-service training in Physical Education and providing information on appropriate external in-service courses.

Any school with a willing and professional staff, and a curriculum consultant who effectively fulfils the above role, will provide the children in the school with an excellent physical education.

Where a school does not have a Physical Education specialist on the staff, it is important to ensure that the curriculum consultant has at least a strong interest in Physical Education and sport. It is then possible for that individual to develop partnerships with relevant groups or organisations to assist where expertise is not available. One very valuable partnership can come out of communication with the local secondary school Physical Education department. This is of benefit to both parties. The primary school can benefit from the expertise of a specialist teacher and the secondary department can have knowledge of and, where appropriate, influence the Key Stage 2 curriculum, thus gaining a clearer understanding of the starting point of pupils moving into Key Stage 3. The non-specialist curriculum consultant should act as a catalyst for developing partnerships where required by the school.

Although the role of the curriculum consultant is a very important one, the contribution of individual class teachers is the most influential factor in the quality of the Physical Education learning experience. All teachers should give careful consideration to their own effectiveness in Physical Education lessons. Personal standards adopted by the teacher will reinforce attempts to raise standards in the children. Teachers should consider their readiness for each lesson by giving consideration to wearing appropriate clothing, particularly footwear; being prepared for the lesson in terms of organisation, planned content, subject knowledge and the provision of teaching resources; giving due care and consideration to aspects of safety by always checking the working space and equipment; and showing enthusiasm for the lesson.

Considerations during the lesson should include establishing clear and achievable standards of behaviour from the children. Teachers should also be seen by the children to value those factors included in the general cross-phase Programme of Study, especially those which bear on the safety of pupils: if teachers value factors such as quality of performance and presentation, effort, and co-operation and consideration for others' safety, the children will also see these as important. Careful selection of a range of teaching styles and teaching presentation, which allows for the range of potential talent and ability within the class, will lead to all children getting a positive and successful learning experience from their Physical Education lessons. Many children have suffered in the past through experiencing humiliation and failure and have consequently been alienated from all forms of physical leisure pursuits in adult life. Some of these individuals have become teachers and their own negative experiences of Physical Education have resulted in a lack of confidence and a consequent reluctance (and often fear) about teaching this area of the curriculum.

Within reason, all practising and student teachers should ensure that their knowledge and understanding of the subject areas they are working with are sufficient to enable them to provide a positive and healthy learning situation. They must *teach* the subject and not rely on the natural movement and physical potential of their pupils.

3.2 The class

To facilitate the use of equipment, apparatus and teaching resources, classes can be divided into groups for a series of lessons. Four, five or six groups are best (depending on the area of activity), each group consisting of six, seven or eight children. This caters for classes of 24 to 32 in number. Each group should be named as a colour or letter, and may be allocated a specific area to work in. The groups should be mixed gender and mixed ability, and care should be taken to avoid clashes of personality within a group. Groups should be encouraged to co-operate and work together and these qualities should be recognised and rewarded by the teacher and the children.

Children enjoy competition providing it is well managed and success is achieved by all. 'Healthy' competition can be developed by using a system which awards *points* to individuals and groups that demonstrate desirable behaviour and skills. These include effort, efficiency, good organisation, co-operation, teamwork and achieving individual potential in any particular activity. Adopting the *points* system may not be appropriate in all the areas of activity, but its use is recommended where teachers feel it will enhance learning and development.

3.3 Facilities

Schools should ensure that they have the minimum facilities to present the areas of activity. It is unlikely that many schools will require additional facilities to those already being used, but where this is necessary every effort should be made to gain access to facilities through initiatives such as partnership development – sharing other schools' facilities or using local community venues. The minimum facilities required to teach the six areas of activity are:

Athletic Activities:	grass area/playground and hall/gymnasium
Dance:	hall/gymnasium
Games:	grass area/playground and hall/gymnasium
Gymnastic Activities:	hall/gymnasium
Outdoor and Adventurous Activities:	hall/gymnasium, school buildings and playground, local park/wood
Swimming:	school/local swimming pool

Consideration during planning should be given to the selection and timetabling of the most appropriate facility for the activities to be taught. Safety is of prime importance and each work area should be checked before the class begins working, particularly when outdoor areas are used, or when an indoor facility has several uses (for example, where a school hall is used as a gymnasium and as a dining hall). Where at all possible, selection and timetabling of facilities should take into consideration likely weather conditions so that teaching may continue indoors during inclement weather. Indoor facilities should be kept at a safe and comfortable temperature.

Games and Athletic Activities should, when at all possible, be taught outdoors. Grass and playground markings greatly assist organisation. A grid system may be marked out or is easily adapted from the existing lines of a netball court (see figure 3.1): two or three grid areas are immediately available, and a line drawn down the middle with playground chalk provides four or six grids, one per group. Such organisation of the playground into group spaces demonstrates that classes of 28 to 32 children may be accommodated in a space which all schools have available.

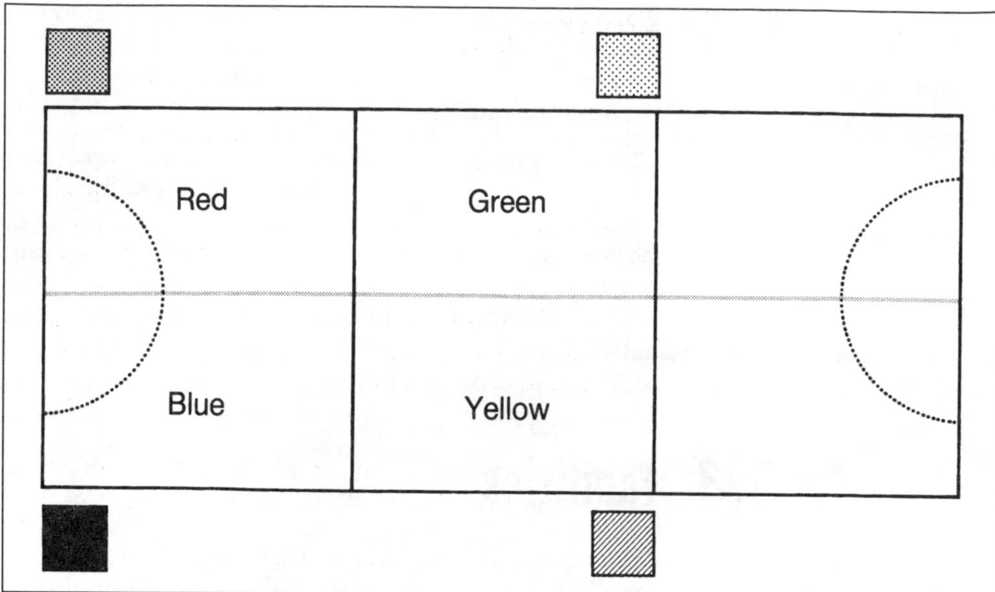

Figure 3.1
A suggested grid system

In planning activities, it is important to consider the position of suitable wall spaces and existing structures which may be used to secure nets, etc. Careful thought and planning of equipment positions in relation to playground grid areas will greatly assist the smooth running of outdoor lessons.

As indicated above, the class can be divided into colour groups. It may also help with organisation if the children wear coloured bibs. Line the groups up and show each group its area. The following activities may help young children to familiarise themselves with the grid system and their own areas.

- walking along the outside lines. Younger children may need more teacher guidance and may need to be taken in turn around their grid lines while the other groups watch
- other ways of travelling along the grid lines (walking, running, jumping, skipping, etc)
- stopping on the lines on a given signal
- running to touch the four corners of their grid
- running to touch the four lines of their grid
- finding a space and moving on the spot in their grid
- moving around their grid space using changes of speed, direction and pathways, always looking for spaces.

This introduction may well take a whole lesson and could be repeated more quickly at the beginning of the next session. If working in grids becomes a whole school policy, at the beginning of a new school year the children will only need to remember their new groups and their grid area, as the system will be familiar.

Access to fixed facilities for athletics, e.g. jumping pits, running areas, take-off boards, etc., is highly desirable but not essential to the delivery of the curriculum. Every effort should be made to maintain any fixed facilities that are available, and they should be checked for safety before each lesson.

3.4 Equipment

Stated in simple terms, it is not possible to teach the National Curriculum without a certain minimum of equipment. Where this equipment is not already available in a school it is strongly advised that a policy for equipment resource development be drawn up and instigated. This should include a list in order of priority of all equipment identified as necessary to teach the curriculum. Its acquisition should then be planned over a realistic period of time, together with a manageable budget. Thereafter, plans should be made to update equipment on an ongoing basis so that the school is not faced with replacing a large quantity of expensive equipment all at once. Other strategies, such as swopping unwanted or surplus equipment with other schools, is an excellent way of improving equipment resources.

It is best if a whole school policy can be developed for the storage and use of equipment for all the activities. Teachers should ensure that they know how to handle and use all apparatus and equipment safely and correctly (from small balls to climbing frames or music centres). Nothing causes deterioration of equipment more than misuse and mishandling through ignorance. Establish common storage spaces for all equipment which take into account safety and the need for easy access when equipment is required for lessons. It is good practice to mark the storage positions to which pieces are to be returned every time after use. Establish correct methods of lifting and carrying equipment so that lessons learned in the early years can be used throughout the school. Procedures for checking equipment before and after it is used will identify maintenance requirements and reduce the likelihood of accidents. This includes small games equipment as well as gymnastic apparatus. In games, group leaders may be appointed to check the contents and positioning of games containers, blow up balls and report any shortage or damage of equipment to the teacher. Regular maintenance and safety checks of all equipment should be carried out by the teacher responsible for Physical Education in the school.

Equipment for Physical Education is very subject-specific and will be used by all classes and teachers in the school. Therefore, it is most efficient to compile a stock of equipment which will allow children at both ends of the age range to be presented with a varied and creative learning experience.

Listed below is the recommended minimum required to teach the six areas of activity. (Equipment for extra-curricular activities is not included.)

DANCE

A good cassette recorder with an index counter.

A range of percussion instruments.

Taped edited music.

Additional stimuli as required by any particular theme, e.g. poetry books, photographs, sculpture, etc.

GAMES

For ease of transport and dispersal, wire baskets are recommended for Games equipment. (The same basket system can be used for Athletic Activities.) Each basket should contain a variety of small equipment in sufficient quantities to allow one of each item of equipment per child, or where appropriate, one per pair. The example below is based on a school with maximum class sizes of 32 children. Classes should be split into four groups, each named for a colour, e.g. red, blue, green and yellow. There should therefore be four wire (or equivalent) baskets, preferably sectioned, each containing:

- 8 bean bags
- 8 tennis balls
- 8 airflow balls (or sponge balls)
- 8 skipping ropes
- 8 quoits
- 8 small bats
- 2–4 cricket bats (small)
- 4 skittles
- 4–8 shuttlecocks

Where possible, the apparatus in each basket should be the appropriate colour, e.g. balls, bean bags, etc in the red group's basket should be red, and where not possible, e.g. skipping ropes, bats, etc, should be marked with a coloured dot or a piece of coloured insulating tape for easy identification. It is helpful to list the contents of each basket on a coloured card attached to the basket for easy checking at the beginning and end of each lesson.

Additional equipment

- 4 nets containing 8 large or medium balls (in each of the colours).
- A minimum of 2 large or medium hoops of each colour.
- One set of 8 bibs or bands of each colour.
- A set of coloured cones or skittles to use as markers for positions or obstacles.

The purchase of other equipment, such as footballs, netballs, wickets, netball stands, rounders posts, hockey sticks, etc, is at the discretion of the school.

The equipment should be stored where it is easily and safely accessible to the children. The nets of large balls and the hoops should be hung on a hook for easy storage. Leaders may be appointed for each group and two pupils per group can be given responsibility for the transportation of the basket from the storage area to the hall or playground and for its return. Checking equipment and tidying the basket at the beginning and end of each lesson in addition to these duties, if clearly explained to the children, will ensure that the equipment is kept in good condition. More importantly, it will stimulate a sense of responsibility and pride. It may be helpful to display in the classroom a plan of the playground or hall showing group places and basket positions. It is also advisable to display the storage positions of the baskets, nets of balls, hoops and other items in the apparatus store in order that every user knows the position they should be returned to. It may be useful to appoint, in rotation, Y6 children to be responsible for tidying the equipment store once a week.

The children will need to practise lining up to choose a piece of equipment out of the basket, but if there is enough variety of equipment then this should only take a very short time. They are ready then to use their choice of equipment in a space in their grid area. At the beginning of a lesson this free choice allows free practice, which will become more varied as the children become skilled in the use of a variety of equipment.

GYMNASTIC ACTIVITIES

The following is the recommended apparatus for teaching Gymnastic Activities.

Apparatus	Recommended minimum	Desirable
Large mats (2m x 1.5m)	12	20
Benches (with hooks)	6	8
Springboards	1	2+
Nest of 3 movement tables	1×3	

Trestle frames	2	
Sectioned bar box	1	2
Sectioned box	1	
Wooden planks with hooks	2	
(Wooden) climbing frame	1	
Ropes (wall mounted)	6	
Agility mats (2m long)		2+
Safety landing mats		1+
Buck or vaulting horse		1

The apparatus listed under the 'desirable' column is not essential but will greatly assist teachers to enhance further the learning experience of children in Gymnastic Activities.

Again, a whole school approach is the best method for apparatus organisation. All staff need to know where the apparatus is stored when it is not in use. It is helpful to display in the hall or gymnasium a plan of the storage positions so that every teacher knows where the apparatus should be returned. Where possible, the apparatus should be stored where it is easily and safely accessible by the children for use by every class. Where this is not possible the teacher should position the apparatus to be used round the edge of the hall or gymnasium before each lesson. (It is possible to train older children to do this during a playtime, end of lunchtime or after school for the following morning.)

Each group should be taught the apparatus layout for a series of lessons and should be responsible for moving the apparatus to the correct place in the hall and returning it to the correct storage position as an integral part of the lesson content. Checking equipment at the beginning of each lesson, together with other apparatus handling skills clearly explained to the children, will ensure that the equipment is kept in good condition. Most importantly, it will ensure a safe working environment and will stimulate a sense of responsibility and pride.

The following information should be used as guidelines for teaching children how to handle the Gymnastics apparatus safely.

- Four children to each piece of apparatus (including mats) are necessary, except with lighter items which two can handle (trestles).
- Teach the children to stand ready (but not lift) until everyone is in position and attending to the task. The technique of lifting using bent knees and not a bent back should be emphasised at all times.
- The hand position is always with fingers underneath and thumbs on top with the hands shoulder width apart.
- Benches should be carried with one child at each end (hands round the side to prevent it toppling over) and one at each side, just off centre. The carriers at the sides place one hand on each side of the bench and always face in the same direction as they are moving. As children grow older and stronger (by ten or eleven) they should be able to carry benches and light mats in pairs.
- When carrying nesting tables or trestles the children at the ends should hold on to the legs about half way down with the thumbs on the inside so that their wrists are not twisted.
- When children are carrying heavier pieces (such as bar boxes) it is advisable for the teacher to assist and emphasise that they do it slowly.

- The children should always know where they are going to place the apparatus before they begin to lift it.
- The children should be trained to check that apparatus is safely secured and stable, e.g. that hooks on benches or planks are in the correct position and don't wobble.
- When positioning apparatus prior to use, the teacher should check that there is sufficient landing space away from doors, windows and nearby pieces of apparatus.
- Children will develop a sense of responsibility if the safety aspect of correct handling is explained to them. At no time should a 'game' be made out of apparatus positioning and great care should be taken when trying to encourage the groups to position the apparatus quickly and independently.

At no time should the hall be 'pre-set' at the beginning of the day with equipment which is then left out in the same arrangement for several classes to use. Careful planning of the apparatus to be used and its positioning, specifically related to the content of lessons, is necessary. There are two methods of using apparatus during the apparatus section of the lesson:

- A rotation system whereby each group of children works at a specified arrangement of apparatus for a specified period of time. The groups can then be rotated to two or three different sets of apparatus during a lesson, and return to their own apparatus to put it away at the end of the lesson. They begin the next lesson on the arrangement where they left off the week before.
- A free use system, where the children are free to move to any piece of apparatus, have one turn, then move on. This must be introduced carefully to eliminate queuing or hogging of popular pieces.

Whichever system is used, always encourage the children to approach the apparatus from different angles without queuing and to use all the floor space and mats around the apparatus. Children need to be taught that the largest piece of apparatus in the room is the floor. It is an important part of their social development to learn to co-operate and share the space effectively with each other.

ATHLETIC ACTIVITIES

The Games equipment listed above, and its method of storage, is excellent as a basis for teaching Athletic Activities. Careful selection and use of gymnastic equipment is also appropriate to assist the teaching of some activities. In addition, specific equipment for Athletics should include the items below:

30m measuring tape	1+ stop watch(es)
8 relay batons	8 skittles + lightweight cross bars (for hurdles)
1 set high jump stands	elastic cross bar and/or 5m rope

It is not necessary for the equipment to be expensive and in many cases it may be adapted or manufactured from everyday materials. For example, additional measuring tapes may be made by the children, using string marked off at intervals and wrapped round a stick. Relay batons may be manufactured from a broom handle cut to appropriate lengths. Indeed, teachers may wish to build into their science and technology curriculum an aspect of equipment design specifically for the teaching of Athletic Activities. It is essential, however, that all equipment is safe and adequate for the purpose it is put to.

OUTDOOR AND ADVENTUROUS ACTIVITIES

The recommended minimum Gymnastics equipment listed above will provide an excellent resource for teaching this activity. The apparatus can be used in the gymnasium or playground for teaching a selection of basic independence and survival skills, adventurous activity skills and problem-solving skills. Other useful activity-specific equipment that the school should acquire might include a quantity of navigation compasses (one between two pupils for a class of 32 children is the ideal, but since they are expensive, one per working group is a good starting ratio). Maps of the local area including any local parks or wooded areas nearby and plans of the school grounds and school buildings are all essential for teaching navigation skills to the children. These can usually be obtained from the local tourist information centre, the local authority planning or parks department or Ordnance Survey, although the latter can be quite expensive.

It is not necessary for individual schools to acquire much specialist Outdoor and Adventurous Activities equipment, since most centres where the activities are taught have a comprehensive loan service available. However, a climbing rope is a very useful piece of equipment for a number of activities within this area of the curriculum. Some Local Education Authorities have local centres and advisory staff who can provide facilities, equipment and expertise to assist with teaching this area of the curriculum. It is well worth a few telephone calls to determine if local advice and even perhaps assistance with content delivery is available.

SWIMMING

Equipment for swimming is likely to be supplied at the facility used. This will include buoyancy aids, diving objects, etc. Other equipment needed will include articles of clothing such as pyjamas or shirts and trousers for use during the development of survival swimming skills. These can be supplied by pupils as the content of lessons require.

In all activities the equipment for a Unit of Work should be selected to meet the aims and the teaching content, and the Forward Plan should show the equipment or apparatus that will be used. In some activities it is useful to have a diagram of the apparatus/equipment layout and cards that each group of children can use to assist with organisation.

3.5 Dress

Clothing for Physical Education lessons should be comfortable, practical and safe. Warm clothing should be encouraged if the children are working outdoors or if indoor facilities are cold. It is helpful if schools provide parents with a list of clothing that the children will need. This should include:

- shorts and t-shirt and/or leotard
- indoor pumps and outdoor training shoes or pumps
- tracksuit or jogging suit
- optional gloves and hat
- swimming costume and towel.

The recommended dress for outdoor Games and Athletics lessons is a t-shirt or vest, shorts, a change of socks, pumps or light training shoes, and a tracksuit or jogging suit if it is cold. For indoor Games, Dance and Gymnastics lessons a t-shirt or vest, shorts, and bare feet is the recommended clothing and again a tracksuit or jogging suit should be worn if it is cold. A leotard is an acceptable substitute for t-shirt and shorts if preferred. Additional clothing for specific activities (such as Outdoor and Adventurous Activities) should be suggested by the teacher as the activity and environmental conditions require.

At the beginning of Key Stage 1 it is important for classroom time to be spent on dressing and undressing skills. It helps not only to develop finger dexterity but to give children a greater degree of independence, and in the long term will allow more teaching time. If these skills are not learned during Key Stage 1, it is important that Key Stage 2 teachers identify this as a priority at the beginning of Y3, so that all the children can undress and dress themselves independently and quickly. Many teachers encourage dressing techniques by displaying charts of ribbons, laces or ties for children to practise tying them correctly. Shown below is a suggested strategy which will teach children to dress and undress most efficiently.

Undressing

- take off shoes/boots and socks
- put socks inside shoes placed neatly under chair
- take off trousers, skirts, pinafores or dresses
- take off top of body clothes such as jumpers, shirts, blouses
- take off vest
- put on shorts
- go to the toilet.

All clothes should be piled neatly right side out in the order they came off. This makes dressing easier and quicker.

Dressing

- put shorts, etc into kit bag
- put vest on
- put tights or socks on
- put blouses, shirts, jumpers, skirts, dresses etc on
- shoes go on last
- hang up kit bags.

After the first term there should be no need to help the children dress or undress; they can help each other by lining up, for example, to do up the buttons or zips of the one in front. The ones who are quickest at dressing should help those who are slower. All children should have a kit bag in which to keep their clothing and footwear and wherever possible, all clothing should have each child's name clearly marked.

Showering after lessons, if facilities are available, should not be compulsory. There are health advantages associated with showering following strenuous exercise, and these should be explained to children. However, some children are sensitive about exposing their nakedness to others in conditions lacking privacy, and an insistence on public showers can be psychologically damaging and counter-productive. It is recommended, therefore, that showers should be optional, and this part of the lesson should be approached with sensitivity and care.

3.6 Safety

All teachers should be familiar with the booklet *Safe Practice in Physical Education* (BAALPE 1991). The general cross-phase Programmes of Study also make particular reference to requirements relating to aspects of safety. For safety in any practical subject it is necessary to establish high standards and to make every effort to maintain them. Teachers have a legal and moral obligation to ensure safe practice and this should establish the pattern throughout all areas of activity. This will have a bearing on dress, tidiness and equipment care and handling and will reap dividends in the quality of work from the children.

All pupils should be appropriately dressed. All jewellery should be removed (and kept in a valuables box) and long hair tied back. (It is a good idea for teachers to have a container with hair bands, but encourage children with long hair to tie it back on days when they have Physical Education lessons.) The facility (hall, playground, etc) and all equipment to be used should be checked to ensure that they are safe before use. Teachers should be aware of any medical problems that pupils may have that will affect their participation in lessons. The class should be taught expected standards of behaviour and safety, especially in relation to equipment and apparatus handling. A first-aid kit should be on hand and the teacher should know procedures to follow in the event of an accident. It is strongly advised that relevant safety precautions are recorded in planning documents.

Safety considerations specific to individual areas of activity and the teaching content will be included in the relevant chapters.

Games

4.1 Introduction

GAMES

'Competitive games, both individual and team, are an essential part of any programme of Physical Education. They are part of our national heritage and offer a range of educational opportunities. To explore to the full these opportunities it is necessary to offer pupils a balance of games experiences.'
(DES 1991, page 75)

The Physical Education National Curriculum (NC) Statutory Orders require that Games be taught as one of the six areas of activity within a balanced programme of Physical Education at Key Stage 2 (seven to eleven). In addition, the NCC recommends that Games be taught throughout all four years within the Key Stage. This section outlines suggested curriculum content that should be taught in order to deliver the NC general and Games Programmes of Study for Key Stage 2 that are presented in the Statutory Orders for Physical Education.

4.2 Games Scheme of Work

The following pages contain a suggested format and content for a Games Scheme of Work for Key Stage 2, based on the model for whole curriculum planning suggested in Chapter 2. The scheme is presented in the form of a curriculum planning document that a school could use to record what it will teach to a particular cohort in each year of Key Stage 2. This shows:

- The length and timing of the units of teaching.
- The teaching aims, reflecting the processes of planning and composing, participating and performing, and appreciating and evaluating.
- An outline of the teaching content for each Unit of Work throughout the four years.

More detailed information about the Games teaching content for the primary curriculum is contained in section 4.5 of this chapter.

The scheme also has sections which describe planning considerations under the headings of organisational strategies; staff, facilities and equipment requirements; safety precautions; special educational needs; and record-keeping and assessment procedures. The end-of-Key-Stage statements that the children will work towards throughout the scheme are listed and, since ongoing evaluation is an essential part of the teaching process, there is space for recording evaluations. A section for teachers' summary of the scheme, with recommendations for planning for future cohorts, is provided.

Using this format schools may develop their own Scheme of Work specific to their own needs and circumstances. The information in section 4.5 should be used for reference when planning the curriculum content. A blank Scheme of Work document is provided in the Appendix (pages 170–173) for schools to use for their own planning.

Scheme of Work

Key Stage: 2 | **Area of activity:** Games | **Cohort:** 1994-95

Units of Work (length of unit x length of lessons)

	Autumn	Spring	Summer
Year 3	8x40 mins	7+6 x40 mins	6+6 x40 mins
Year 4	8x40 mins	13 x40 mins	12 x40 mins
Year 5	15x40 mins	13 x40 mins	12 x40 mins
Year 6	15x40 mins	13 x40 mins	12 x40 mins

Process aims

The Scheme of Work will work towards enabling the pupils to carry out the following:

PLANNING AND COMPOSING

- plan appropriate responses to Games tasks set by the teacher
- plan, refine and adapt practices and games alone and with others in response to prescribed limits set by the teacher
- plan simple tactical responses in a variety of types of games.

PARTICIPATING AND PERFORMING

- perform appropriate and safe body preparation as warm-up and warm-down activities
- explore safely a variety of games-related tasks set by the teacher and present different responses
- work alone and with others to develop, consolidate, refine and link games skills through practice and rehearsal
- remember, select and repeat a range of games skills and apply them tactically in small-sided games situations
- care for, select and use games equipment appropriately and safely.

APPRECIATING AND EVALUATING

- appreciate the importance of correct body position in the efficient performance of games skills and actions
- make simple constructive comments and judgements on their own and others' performances
- be able to appreciate, apply and evaluate the rules and scoring systems used in a range of simplified games.

Programme of Study requirements

'Pupils should individually, with a partner and in small groups:

- *explore and be guided to an understanding of the common skills and principles, including attack and defence, in invasion, net/wall and striking/fielding games.*
- *be helped to improve the skills of sending, receiving and travelling with a ball for invasion, net/wall and striking/fielding games.*
- *be given opportunities to develop their own games practice, working towards objectives decided sometimes by themselves and sometimes by the teacher.*
- *make up, play and refine their own games within prescribed limits, considering and developing rules and scoring systems.*
- *develop an understanding of and play games created by the teacher, as well as small sided simplified versions of recognised games, covering invasion, net/wall and striking/fielding games.'*

Teaching Content Outline

Year: 3 **Unit:** 1

Autumn 2nd half term

Title: Review of apparatus handling

8 x 40 minute lessons

Outline: Review of apparatus handling skills with sub-theme consolidation and refinement. Develop using full range of games equipment, co-operative practices and games. Emphasis on developing quality and consistency of skills and team co-operation.

Year: 3 **Unit:** 2

Spring 1st half term

Title: Developing dribbling and pushing skills – large balls and invasion games

7 x 40 minute lessons

Outline: Dribbling and pushing skills with hands, then feet, then bounce dribbling using large balls. Individual, partner and co-operative group practice. Invasion games, such as *invader dribble ball* - using the skills learned.

Year: 3 **Unit:** 3

Spring 2nd half term

Title: Introduction to throwing and catching skills – large balls

6 x 40 minute lessons

Outline: Shoulder pass, chest pass and bounce pass. Catching skills, practice and teaching points. Co-operative and non-invasive competitive games.

Year: 3 **Unit:** 4

Summer 1st half term

Title: Development of throwing and catching skills – large balls/ invasion games

6 x 40 minute lessons

Outline: Selecting best pass to use in given situations. Using throwing skills under pressure. Co-operative practice and games and invasion games - *invader pass ball.*

Year: 3 **Unit:** 5

Summer 2nd half term

Title: Development of throwing and catching skills – bean bags/small balls/quoits

6 x 40 minute lessons

Outline: Shoulder pass throwing for accuracy and throwing for distance. Catching skills, practices and teaching points. Co-operative and non-invasive competitive games.

Year: 4 **Unit:** 6

Autumn 1st half term

Title: Introduction to striking – large balls and striking/fielding games

8 x 40 minute lessons

Outline: Using the hand and feet to strike and pass the ball. Bowling skills and catching skills revision. Rounders using striking skills and throwing and catching (fielding) skills. Team co-operation and full participation of all teams. Introduction to tournament play.

Year: 4 **Unit:** 7

Spring term

Title: Development of dribbling and striking skills – large balls/small ball & stick

13 x 40 minute lessons

Outline: Development of dribbling and passing using feet with large ball and medium/small balls using stick/bat. Introduction of the games of small-sided football and shinty/unihoc/hockey. Developing skills and tactics to play small-sided invasion games.

Year: 4 **Unit:** 8

Title: Consolidation of dribbling and striking

Summer term

12 x 40 minute lessons

Outline: Small-sided tournaments to allow revision, practice and consolidation of previously learned skills. Rounders variation, Invader Ball variations and football and hockey variations. Emphasis on understanding rules, tournament play, team tactics and co-operation. Introduction to understanding of fitness for games.

Year: 5 **Unit:** 9

Title: Consolidation of throwing and catching skills and invasion games

Autumn term

15 x 40 minute lessons

Outline: Revision of throwing and catching using large balls with variations of types of equipment and throwing skills. Practice and tactical developments in invasion games. Small-sided games designed to develop towards national games of netball, basketball, handball. Introduction of New Image Rugby and mini-rugby. Development of understanding fitness for invasion team games.

Year: 5 **Unit:** 10

Title: Introduction to bat and ball striking skills

Spring term

13 x 40 minute lessons

Outline: Introduction to basic bat and ball work. Development of tennis/badminton/squash type strokes of forehand, backhand, under-arm serve. Practising individually, in pairs and small groups the learned skills. Introducing game-type situations without a net and using the wall, such as *keep the rally going, how many times?*, to practise the skills.

Year: 5 **Unit:** 11

Title: Development of bat and ball striking skills – net and wall games

Summer term

12 x 40 minute lessons

Outline: Review and consolidation of previously learned strokes. Introduction of the forehand and backhand volley and over-arm serve (if appropriate). Variations of fun games that increase skill under pressure and allow practice and consolidation of skill in bat and ball work, e.g. *round robin*, *hit and follow behind*. Introduction of the net, simple rules and scoring systems, and tactics in singles and partner play.

Year: 6 **Unit:** 12

Title: Development of net games – mini volleyball

Autumn term

15 x 40 minute lessons

Outline: Introduction of skills of volleyball: catch, volley-throw, dig-throw, under-arm serve. Introduction of game of mini-volleyball. Develop towards use of spike and blocking. Simple tactics of defence, attack and formations of play. Mini-tournament. Introducing children to officiating and game/tournament organising.

Year: 6 **Unit:** 13

Title: Introduction to 'games making' and development of tournament organising

Spring term

13 x 40 minute lessons

Outline: Review with children the skills and types of games they have learned. Introduce basic principles for making their own games, giving appropriate examples. Set tasks for children to make games in groups. Develop game/tournament organisation with roles of 'officials' and players. Run mini-tournaments and set tasks for final term's 'mini-Olympics' sports festival.

Year: 6 **Unit:** 14

Title: The mini-Olympics sports festival

Summer term

12 x 40 minute lessons

Outline: Presentation of the children's planned sports festival where children plan, organise, officiate and take part in their 'mini-Olympics sports festival'.

Organisational strategies

The organisation is based on a class of 32 children split into four colour groups of eight of mixed gender and mixed ability. The equipment should be organised into four sectioned wire baskets colour-coded red, blue, green and yellow. Children should be taught to collect, check and return the equipment used during the lessons.

Staff, facilities and equipment required

Lessons will be taught by the class teacher with occasional input from students or visiting teachers to the school. Where possible and appropriate Games lessons will be taught outdoors, using the playground and grass areas as the curriculum content demands. A wet weather alternative in the school hall should be available if required.

The equipment stored in each basket for use and access during the Games lesson is listed below.

- 8 bean bags
- 8 tennis balls
- 8 airflow balls (or sponge balls)
- 8 skipping ropes
- 8 quoits
- 8 small bats
- 2–4 cricket bats (small)
- 4 skittles
- 4–8 shuttlecocks

Where possible, the apparatus in each basket should be the appropriate colour, e.g. balls, bean bags, etc in the red group's basket should be red, and where not possible, e.g. skipping ropes, bats, etc, should be marked with a coloured dot or a piece of coloured insulating tape for easy identification. (It is helpful to list the contents of each basket on a coloured card attached to the basket for easy checking at the beginning and end of each lesson.)

Additional equipment

- Two nets of large or medium balls (one containing 8 blue and 8 green, the other 8 red and 8 yellow).
- A minimum of 2 large or medium hoops of each colour.
- One set of 8 bibs or bands of each colour.

Safety precautions

Ensure that appropriate dress is worn and that all jewellery is removed before each lesson. Check that pupils understand the reasons for these simple rules. Establish a code of conduct and safety requirements at the beginning of each unit and remind pupils of them regularly throughout the scheme. Check and record any medical conditions that may affect the activity. Carry out an appropriate evaluation of skills competence and group pupils accordingly during the first lesson of each unit. Ensure that codes of behaviour and safety are clearly understood before the pupils begin the units.

Special needs

(It is likely that a wide range of ability levels will be apparent from the beginning of the first unit. Some children may have special needs that require special provision and it may be necessary to enlist knowledgeable advisory support to help with ideas to cater for children with special needs in the early stages. Nevertheless, the teaching content is designed to cater for all ranges of ability. Individual special needs should be assessed at the beginning of the first Unit of Work and specific provision should be outlined in each Unit of Work Forward Plan.)

Record-keeping and assessment procedures [see also Chapter 10]

Record-keeping with reference to teaching content should include:

- a Scheme of Work with recommendations for future planning and content
- a Forward Plan for each Unit of Work within the scheme with a summary and recommendations for future teaching content in subsequent Units
- for more experienced and specialist teachers, an ongoing record and formative evaluation of individual lesson content used to inform the planning and teaching of subsequent lessons
- where necessary and appropriate, individual lesson plans based on the content outline in the Forward Plan with an evaluation and recommendations for the next lesson.

Assessment procedures should include:

- ongoing evaluation of class progress in relation to aims and objectives throughout the teaching units
- ongoing observation and recording of each pupil's progress in relation to the Unit of Work aims and pupil targets using a Unit of Work record and assessment document
- school summative records for individual pupils with reference to end-of-Key-Stage statements updated at the end of each year and at the end of each Key Stage.

End-of-Key-Stage statements

'By the end of the Key Stage, pupils should be able to:

- *plan, practise, improve and remember more complex sequences of movement.*
- *perform effectively in activities requiring quick decision making.*
- *respond safely, alone and with others, to challenging tasks, taking account of levels of skill and understanding.*
- *evaluate how well they and others perform and behave against criteria suggested by the teacher and suggest ways of improving performance.*
- *sustain energetic activity over appropriate periods of time in a range of physical activities and understand the effects of exercise on the body.'*

Evaluation of scheme

(A record of class progress at the end of each Unit of Work should be made to assist with future planning (as described in Chapter 10) and a summary of the whole scheme should be recorded here.)

Recommendations for future planning

(A statement of any recommendations that become apparent during the teaching should be recorded in order to inform future planning and teaching for other cohorts of children.)

4.3 Sample of Games Unit of Work Forward Plan

The following section is a sample Forward Plan for Unit 3 (shown on page 24) in the Games Scheme of Work. A similar blank master document which teachers can use for their own curriculum planning can be found in the Appendix (pages 174–177).

Unit of Work Forward Plan

Area of Activity: Games

Unit: 3 | **Title:** Introduction to throwing and catching skills – large balls

Spring 2nd half term | 6 x 40 minute lessons | **Day:** Thursday am

Class: 3ER **Age:** 7/8 | **No. in class:** 15m, 17f | **Teacher:** E Robertson

Previous knowledge and experience

The children have been taught apparatus handling skills in the early years and have worked during Unit 2 on dribbling and pushing skills using large balls. They have played *invader dribble* and so have an understanding of a simple invasion game. They have used the colour group and basket system and the points system for team scoring. The class needs to work on developing team co-operation and encouraging each other in co-operative situations.

Aims of the Unit of Work

- to introduce shoulder pass, chest pass, bounce pass and two-handed catching skills using large balls
- to consolidate previously learned skills and understanding of co-operative situations
- to develop understanding of practising in pairs and in small groups
- to improve the accuracy and consistency of throwing and catching skills
- to encourage children to begin to evaluate their level of skill and how to improve.

CONTENT OUTLINE

LESSON 1 Introduce class to work that will be covered in the unit. Free choice of basket apparatus with task to practise apparatus handling skills. Skill learning and practice: individually, two-handed bouncing and catching, throwing up and catching; in pairs, shoulder passing and receiving; co-operative group *pass and follow* and *pass* and *follow behind*. Game: non-invasive game against time and other groups.

LESSON 2 Free choice of basket apparatus with task to practise apparatus handling skills. Skill learning and practice: revision individually of two-handed bouncing and catching, throwing up and catching; in pairs shoulder passing and chest passing; co-operative group pass and follow and pass and follow behind using chest passes. Game: passing rounders using chest pass.

LESSON 3 Free practice using large balls individually or in pairs. Skill learning and practice: revision in pairs of shoulder passing and chest passing: introduction of the bounce pass; co-operative group *pass and follow* and *pass* and *follow behind* using chest passes. Game: passing rounders using shoulder pass and bounce pass.

LESSON 4 Free practice using large balls individually or in pairs. Skill learning and practice: revision in pairs of shoulder passing, bounce passing, and chest passing; introduction of the two-handed rugby pass and receiving the pass; co-operative *group passing on the move*. Game: *how many passes without dropping?*

LESSON 5 Free practice using large balls individually or in pairs. Skill learning and practice: revision in pairs of shoulder passing, bounce passing, chest passing and two-handed rugby pass; co-operative group *passing on the move*. Game: introduction of simplified New Image Rugby.

LESSON 6 Free practice using large balls individually or in pairs using all throwing and catching skills. Skill learning and practice: revision in pairs of shoulder passing, bounce passing, chest passing and two-handed rugby pass; co-operative group *passing on the move*. Extended game: simplified New Image Rugby mini tournament.

Organisational strategies

Children change in classroom, walk to hall with pumps on and take them off in hall. Class splits into four groups of eight with group positions during the first lesson, once ability has been assessed in hall. Hair band and grips box and valuables box will be ready for use.

Facilities and equipment required

School sports field/playground and hall/gymnasium (in case of bad weather).
Grids and cones/skittles for markers. Colour baskets and bibs; four nets of large coloured balls; four rugby balls (if available).

Safety precautions

Dress – t-shirt and shorts or leotard, bare feet or light indoor pumps; tracksuit or jogging suit and outdoor pumps in case of bad weather. No jewellery. Hair tied back. Check field/hall is safe and make equipment baskets ready. Check on medical problems. Remind class about rules of behaviour and safety. Take first-aid kit.

Special needs provision

(This section should be used to help plan and record provision for children with special educational needs in Physical Education. This may include catering for children with physical and mental disabilities, children with emotional difficulties and the physically gifted. Three examples are given below.)

- One child (Peter) with hearing impairment but can lip read – make sure he can see you and speak clearly. He is also good at copying other children to interpret the task but may need some individual reinforcement.
- One child (Darren) with learning difficulties who can be disruptive but responds well in P.E. if interested and motivated. Responds well to praise but tends to seek attention if firm control is not exercised.
- One child (Joanne) with an artificial leg. Shy about P.E. but is very able and copes with most tasks well. Some encouragement needed but is aware of own capabilities and understands well about safety. Keeps artificial leg on in lessons and wears tracksuit bottoms.

Equipment and group positions

The names of group members can be recorded if they are to remain the same for the whole unit. In Games this is acceptable, particularly if a competitive element is used as an organisational strategy.

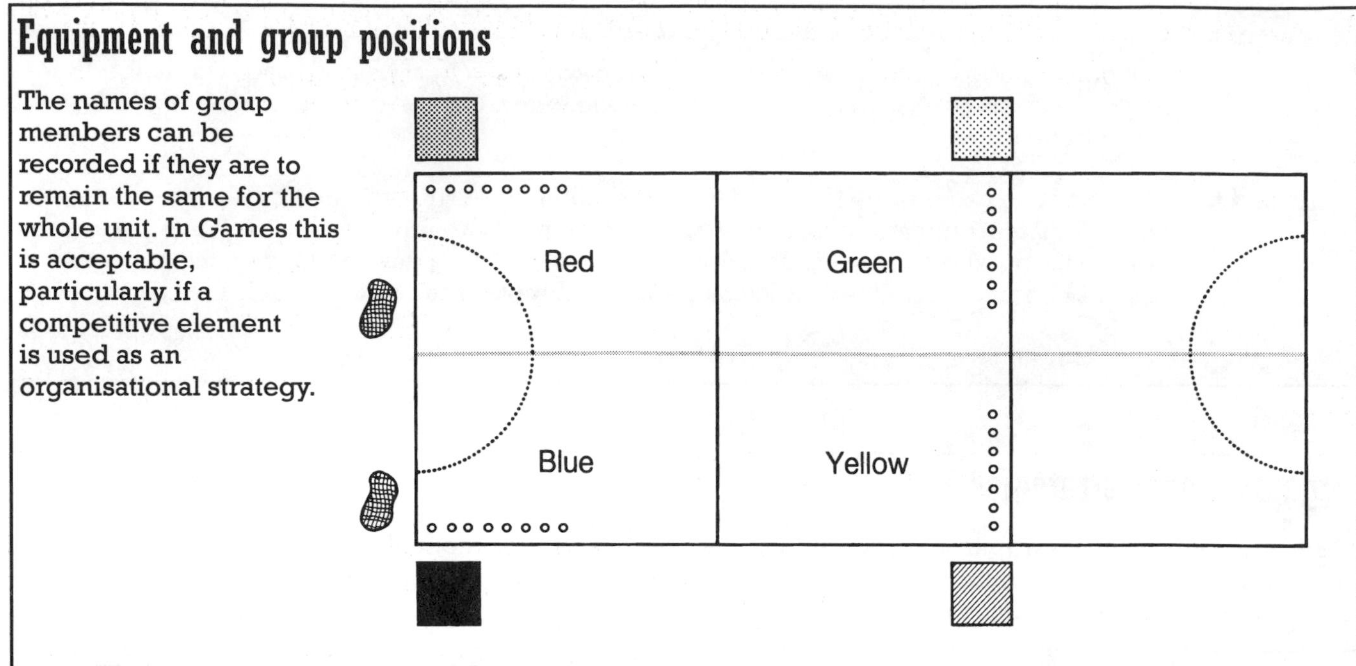

Evaluation of lessons

(The date should be entered beside the lesson number once the lesson has been taught. If individual lesson plans are not used by teachers, a highlighter pen can be used to indicate the work that has been covered in each lesson in case adjustment decisions need to be made. This records what is actually taught relative to what was planned.

Notes should be made in this section each week, with recommendations for future lessons. This is useful for future planning and for record-keeping purposes.)

Summary and recommendations for next unit

(A record of class progress at the end of the Unit of Work should be made to assist with future planning. Individual pupil progress should also be recorded at appropriate times using the method described in Chapter 10.)

4.4 Sample Lesson Plan

A sample plan for Lesson 1 in the above Unit of Work, showing details of tasks and activities, corresponding teaching points and the organisation of children, equipment and space, has been included on the following pages. Experienced teachers may feel this level of planning is not necessary and that they can work from the lesson outlines in the Forward Plan. Some teachers may find that the children have a better learning experience if they plan individual lessons in the detail shown.

Games Lesson Plan (1)

Key Stage 2 **Unit of Work 3: Introduction to throwing and catching skills – large balls**

Lesson number in unit: 1

Date: Thursday 2nd March 1995

Time: 2.10 – 2.50pm

Length of lesson: 40 mins

Class: 3ER **Age:** 7/8

Teacher: E Robertson

No. in class: 5m, 17f

Venue: Playground

Lesson objectives

(S = social, E = emotional, C = cognitive, P = physical)

P: to introduce class to two-handed bouncing and catching skills and the shoulder pass
E,S: to work in pairs and understand the importance of sympathetic passes
S: to co-operate as a group in practising *pass and follow* and *pass and follow behind*
C: to understand the simple rules of group activities and non-invasive competitive games.

Facilities and equipment

- School sports field/playground and hall/gymnasium (in case of bad weather)
- Grids and cones/skittles for markers
- Colour baskets and bibs
- Four nets of large coloured balls
- Four rugby balls

Lesson evaluation

Games Lesson Plan (2)

Phase	Tasks/activities	Teaching points/coaching feedback	Organisation and resources
Pre-lesson preparation	Check that the facilities are safe and clean and ensure that the baskets of equipment are ready to use. Children will change in the classroom where jewellery and valuables will be collected and long hair tied back. Delegate team leaders to take out the equipment and to keep the team scores for the lesson. Remind class about noise levels and safety and behaviour.		
Introduction	Introduce class to work that will be taught in the unit. Free choice of basket equipment and practise any apparatus handling skills. Set a target to work towards. Stop and put equipment away. Take out a large ball each.	Explain the skills and their use in types of games. Use questions and answers to find out what the children already know about these. Make sure the basket is tidy first. First team with everyone working will get 4 points, next 3, etc. Take equipment out of basket, a piece at a time. Work in your own space and keep control of your equipment. Make sure the equipment is neat and tidy. Take your time.	Talking to the whole class. Baskets in corner of grid square. Line up at basket. Line up and work one at a time.
Skill Practices Individually In pairs Small groups	a) Two-handed bouncing and catching b) Underarm throw in air – bounce – catch c) Underarm throw in air and catch d) Tricks – e.g. from sitting, clap hands, etc. Shoulder passing and receiving (aim to get 10 throws without dropping) *Pass and run round* *Pass and move* *Pass and follow* *Pass and follow behind*	Watch the ball; make a cup with the hands; reach out to catch the ball; move your feet into the correct position. Take your time – don't try anything too fancy! As above; be accurate with your throws; get behind the ball; make sure your partner is ready. Wait till your partner is back in position. Pass the ball then move. Concentrate on what you need to do next. Stop before you throw. (Reinforce the above teaching points.)	Individually working in a space in team grid square.
Games	Non-invasive games against other groups. *Pass and follow behind* Each team competes against the others to be the first team to reach a target of 10/20/30 catches without dropping the ball.	Help one another with accurate passes and encourage each other. The team must count. It's better to take time than have to start again.	
Conclusion	Line up at basket and put equipment away. Count up team points for lesson and decide winning team for the week. Debrief the activities with question and answer.	Make sure basket is tidy. Award points for tidiest basket and best organised team.	Return baskets and equipment to store. Return to classroom and change.

4.5 Games teaching content

In order to fulfil the Games Programme of Study it is advantageous to categorise the vast number of skills, tactics and games into a logical and progressive structured curriculum. Consequently, the teaching content has been presented in the form shown in figure 4.1, which uses a Skill Themes and Game/Type approach to the teaching of Games.

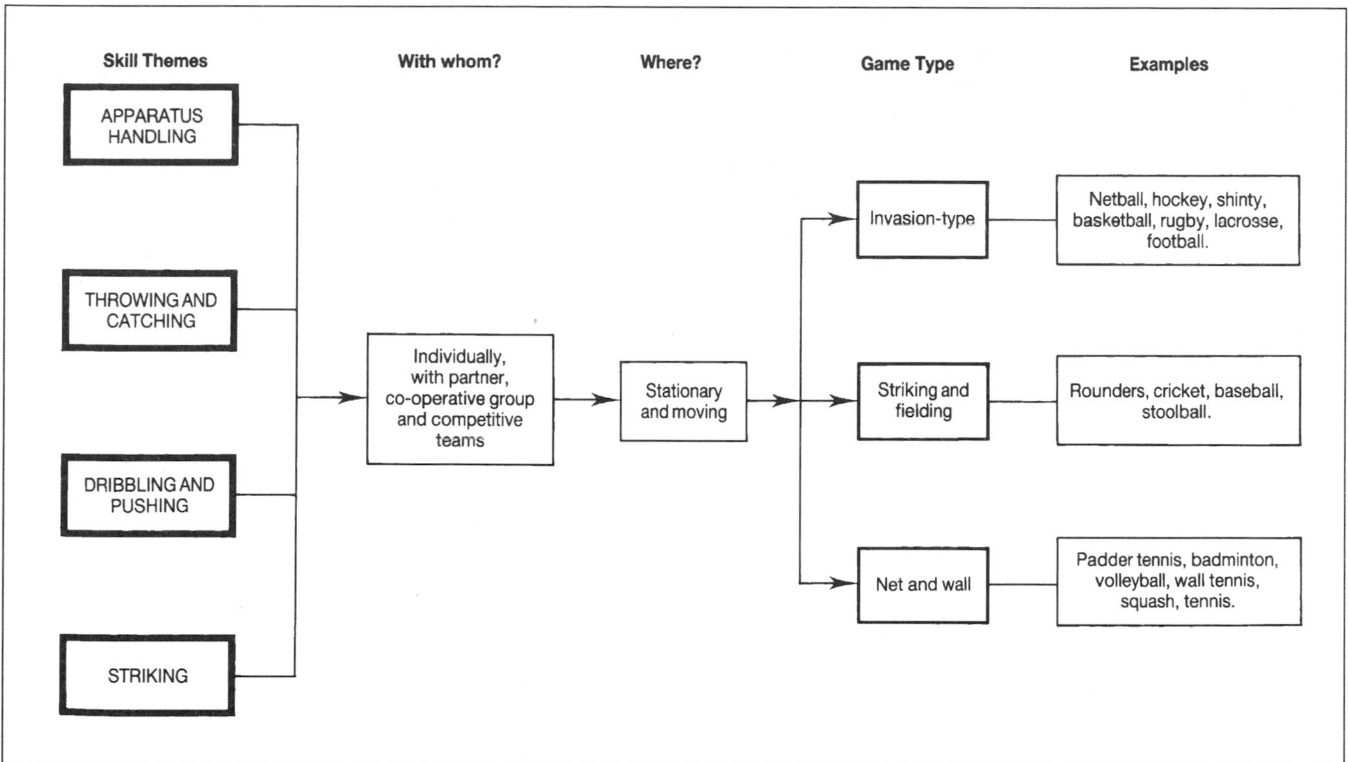

Figure 4.1
Games Skill Themes

The advantages of this approach over a curriculum based on teaching individual games are many. A good analogy comes from classroom practice: children are taught the skills of writing – letter forming, word construction, grammar, punctuation, etc – and these skills are practised, consolidated and developed and then applied in many forms of writing, such as poetry, letter-writing, stories, etc. The Skill Themes and Game/Type approach to teaching Games is very similar. Each theme places the emphasis on developing **skills** that, once mastered, can be applied when playing a number of different games.

The Skill Themes used are:

- apparatus handling
- throwing and catching
- dribbling and pushing
- striking.

Each theme begins with basic skills and simple practices and progresses to more advanced skills and concepts. Figure 4.1 indicates that progressive learning and practice should take place:

- individually – stationary then moving
- with a partner – stationary then moving
- in small groups working co-operatively – stationary then moving.

Tactics and positioning should develop as an integral part of the curriculum, using:

- small-sided competitive situations
- modified versions of recognised national games
- full-sided national games.

These should be flexible in terms of rules, and a balance should be presented during lessons. The emphasis of all these games is on active participation and 'healthy' competition while learning and consolidating skills. Throughout the teaching, children should be given opportunities to be creative, adapting the skills, tactics and rules to invent their own practices and games.

Listed below are examples of the Game-Types which are referred to in the Programme of Study and which are shown in figure 4.1. This method of classification groups together games that have common tactics and game plans and these should be emphasised once basic playing skills have been mastered.

'INVASION' GAMES

Invasion games are primarily concerned with the tactics of gaining and retaining possession, dodging and marking against an opponent and attacking and defending a goal area. They also involve a dominant element of team co-operation. Games include:

Ground handball	Benchball	Invader ball/strike
Unihoc	Hockey	Netball
New Image Rugby	Mini-rugby	Rugby
Five-a-side football	Football	
Basketball		

'STRIKING AND FIELDING' GAMES

Striking and fielding games involve the tactics of 'setting' a field (effectively positioning players in the team so that all areas in the field are covered), and 'reading' a field (knowing where to hit the ball so that it is difficult for the fielding team to collect), and involve co-operation between team members. Games include:

Tunnel rounders	Running rounders	Team rounders
French cricket	Continuous cricket	Cricket
Baseball	Stoolball	

'NET/WALL' GAMES

These games are primarily concerned with tactics involved in playing for position (being in the best position to play a return shot) and outwitting an opponent or team (playing a shot where it is most difficult for an opponent to make a return). They can be played in teams, with a partner or individually. Games include:

Newcombe (junior) volleyball	Hand wall tennis	Target tennis
Wall target tennis	Quoit tennis	Hand tennis
Padder tennis	Battington	Squash
Racquet ball		

Many of the larger games listed should only be played once a good level of skill has been acquired and much skill practising has taken place. Otherwise, the children's lack of skill will result directly in a lack of activity, leading to frustration and boredom.

The following sections attempt to provide teachers with reference material for each skill theme when preparing to teach the Games curriculum. It is organised to reflect progressive development, but can be dipped into as required.

Each section includes:

- a description of the basic skills and their associated teaching points
- a selection of individual, pair and small co-operative group practices that can be used to develop and master the skills
- a number of competitive games.

Descriptions have been kept as simple as possible and diagrams have been drawn to reflect accurate arm, leg and body positions that children should aim to achieve. A variety of alternative teaching and learning styles should be used, including formal skills teaching and reciprocal, self-check and discovery learning. Readers are also directed towards the selected bibliography on page 184 for texts that may be of use for additional reference when preparing teaching material.

Apparatus handling

The 'apparatus handling' theme is designed as the first theme to be taught, and is most appropriate for younger children. The content introduces basic skills and the concept of control which are pre-requisites for more advanced skills and group practices.

An example of how the contents of the 'apparatus handling' theme can be presented and developed is shown in table 4.1. The teaching content is presented in the form of 'skill tasks' and the suggested method of presentation is shown as 'sub-tasks' or 'questions to ask the children'. This method allows for a problem-solving, question and answer approach to teaching and facilitates a balance between 'direct teaching' and 'exploration' by the children.

For younger children, emphasis should be placed on enjoyment followed by acquisition of skill, since from enjoyment skill will emerge. Much opportunity should be given for practice and consolidation of skills, and teaching should emphasise active participation at all times. Many of the basic apparatus handling skills that children learn in the early years are developed to a much higher level of skill performance through the content of the other three skill themes during Key Stage 2. If the 'apparatus handling' theme is not fully covered at Key Stage 1 then it should be presented comprehensively at the beginning of Key Stage 2.

Table 4.1 A GUIDE TO TEACHING APPARATUS HANDLING SKILLS

Skill task with progressions	Sub tasks (questions to ask the children)	Teaching points that can be given	Associated Game-Type theme	With whom?
Bean bags then quoits	**A mixture of exploration and direct teaching**	**Children should be able to run, jump, skip, hop, without dropping the apparatus**		
Explore what can be done with apparatus a) Drop it! b) Throw it up and let it drop!	What can you do with the apparatus in your own space? What does it feel like? How does it move in the air? Does it bounce? Does it roll?	Make sure they don't move from their own space. Keep watching the apparatus. Encourage them to throw so that the apparatus lands near their feet.		Individually
Dribbling a) Balance apparatus on body parts b) Dribbling apparatus with body	How many parts of your body can you balance the apparatus on? Can you walk, run, jump, without it falling? Which parts of your body can you push the apparatus with?	Keep watching the bean bag. Move slowly to begin with and try to watch where you are going.	Invasion e.g. hockey, football	
Throwing and catching a) 2 hands to 2 hands b) 1 hand to 2 hands c) 2 hands to 1 hand d) 1 hand to 1 hand and back again e) Foot to hands f) Other body parts to hands g) Hands to other body parts	Sitting, then kneeling down, then kneeling up,then standing (demonstrate). Can you pass the bean bag/quoit from one hand to the other without dropping it? Can you throw it up and catch it? How many hands do you need? Can you toss it with your foot and catch it? What other parts of your body can you use to throw it up? Can you catch it on any other body part? Foot, back, knee?	Kneeling down = hips bent. Kneeling up = hips straight. Begin with little throws. Hands in a 'cup' shape, keep watching the apparatus. Hands go to meet the apparatus. Small toss only in own space. Balance it first, use elbow, knee and keep watching the bean bag.	Invasion e.g. netball, basketball	Individually
Aiming and Throwing In pairs throw bean bags into partner's 'leg hoop', through 'arm hoop'. a) Underarm throw into leg hoop b) Underarm throw through arm hoop c) Overarm throw into leg hoop	Can you make a 'hoop' with your legs (sitting down)? Can you make a 'hoop' with your arms? Can you throw the bean bag/quoit onto a line, into a hoop? Can you hit a wall target? Can you throw it overarm? (demonstrate)	Partner makes a 'hoop' with their legs, sitting down. Do it gently, smooth arm action. With an arm action not a wrist action.	Invasion e.g. netball, basketball	Partner

Table 4.1 cont

Skill task with progressions	Sub tasks (questions to ask the children)	Teaching points that can be given	Associated Game-Type theme	With whom?
Balls (stationary)	**(Start with large balls then medium then small as the children improve)**			
Picking the ball up a) Sitting on floor with legs wide apart b) Kneeling down c) Kneeling up d) Crouching e) Standing f) 1v1 'Get the ball first'	Can you make the ball stay still? Can you hold it in front of you; above your head; out to the side? How many hands do you need to pick the ball up? Can you grab it and hold the ball high when I say 'go'? Can you put the ball in front, behind, at the side of you and pick it up when I say 'go'?	Make sure that children: a) watch the ball all the time b) pick up and hold the ball with 'big' hands and 'hug' it tight.	Batting and base running, e.g. cricket, rounders	Individually
	Can you get to the ball before your partner and hold it up?	Both partners are equal distance from the ball when you say 'go'.		Partner
Handling the ball Sit on floor with legs apart a) Roll ball from hand to hand b) Roll ball round your body c) Lift ball inside and outside of legs d) Spin the ball and stop it e) In pairs roll ball to partner	Can you keep the ball near your hands? Can you use one hand then the other? Can you hide the ball behind you? Can you put the ball beside you – both sides? Can you keep the ball on the same spot? How many hands do you need? Always 2?	Ball should be kept close to hands. Follow the ball with the hands. Use spread fingers. Keep reminding the children to keep their eyes fixed on the ball.	Invasion (skills developed in dribbling theme)	Individually
	Can you use 2 to spin and 1 to stop? Can you roll the ball into your partner's legs?	Start very close together then move apart as children get more skilful.		Partner
Throwing and Catching a) 2 hands to 2 hands b) 1 hand to 2 hands c) 2 hands to 1 hand d) 1 hand to 1 hand and back again e) Drop and catch	Sitting, then kneeling down, then kneeling up then standing (demonstrate). Can you pass the ball from 1 hand to the other without dropping it? Can you throw it up and catch it? How many hands do you need? Can you throw the ball up, let it bounce and catch it? Can you drop the ball and catch it?	Kneeling down = hips bent. Kneeling up = hips straight. Begin with little throws. Hands in a 'cup' shape, keep watching the apparatus. Hands go to meet the apparatus. 'Gently' throw it up, use 2 'big' hands and 'hug' the ball to catch it.	Invasion (skills developed in throwing and catching theme)	Individually in own space

Table 4.1 cont

Skill task with progressions	Sub tasks (questions to ask the children)	Teaching points that can be given	Associated Game-Type theme	With whom?
Balls (moving)				
Explore what can be done with the ball still on floor: Round: run, jump, hop, skip	How can you move round the ball, over it? Can you change direction? Can you change speed?	The ball must be still. Movements should be light and springy. All movements must be controlled.	All games: develops co-ordination, fitness and dexterity	Individually in own space
Moving with the ball a) In both hands b) Other body parts	How many ways can you move without dropping it? What other parts of your body can you hold the ball with? Can you touch a target with the ball, e.g. basket, wall, bench?	Watching the ball, looking and listening, spacing, light footwork are all important. Explore many ways, e.g. between knees, ankles; jumping about the hall/grid; different directions, etc.		
c) Ball on the ground Explore what parts can be used	Which parts of your body can you push the ball with? What parts of your body can you use to dribble the ball and keep it close to you? Can you stop and be still? Can you turn with it?	Keep the ball close. The children should have already covered stationary dribbling skills with various apparatus in 'apparatus handling skills' theme.	Invasion	
Dribbling with hand(s)	Can you dribble the ball with your hands and keep it close to you? Can you use both hands – one then the other? Can you stop it with your hand without it rolling away? How many directions can you move in? Can you change direction and keep it close to you? Can you change your speed (walking, then running)?	Emphasise keeping the ball close to the body. They must keep their body in the correct position – knees bent, head up, fingers apart and hands round the side of the ball. Trap the ball with a flat hand on top of the ball. Feet should move first when changing direction. Keep the ball close, move your body into position at all times – ball at side and in front all the time.	'Invasion type' (skills developed in dribbling theme)	Individually
Practise in pairs with a ball each	Dribble round your partner and back to your place – each partner do it 3 or 5 times.			With partner
Dribbling with feet	Can you dribble the ball with your feet and keep it close to you? Can you use both feet – one then the other? What parts of your feet do you use to keep the ball close? Can you trap it with your foot without it rolling away?	Emphasise keeping the ball close to the body. They must keep their body in the correct position – keep on balance, head up, use inside and outside of foot, 'gently push', don't kick.	'Invasion type' (skills developed in dribbling theme)	Individually
Rolling and collecting a) Individually b) Partner	Can you roll the ball into a space and follow it, keeping close, and collect it/pick it up? Can you roll it to your partner and change places with them? Now the other partner rolls.	Roll it gently. Watch the ball, keep close to it. Run ahead of the ball. Pick it up and hold it high. Collect the ball, pick it up then move.	Batting and base running, e.g. cricket and rounders	a) Individually b) In pairs rolling to partner

Table 4.1 cont

Skill task with progressions	Sub tasks (questions to ask the children)	Teaching points that can be given	Associated Game-Type theme	With whom?
Ropes				
Explore ways of moving with rope on floor, e.g. jumping, hopping: a) across middle of rope b) sideways from end to end c) into and out of rope 'hoop'	How many shapes can you make with the rope on the floor: straight line, snake shape, circle (hoop)? Can you do little jumps/hops? Can you do it lightly? Can you go sideways, forwards and backwards? Can you make an interesting floor pattern?	Make sure children hop, jump lightly on balls of feet.	All games: develops co-ordination, fitness and dexterity.	Individually
Learning to skip a) Jumping b) Swinging rope c) Swinging rope overhead d) Skipping e) Fancy steps, crossing the rope f) Moving into a space	Can you do a big jump then a little jump? Can you swing the rope back and forward? Can you step or jump over it as it 'slaps' the floor? Can you swing the rope backwards and forwards over your head? Can you step or jump over it as it 'slaps' the floor? Can you go a bit faster? How many can you do without stopping? Can you skip without a rebound jump? Can you do it with any fancy steps or swings? Can you travel to a different space?	Make sure children hop, jump lightly on balls of feet. Hold rope between fingers and thumb. Wrists do circling movements. The whole arm swings from the shoulder. Young children may need to keep arms straight. This takes practice in young children.		
Tying up a rope	Can you put both ends together, same again? Make a circle/hoop in the middle, tuck one end through the, hoop then pull the ends tight.	Young children may find this difficult and can use their foot to help them make a loop. Put the rope under the foot and cross the ends over.		

SOME GAMES INVOLVING APPARATUS HANDLING SKILLS

Some simple games involving apparatus handling skills are explained below. Even very young children, however, can cope with, understand and enjoy many of the games included in the other skill groups, but they may require some adaptation to reduce the level of skill difficulty required.

How many times? Series of games involving application of simple skills through the instruction 'how many times can you ...?' e.g. 'how many times can you bounce the ball and catch it without moving your feet?', or '... before I shout stop!', or in a given time, e.g. fifteen seconds. (The children should be encouraged to score, then to try to beat their own score.)

Keep the basket tidy The teacher scatters the contents of each group basket, e.g. bean bags, balls, quoits, skipping ropes, etc, over a defined area. The children gather these and refill the basket, putting the equipment in the correct places as quickly and neatly as possible. The class may work in their colour groups, which may compete against each other to score points for tidiness, speed and co-operation within the group.

Ball tag As for ordinary tag or 'it', but 'it' carries a ball with which to touch any of the 'free' children – 'it' must hold the ball not throw it. When caught, that player takes the ball and becomes 'it'. More than one ball can be used, large or small, and the game can also be played in pairs.

Musical ropes/hoops Each child stands within a hoop or rope circle in a space. On a signal from the teacher, the children leave their hoop or circle and run/skip about the area without touching the hoops/ropes. When the music stops, or the teacher shouts 'stop', the children must find the nearest empty circle and stand in it, one child per circle. The teacher takes hoops/circles away after each round, so some children will be unable to find a circle to stand in – they lose a 'life', but continue in the game. The numbers of 'lives' lost are noted at the end of the game.

Scoring runs On a signal from the teacher, the children run between two markers using a piece of small apparatus, e.g. a rope, quoit, ball or bat.

Aiming on the move Skittles or hoops are placed in a line down the centre of the team square, and the children work in pairs. The first child runs down one side of the team square and tries to knock down the skittles or land the ball/bean bag in the hoop. The second child, who watches from the other side of the square, collects the ball/bean bag and repeats the activity. Successful hits at the target are counted up after an equal number of attempts each.

Throwing and catching

As a general rule in most throwing and catching situations, efficient learning will be optimised if progression from the easiest piece of equipment to the more difficult occurs in the correct order. At Key Stage 2 this order is:

- large balls
- bean bags
- small balls
- quoits.

Descriptions of the techniques and the teaching points of basic throwing and catching skills are outlined below.

Figure 4.2
Underarm throw or bowling action

One foot in front of the other – opposite foot to arm forward; throwing hand underneath the ball, fingers spread, holding it beside the hip; other hand steadies the ball; swing the throwing arm forward and point the arm where you want the ball to land.

Figure 4.3
Overarm shoulder pass or javelin throw (large ball)

One foot in front of the other, standing side on – opposite foot to arm forward; throwing hand underneath the ball, fingers spread, holding it beside the shoulder with the elbow bent; use the other hand to steady the ball; throw the ball by straightening the arm and finish the throw by pointing where you want the ball to go; use the wrist and fingers to assist the throw.

Figure 4.4
Overarm shoulder pass or javelin throw (small ball)

One foot in front of the other; sideways stance with the opposite foot to arm forward; weight on back foot; ball held between fingers and thumb; elbow bent and the arm behind the head; throw the ball by straightening the arm and finish the throw by stepping forward; finish the throw by pointing where you want the ball to go; use the wrist and fingers to assist the throw.

Figure 4.5
Chest pass

One foot in front of the other – opposite foot to arm forward; hold the ball in two hands, fingers spread, thumbs pointing towards the body; pull the ball up the mid line of the body to the chest; elbows out and fingers behind the ball; throw the ball by straightening the arms and snapping the wrists quickly and finish the throw by pointing where you want the ball to go.

Figure 4.6
Bounce pass

As above, but throw the ball using a chest pass action to bounce on the ground two thirds of the way to where you want it to go.

Figure 4.7
Overhead pass (two-handed)

Hold the ball above and behind the head using two hands; fingers behind the ball, thumbs pointing towards the back of the head, elbows out to the side; throw the ball by straightening the arms so that the hands finish pointing up to the sky. The ball should travel in a high looping pathway towards the intended destination.

Figure 4.8
Overarm bowling action

One foot in front of the other, standing side on – opposite foot to arm forward; throwing hand underneath the ball, fingers spread, holding it behind the body with a straight arm; throw the ball using a straight arm bowling action over the throwing shoulder; more power can be developed if desired by stepping forward with the back foot to allow the body movement to assist in the throw.

Figure 4.9
Two-handed pass (usually sideways)

Hold the ball in both hands close to the stomach with the fingers spread round the ball and the arms bent; stand side on to the destination; throw the ball by straightening the arms and sending the ball sideways from the hips.

It is important that catching skills be taught alongside throwing skills so that children experience success in both aspects. Often the catcher experiences difficulty, not because their catching skills are poor, but because the throw is inaccurate.

Catching can be achieved using two hands or one hand, and in the case of the latter, using the preferred or the non-preferred hand.

Figure 4.10
Two-handed catch

Look at the ball all the time; hold out the hands as a target for the thrower; move the feet so that the body is behind the ball and well balanced; reach out for the ball and then hug it to the body. (Once the skill level improves the ball can be caught in the hands without pulling it to the body.)

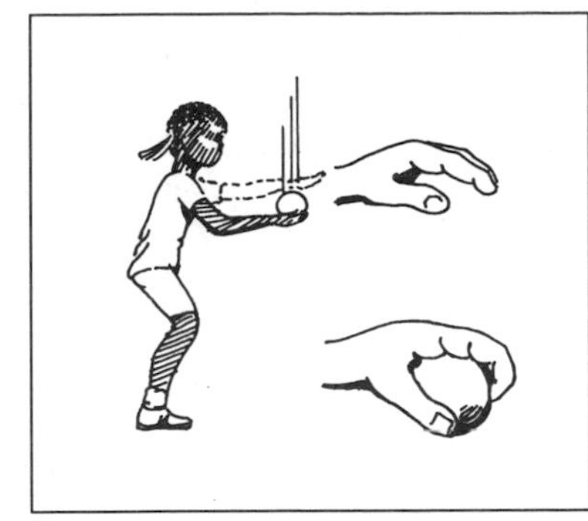

Figure 4.11
One-handed catch (small ball)

This can be achieved using the hand either as a cup under the ball for the ball to drop into or as a claw to grip the ball with the fingers. Look at the ball all the time; hold out the hand as a target for the thrower; move the feet so that the body is behind the ball and well balanced; reach out to the ball and as it comes into the hand move the hand and arm to 'cushion' the ball so that it doesn't bounce out of the hand.

There are a number of individual, partner and group practices that can be used when teaching games skills and some examples of these are listed below. These may be adapted in many ways and can involve a variety of skills. As a general rule practices begin with the children stationary, and movement should only be introduced once success is high.

INDIVIDUAL PRACTICES INVOLVING THROWING AND CATCHING

- Bounce and catch
- Underarm throw in air – bounce–catch
- Underarm throw in air – catch
- As above, but with tricks, e.g. from sitting, clap hands, turn round
- As above, progressing to use of one hand to catch
- Throwing and catching against a wall.

SKILLS AND PRACTICES WITH A PARTNER INVOLVING THROWING AND CATCHING

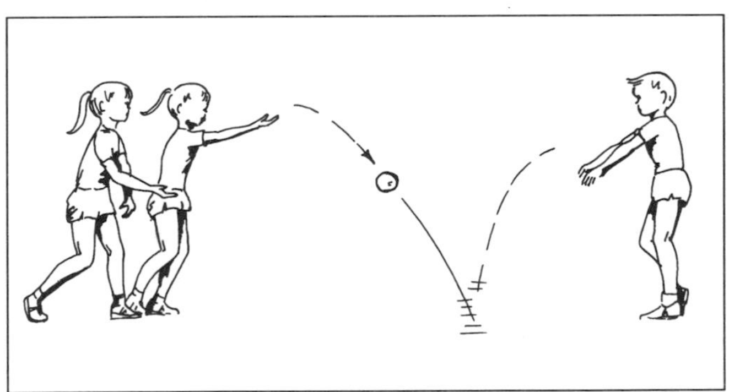

Figure 4.12
Underarm throw (bounce)

Underarm throw to partner, let it bounce then catch with two hands; stationary then moving.

Figure 4.13
Underarm throw (catch)

Underarm throw to partner – catch with two hands; stationary then moving.

Figure 4.14
Underarm throw (bounce and catch)

Underarm throw to partner – bounce–catch with two hands; moving forwards, backwards, sideways.

All the above can be practised using one hand to throw and catch if a small ball, bean bag or quoit is used. An overarm throw first with a large ball and then with a small ball, can also be practised as the skill level progresses.

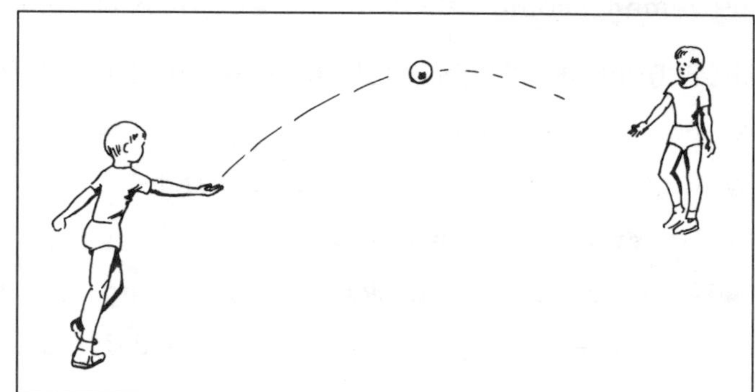

Figure 4.15
One-handed throw

Using one hand to throw and catch with a small ball.

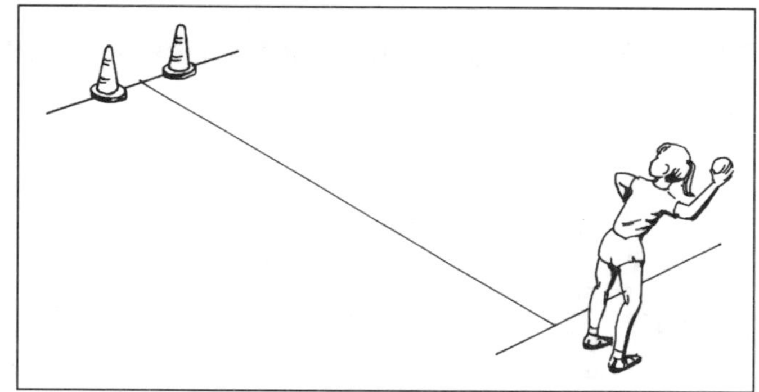

Figure 4.16
Overarm throw

Overarm throws can be practised, throwing for accuracy with a partner or throwing for distance as an athletic activity.

Practices involving movement can include:

Figure 4.17
'Pass and run round'

Partner number 1 throws the ball to 2 and then runs round partner 2 and back to their own place. Partner 2 waits until partner 1 has returned and the practice is repeated.

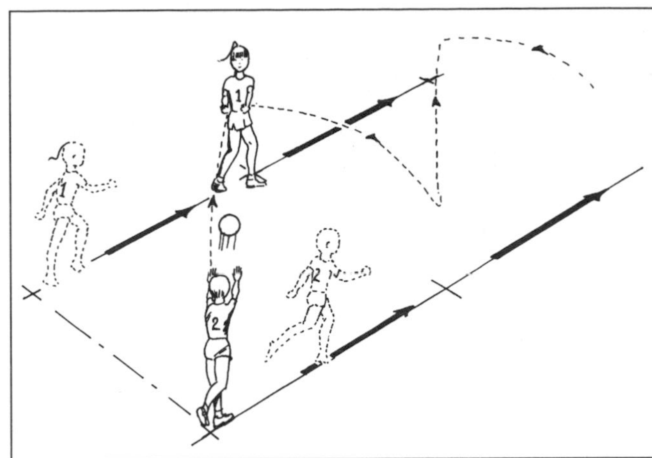

Figure 4.18
'Pass and move'

Partner 1 throws the ball to partner 2 as they move to a new position to receive the ball. Partner 2 catches the ball and returns the pass once 1 has progressed to a new position. Footwork can be introduced in this practice and a *target* or *goal* can be positioned at the end of the playing area to *score* a point.

CO-OPERATIVE GROUP PRACTICES INVOLVING THROWING AND CATCHING

The emphasis in these practices should be on group members working together to carry out the practice and improve the collective skill level. Throws should be 'sympathetic' to the catcher and the children should be taught to encourage one another.

Figure 4.19
'Circle pass ball'

Children form a circle of about three or four metres diameter. The players pass the ball/bean bag back and forth across the circle (not to people beside them). Eventually two balls or bean bags may be introduced. Practice for younger children involves passing the ball round the circle.

Figure 4.20
'Pass and follow'

This can be done with any number and in a square, circle, line etc. Throwing, pushing and striking skills can be practised in this way.

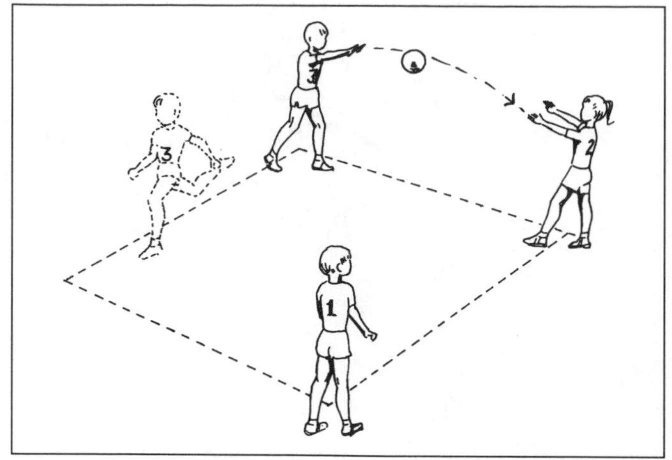

Figure 4.21
'Pass and move back'

A practice exercise for a group of three working in a square. Each child must throw the ball in one direction round the square and then run in the opposite direction to the available free corner of the square. This teaches them to move to a free position once they have made a pass.

Figure 4.22
'Pass and follow behind'

In groups of six the children line up as shown in the diagram. Numbers 1, 3 and 5 stand some distance apart from 2, 4 and 6. Using any throwing, dribbling or striking skill, 1 passes to 2 and follows to take up a position behind 2, 4 and 6. Child 2 collects the ball, passes and follows behind to take up position behind 3 and 5,and so on. The distance between the two lines of children can be varied depending on the skill being practised.

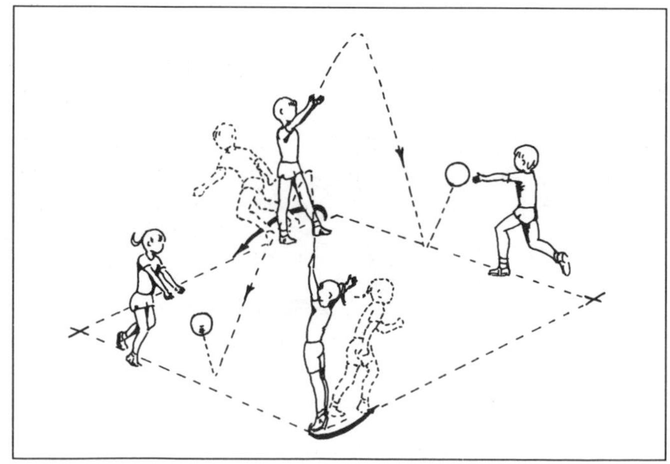

Figure 4.23
'Throw up and move'

Number 1 and number 3 throw their ball up and run. Numbers 2 and 4 run to catch the ball after it has bounced only once. The practice can also be done with a small ball and a high throw.

Number 1 and number 3 have a ball each and they bounce their ball up and run to the next corner of the square. Number 2 and 4 run to catch the ball before it bounces again.

Figure 4.24
'Bounce and move'

Once the groups are working together successfully a measure of *non-invasive* competition can be introduced by allowing the groups to compete alongside one another, providing they are of mixed ability. For example, a number of catches can be set as a target for each team to achieve and the first team to reach the target is awarded four points, the next three, and so on. The last team to reach the target is awarded one point. This encourages 'healthy competition', since everyone is rewarded and good teamwork is essential for success.

GAMES INVOLVING THROWING AND CATCHING

Hit the target A basket or tub is placed in the centre of the grid or team square as a target, and hoops are positioned at varying distances away from the 'target'. Each child stands in a hoop to throw a piece of apparatus (bean bag, ball, quoit) and tries to get it into the 'target'. (All children should throw then collect together). Successful attempts should be scored. Other targets, such as skittles, can be used as the children improve and the hoops can be moved further away.

Circle dodge ball As above, but instead of a tub the target is a player who is a 'dodger'. The outside players pass the ball and throw it to hit the dodger below knee height. When the dodger is hit, she or he is replaced by the player who scores the 'hit'.

Team dodge ball As above, except that one, two or three players or a whole team may be placed within the circle or team square as targets for the other team, who form a circle around them or are standing around the edge of the team square. The ball can be rolled or bounced and a 'hit' is only successful if it has been made below the knee. Points are scored for every 'hit' recorded in a certain time. This game is popular with all ages.

Pass and duck The children form teams of four and line up so that number 1 stands three metres from, and facing, the rest of the team who are lined up one behind the other. Number 1 passes the bean bag or ball to 2 who returns it to 1 and ducks (crouches on ground). Number 1 now passes bean bag to number 3 who also ducks after passing it back. Once number 4 has done the same, number 1 runs to the back of the line and number 2 runs out to face the team who all move up one place. When everyone is back in their original place, the game has finished. The number of passes to each child can be set and the game played competitively.

Circle skittle ball A group of children are spaced around the outside of a large circle. A skittle is placed in the centre of the circle, which one player defends as the outside players pass the ball and shoot at the skittle. A player who makes a successful hit changes places with the defender.

Invader play Three children form a triangle with a fourth 'invader' in the middle. The 'invader' has to try and prevent (by interception) the other children from passing the ball, bean bag, quoit, etc to each other. If a successful interception is made, or a catch is dropped, then whoever had possession last must become the 'invader'. Children should be encouraged not to pass the ball over the head of the 'invader' but to the person who is 'free', i.e. the players in the triangle must keep moving. The 'invader' is changed after a successful invasion or six passes.

On the move Each group of children works within its group square. One of the group starts with a ball, and must pass to someone who is on the move. On receiving the ball that child must stop immediately and attempt to pass the ball to a different child who is on the move. Players must keep within their square, and each successful catch counts as a point. (In a confined space the teams can work one or two at a time then change over, each team getting 30–45 seconds each.) This game is particularly suitable for older children. It encourages the ability to catch and pass on the move and also helps to develop anticipation of the path of the ball. It also develops children's concentration if their turn is over when they drop the ball.

Invader on the move This game combines the two above. Each member of each team is given a number, from 1 to however many there are in the largest team. One team takes the 'court' or playing area and plays *on the move.* The teacher calls a number and each team member with that number from the three remaining teams (who are sitting at their baskets ready) then 'invades' the playing area and tries to intercept the passes. If the 'invaders' are unable to intercept, another number can be called and so on. The initial invaders can either sit down or can remain on 'court', whichever is appropriate to the skill level of the class. Each team has a turn playing *on the move.* (This game can be adapted to allow practice of a number of skills with a variety of pieces of apparatus, e.g. throwing and catching with a large or small ball, and dribbling and pushing with stick and ball.)

Skittle ball This is played in an area equivalent to two grids or one third of a netball court. It is played by two small teams who each try to knock down a skittle at the other's end of the court. Each skittle is ringed by a large hoop or chalked circle with a radius of about one metre, which acts as a restraining circle. No player is allowed within the circle, nor may they run with the ball or dribble it; this encourages them to progress through passing and then running off the ball into space to receive it again. A goal is scored each time the skittle is knocked down.

Corner ball A fairly advanced game played between two teams who may run anywhere within a specified area. Team A has possession of the ball and players attempt to touch any member of Team B whilst still handling the ball – it may not be thrown at the opposition. The player with the ball may not run with it, but by quick passing to team-mates, the opposition player(s) may be cornered and touched. When a player is touched, a point is scored and after a certain time the points are totalled up and the teams change roles.

End ball This game is played over two grids or one third of a netball court by two teams. One player from each team stands on the goal line defended by the opposing team, and may move anywhere along that line, but must not come off it – this player is known as the 'catcher'. The game is then played along similar lines to *skittle ball*, but a goal is scored this time when a team eventually passes the ball successfully to their 'catcher' on the opposition line. An area outside which shots to the 'catcher' should be made may be indicated by a chalked semi-circle. After each goal, the 'catcher' is changed.

Benchball This game is the same as *end ball*, except that the 'catcher' stands on a bench which is on the goal line defended by the opposition.

Cross the river Two children from the same team stand on each side of the team square and two children from another team stand in the middle of the team square. The first two children try to pass the ball across the square to each other whilst the middle two children try to intercept. The children on the two sides may run anywhere along their line: this helps to develop anticipation of the speed and path of a ball, especially if a rule is made that the ball must not be passed over the head of the two interceptors in the middle.

Junior volleyball Two teams, ranging from one to six players, compete on a court of approximately eight by four metres. A net is stretched across the width of the court, a little above head height. A light plastic or sponge ball (size three or four) is served over the net by a rear player in one team, and then passed back and forth among the players and over the net until one team scores by landing the ball in the opponents' court. Initially, players may catch the ball and then throw it to a partner or over the net, but later they should be encouraged to push or strike the ball without catching it. Eventually, correct serving should be taught and the players should rotate their positions clockwise in each half of the court as a new session of serving starts.

New Image Rugby This is a non-contact form of the adult game played with small-sided teams of mixed gender. Official rules exist and can be obtained from the RFU, together with a video.

Mini-rugby This is a mini-version of the adult game played between two teams of up to ten-a-side. The skills of the adult game are practised, including tackling, and there is an emphasis on safety. It is suitable only for older children.

Recognised national games involving throwing and catching skills include netball, handball, rugby and basketball.

Dribbling and pushing

Dribbling skills are ones where a piece of equipment, usually a ball, is kept in contact with, or close to, the body or an implement (e.g. a hockey stick) while the player moves about the playing area. Pushing skills involve propelling a piece of equipment using a pushing action (as distinct from an impact striking action) with the hand or foot or an implement.

In most dribbling and pushing situations and skills the order of equipment progression is:

- a bean bag using the hands and feet
- a large ball using the hands
- a large ball using the feet
- a small ball using a modified stick (i.e. a bat)
- a small ball using a stick.

The basic dribbling and pushing actions are described and shown below.

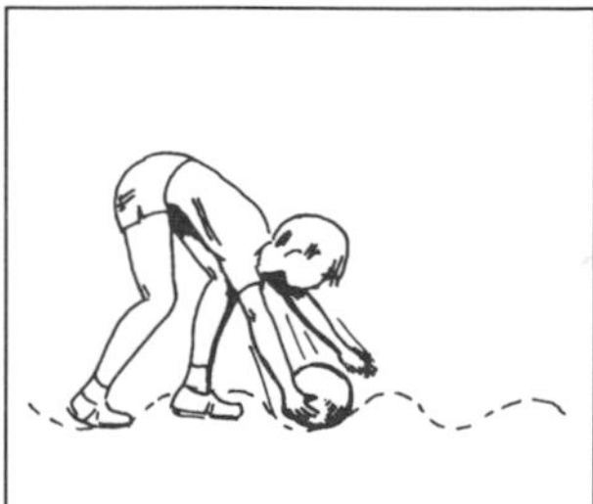

Figure 4.25
Push dribbling with the hand

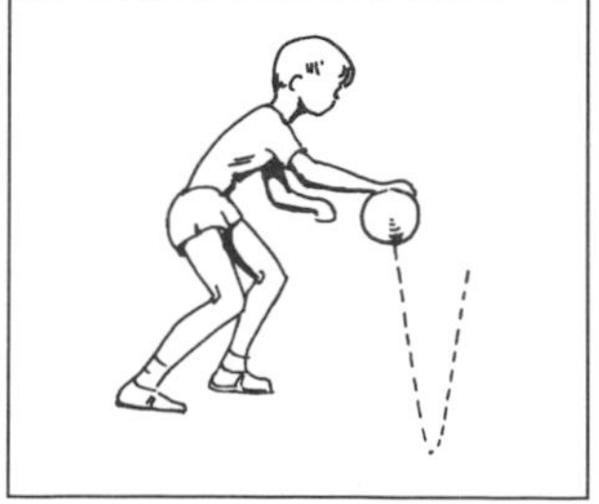

Figure 4.26
Bounce dribbling with the hand

Figure 4.27
Dribbling with the foot

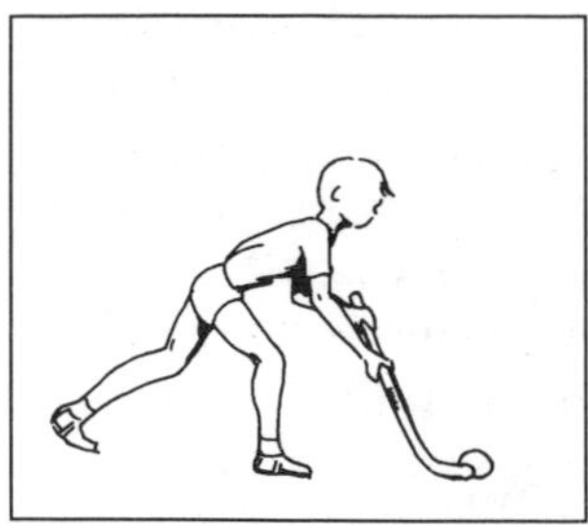

Figure 4.28
Dribbling with a stick (or bat)

Figure 4.29
Pushing with the hand

Figure 4.30
Pushing with the foot

Figure 4.31
Pushing with a stick

PRACTICES INVOLVING DRIBBLING AND PUSHING SKILLS

The practices described in throwing and catching can be adapted by substituting dribbling and pushing skills. Some of these are shown below as examples.

Figure 4.32
'Dribble round'

Dribble round and push pass to partner (all styles of dribbling can be used, and combined with a push pass or a throw).

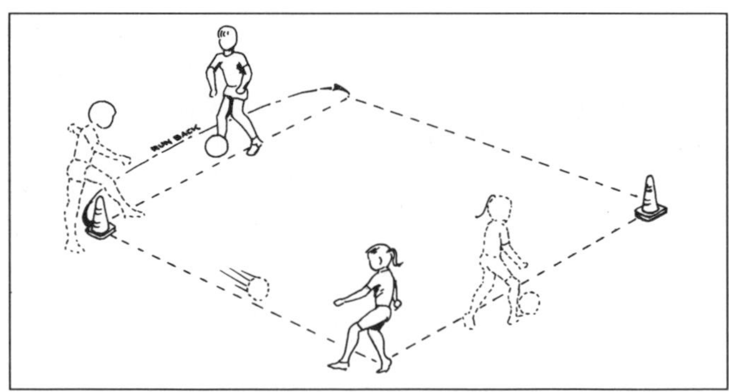

Figure 4.33
'Dribble and push'

Two players work in a square. Dribble to a cone, push pass to partner and run back to your place.

Figure 4.34
'Dribble pass and shoot'

Two players dribble and pass to each other across a space. Introduce a target to push the ball at, once they reach a designated position.

Figure 4.35
'Dribble pass and move on'

Each player dribbles along the side of a square, push passes to the front player in the opposite line of children and then runs to the end of the line they have passed to, ready for their next turn.

Figure 4.36
'Dribble round cones'

The player dribbles round the cones to the opposite line of children and then runs to the end of the line. (All styles of dribbling can be used.)

A selection of progressions and teaching points are listed below.

Practice/ activity	Teaching points
Individually	
■ push dribbling round your body in own space	look at ball
■ walking and stopping with the ball – roll the ball with the hand, chase and stop	keep on balance in the correct position by moving feet
■ turning	begin with a very gentle action
■ running dribble and stopping with ball	
In pairs explore	
■ passing the ball for a partner to collect it under control	try to pass the ball under control to your partner
■ pass and change	move to meet the ball
■ pass and run round	face in the correct direction
■ pass and move	pass the ball sympathetically so that your partner has time
■ pass, move and score	move into position early, ready to play
In small groups	
■ circle pass ball	with bat – shake hands grip
■ pass and follow	with stick – grip with hands spaced apart
■ pass and dribbling relays	
■ pass and move into space	
■ invader pass 3 v 1, 2 v 1 situations; 3 v 3, 5 v 5, 6 v 6 game-like situations	

GAMES INVOLVING DRIBBLING AND PUSHING

Scoring runs On a given signal from the teacher, the children race back and forth between two markers using dribbling skills – the runs may be counted over a given period.

How many times? A series of games involving dribbling skills: e.g. how many times can you bounce the ball on the ground without losing control?

Invader dribble Same as *invader play* (page 48) using the skills of dribbling with body parts or a piece of apparatus.

Unihoc A game similar to hockey but played with adapted sticks, a puck and small sides indoors. There are official rules, but rules can be adapted or created by the teacher and the children.

Recognised national games involving dribbling and pushing skills include hockey, football and basketball.

Striking skills

Striking skills are ones where a piece of equipment, usually a ball, is struck by a body part or an implement such as a bat or a hockey stick in order to make a pass to a team member, a strike at a goal or a strike at a position on a court in order to deceive an opponent. Striking skills involve propelling a piece of equipment using an impact action with the hand or foot or an implement.

The usual order of progression through equipment is:

- a large ball using the hand – batting, or a dig, serve or spike in volleyball
- a large ball using the feet – kicking
- a bean bag or puck using a stick
- a large ball using a stick
- a small ball using a stick – a hit to a partner or at goal in hockey
- a bean bag using a bat
- a light, small ball using a bat – e.g. forehand, serve, etc in tennis
- a tennis ball using a bat then a modified tennis racket.

Below is a description of frequently used striking actions in these categories, together with some skill variations, practices and teaching points that are common to many activities and games.

STRIKING A LARGE BALL USING THE HAND

Figure 4.37
Striking a large ball using the hand

Skill variations: hitting the ball in the game of rounders; digging, serving and spiking in the game of volleyball.

Practice/activity

- hitting the ball for a partner to catch with the inside of the fist
- serve the ball underarm against wall and catch
- serve the ball underarm for partner to catch
- partner feeds for a *digging* action, with both arms used to return the ball
- *dig* the ball back and forward between two
- serve the ball underarm for partner to *dig* return

Teaching points

look at ball

keep on balance in the correct position by moving feet

move into position early, ready to play

begin with a very gentle action

try to hit the ball under control to your partner

face in the correct direction

hit the ball up in the air so that your partner has time to catch it

STRIKING A LARGE BALL USING THE FOOT – KICKING

Figure 4.38
Striking a large ball using the foot – kicking

Skill variations: passing the ball to a team member, kicking at goal, kicking for distance to clear the ball, kicking along the ground, kicking high in the air (a rugby-style conversion).

Practice/activity

Individually

- kick against a wall
- keep the ball in air (also use the knees chest and head)
- keep control of the ball and move about the space using little tap kicks

In pairs explore

- strike and change
- strike and run round
- strike and move
- strike, move and score

Teaching points

look at ball

keep on balance by moving feet

move into position early, ready to play

inside and outside of foot for passing

practise using both feet

control the ball then kick

use of instep to control – 'give' (absorption of force of ball)

control, look, pass

move to meet the ball

STRIKING A BALL USING A STICK

Figure 4.39 Striking a ball using a stick

Skill variations: to hit to a fellow team member or at goal in hockey.

Practice/activity

- hitting the ball for a partner to *field* under control
- keep ball in air
- strike against wall

In pairs explore

- strike and change
- strike and run round
- strike and move
- strike, move and score

In small groups

- circle pass ball
- pass and follow
- pass and dribbling relays
- pass and move into space
- invader strike 3 v 1, 2 v 1 situations

Teaching points

look at ball

keep on balance by in the correct position by moving feet

move into position early, ready to play

begin with a very gentle action

try to hit the ball under control to your partner

face in the correct direction

hit the ball up in the air so that your partner has time to catch it

move into position early

STRIKING A SMALL BALL USING A BAT

Figure 4.40 Striking a ball using a bat/racket

Skill variations: Forehand and backhand drive, volley, serve and smash in net and wall games; batting actions in striking and fielding games such as cricket, rounders and baseball.

Figure 4.41 Hit and catch

Figure 4.42 Throw up, hit and catch

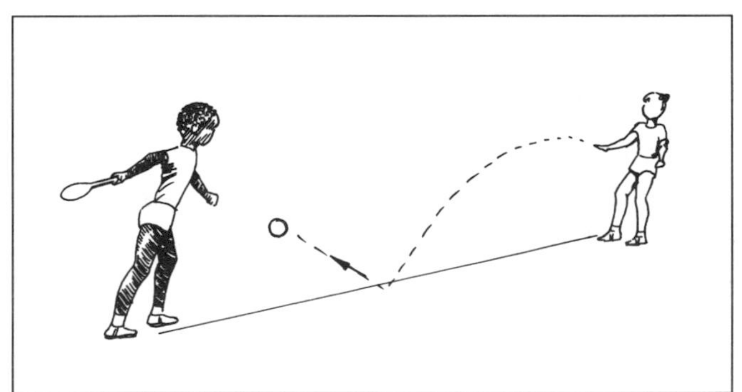

Figure 4.43 Bounce, feed and hit

Practice/activity	Teaching points
Individually	
■ grip	Grip: shake hands – V-shaped
■ lift and bounce – hit in air	hit the ball in the centre of the bat
■ forehand, backhand	strike ball at top of bounce
■ volley in air – forehand, backhand	look at ball
■ pat bounce – hand	keep on balance in the correct position by moving feet
■ pat bounce – bat	move into position early, ready to play
■ pat bounce – forehand, backhand	begin with a very gentle action
■ tricks	try to hit the ball under control to your partner

In pairs and small groups	face in the correct direction
■ keep the rally going	hit the ball up in the air so your partner has time to catch it
■ move, bounce, hit	stand in sideways position
■ move, volley	prepare and get into position early, ready to hit the ball before it is too close
■ wall tennis	hit through the ball – follow through
■ wall target tennis	
■ padder tennis	
■ continuous cricket	
■ French cricket	
■ Rounders	

GAMES INVOLVING STRIKING SKILLS

There are many possible games involving different aspects of striking – using different parts of the body and a variety of sticks and bats. The rules can be adapted to the ability of the children.

How many times? A series of games involving striking skills: e.g. how many times can you bounce the ball on the ground with the bat, without moving? Wall and rebound games are particularly applicable to this type of striking skill and approach.

Pass and follow behind In fours the children line up as follows: numbers 1 and 3 (one behind the other) standing ten metres away from 2 and 4. Using any striking skill, 1 passes to 2 and runs to take up a position behind 4 and so on until all are back in their original places.

Circle pass ball As previously described (figure 4.19), but players pass the ball by striking it with different parts of the body, sticks and various bats.

Invader strike As *invader play* (page 48), but players pass the ball by striking with bats, sticks or different parts of the body.

Cross the river As previously described, but players pass the ball by striking with bats, sticks, and different parts of the body.

French cricket Children play in groups of four, five or six in their own team square. One child becomes the batter and stands in the middle of the square, with a batting shape ready to protect the legs below the knees. The other children are fielders positioned on all sides of the batter with one tennis ball between them. The ball is tossed to try and hit the batter's legs; the batter attempts to protect his/her legs by hitting or deflecting the ball, which should be fielded as soon as possible and bowled from the fielder's position back at the batter. The batter can either be allowed to turn or be obliged to remain continually with feet fixed. If the batter is unable to protect his/her legs and the ball hits him/her below the knees, then whoever tossed the ball becomes the batter.

Team rounders or tunnel rounders Rounders is a good game, but is too often played with large teams, little success in hitting the ball, and a great deal of inactivity. The game should not be played until the children have a good grounding in the skills of throwing, catching and striking. Two mixed teams of about eight children should play *team rounders*, on a pitch adapted to the ability of the children. The ball should be a medium-size playball, and the bat should be a round playbat – this should allow the children to hit the ball more easily! The fielding side take up normal positions; the batting side stand a few metres from the actual batting/hitting area, for safety. After the batter has hit the ball, the whole of the batting team runs around the rounders posts and back to the batting team position. Meanwhile the fielding players have to field the ball and then form a tunnel in the middle of the rounders pitch by standing one behind the other and rolling the ball between their legs to the player at the back of the line, who then runs to the front and holds the ball above his/her head. If the fielding side is able to do this before the whole of the batting side arrives back at their batting team position, then no rounder has been scored. It may be seen immediately that *team rounders* is a very active game.

Running rounders The ordinary game of rounders is often unsuccessful during lesson time due to lack of skill in hitting the ball, and can consequently be tedious and slow. As a curriculum activity *running rounders* is much more active, providing valuable practice, particularly at fielding, with a positive carry-over to the conventional game. About eight players take part in each game. The ball is served so that a good hit is likely to result – this can also be ensured by using a playbat or padder tennis bat. The batter then has to run to each base in turn. The ball is fielded, returned to base 1 and thrown around the bases to base 4. If the batter arrives at base 4 before the ball, a rounder is scored. Each player should have an opportunity of filling each position in the game and a rule should be made for the order of change (bowler to batter, batter to backstop, etc) The change may occur after a prescribed number of hits or when the batter is out.

Five- or six-a-side football The court is the same as for *ground handball* and the game is played in the same way, but with the feet substituted for hands. The ball should not travel above knee height, and if it goes out of play, the non-offending team should roll the ball in by hand. After a goal is scored, the defending side takes possession and the game continues immediately – there should be a minimum of time wasted.

Shinty (Hockey) This game is played with similar rules to five-a-side football, but a small, soft rubber ball is suggested, struck with a shinty stick. The ball should be hit along the ground, and rolled in if it goes out of play.

Wall tennis A horizontal white line is painted or chalked on a wall about one metre above ground level to represent a net. Two players, each with a playbat or padder tennis bat, play a ball against the wall alternately, aiming above the white line. A player scores a point when the opponent fails to hit the ball as it leaves the wall, or after one bounce on the ground, or if the ball is played at the wall below the white line.

Hand wall tennis This game is played in the same way as above, but the hand is used to strike the ball in place of the bat.

Target tennis Two square targets, two or three metres apart, are painted or chalked on the ground – the dimensions of the square being two, three or four metres depending on the ability of the children and the space available. The aim is to hit the ball into the target area belonging to your opponent. When a player fails to do this the opponent scores a point. The game may be played as singles or doubles – the target should be of appropriate size.

Wall target tennis The above game can be transferred to a wall: in this case only one target needs to be used, the size of which may be determined by the ability and number of players. The game may be played by one, two, three, or four players.

Padder tennis Official rules are available for this game, which is played by two or four players on a rectangular court of approximately ten by five metres, with a net across it at a height of about one metre. Using a padder tennis bat or playbat, players attempt to hit the ball across the net into the opponent's half of the court. A point is scored when the opposition fails to return the ball into the appropriate half of the court or allows the ball to bounce more than once on their side of the net. An underarm service should be used.

Hand tennis This game is similar to padder tennis, but the hands are used in place of bats. A larger, lighter ball is suggested.

Battington This game is played with similar rules to padder tennis, but a shuttlecock is used instead of a ball. The net height may be increased to 1.5 metres. Official rules are available for this game, which is often marred by the wind.

Stoolball This game has official rules and is similar to cricket. The aim is for the two batters to score runs by moving between two stoolball wickets placed about fifteen metres apart. A bowler bowls underarm an over of 6–8 balls at each wicket in turn. Batters touch the wicket with the stoolball bat when completing a run, and a batter is out by being bowled, caught or run out.

Continuous cricket A complicated game to explain, but a most enjoyable one to play. The pitch is arranged as follows. The stumps (or skittles) are erected facing the bowler's circle, which is six to nine metres away. A further wicket (or skittle) to which the batter will run is placed nine metres away from the stumps and to the left of the batter as he faces straight on to the bowler's circle. The two teams should comprise about five or six players each. One batter stands in front of the stumps to defend them with a cricket bat shape. The remaining batters stay behind a restraining line which is away from play. The bowler takes up his/her position in the bowler's circle and the rest of the fielding side – these should include a wicket-keeper – take up suitable positions. Every time she or he makes contact with the ball, the batter must run to the skittle and back to the wicket, the completed journey counting as one run. In the meantime, the bowler continues to bowl at the wicket, irrespective of whether the batter is in position to defend it or not. The fielders make their contribution by collecting the ball and returning it quickly to the bowler, who must remain within his/her circle. When the bowler hits the wicket, the batter is out and must drop the bat and retire. The incoming batter must collect the bat and defend the wicket before she or he too is out. When the last batter is out the teams may change roles quickly – as soon as the new bowler has arrived in her/his circle she/he may bowl. If there is time, two innings per side is normal and the runs should be counted up to decide which is the winning side.

Summary

The above information should help teachers to select activities, skills and practices for inclusion in their lessons. The Scheme of Work presented in section 4.2 is one example of how the content can be planned and organised so that children develop their skills, knowledge and understanding of Games through enjoyable and fun activities. Schools and teachers should adapt their scheme and the teaching content to suit the ability of the children they are working with and the individual needs of their school.

4.6 Structure of lessons

For all children, a structured approach to the teaching of Games is required for maximum benefit to be gained from the teaching content. A suggested lesson structure is shown below.

INTRODUCTION

A free choice of apparatus from their own group basket. Emphasis is on use of space in the grid and the use of a variety of pieces of apparatus for practice and exploration. This time may be used by the teacher to encourage children and, if necessary, to organise the distribution of additional apparatus required for the lesson. It should also provide a physiological warm-up activity.

SKILL PRACTICES

This is an extremely important part of the lesson, in which the children use the appropriate equipment to learn specific skills. The teaching style may be a blend of demonstration (by children or teacher), exploration and question and answer. The children may be asked to work individually or with a partner, possibly moving on to small group activities. The children practise with a particular piece of apparatus, or practise a particular activity, or develop a game-like situation, for example, setting themselves a realistic target number of repetitions to consolidate a skill.

GAMES (APPLICATION OF SKILLS)

This section may involve the simplest of games with little competitive element for the youngest children. As the children become older and more skilful, group situations, where the children are working in more complex games involving footwork, hitting, striking, throwing, catching, fielding, passing etc, should be introduced. It is important that this stage progresses naturally from the skills stage, using the skills that pupils have practised earlier. For older children, this part of the lesson will involve participation in modified forms of recognised national games.

CLOSING ACTIVITY

This section should include tidying of the equipment and a settling down activity in preparation for return to the classroom.

4.7 End-of-Key-Stage statements

The above teaching content, when presented progressively using a range of teaching styles throughout Key Stages 1 and 2, will more than satisfy the Games Programme of Study and will lead towards the attainment of a number of the end-of-Key-Stage statements as set out on page 27.

4.8 National governing bodies for Games

Listed below are some addresses and telephone numbers of National Governing Bodies for school sports which fall into the category of Games. A number of these associations provide information and resources which may be useful to school teachers for both curriculum Physical Education and extra-curricular activities. Some of the sports also have performance award schemes and specific leadership and coaching awards for teachers.

The English Schools Basketball Association, 44 Northleat Avenue, Kings Ash, Paignton, Devon, TQ3 3UG. Telephone 0830 842289.

The English Schools Netball Association, 76 Macklands Way, Rainham, Gillingham, Kent, ME8 7PF. Telephone 0634 852341.

The English Schools Football Association, 4A Eastgate Street, Stafford, ST16 2NQ. Telephone 0785 55485.

The National Rounders Association, 3 Denhurst Avenue, Nottingham, NG8 5DA. Telephone 0602 785514.

The Rugby Football Union, The Rugby Road, Twickenham, TW1 1DZ. Telephone 081 892 8161.

British Schools Lawn Tennis Association, c/o A.L.T.A. Trust, The Queens Club, West Kensington, London, W14 9EG. Telephone 071 385 4233.

The Hockey Association, Norfolk House, 102 Saxon Gate West, Milton Keynes, MK9 2EP. Telephone 0908 241100.

Gymnastic Activities

5.1 Introduction

GYMNASTIC ACTIVITIES

'Like dance, gymnastic activities focus on the body. They are concerned with acquiring control, co-ordination and versatility in the use of the body in increasingly challenging situations and with developing strength, especially of the upper body, and maintaining flexibility. These activities are based on natural actions such as leaping, balancing, inverting, rolling and swinging.'
(DES 1991, page 76)

The Physical Education National Curriculum (NC) Statutory Orders require that Gymnastic Activities be taught as one of the six areas of activity within a balanced programme of Physical Education at Key Stage 2 (seven to eleven years). The National Curriculum Council (NCC) further recommends that Gymnastic Activities be taught throughout all four years within the Key Stage. This section outlines the suggested content of the Gymnastic Activities curriculum that should be taught in order to deliver the NC general and Gymnastic Activities Programmes of Study for Key Stage 2 that are presented in the Statutory Orders for Physical Education.

5.2 Gymnastic Activities Scheme of Work

The following pages contain a suggested Gymnastic Activities Scheme of Work for Key Stage 2, based on the model for whole curriculum planning suggested in Chapter 2. As with the other areas of activity, the scheme is presented in the form of a curriculum planning document that could be used to record what will be taught to a particular cohort through Key Stage 2.

Using this format schools may develop their own Scheme of Work specific to their own needs and circumstances. The teaching content described in more detail in section 5.5 should be used for reference when planning the curriculum content. A blank Scheme of Work document is provided in the Appendix (pages 170–173).

Scheme of Work

Key Stage: 2

Area of activity: Gymnastic Activities

Cohort: 1994-95

Units of Work (length of unit x length of lessons)

	Autumn	Spring	Summer
Year 3	7+8 x40 mins	7+6 x40 mins	
Year 4	8 x40 mins	7+6 x40 mins	
Year 5	7+8 x40 mins	7+6 x40 mins	
Year 6	7+8 x40 mins	7+6 x40 mins	

Process aims

The Scheme of Work will work towards enabling the pupils to carry out the following:

PLANNING AND COMPOSING

- plan appropriate responses to Gymnastics tasks set by the teacher on floor and using apparatus
- compose Gymnastics sequences showing creativity and individual interpretation on floor and using apparatus
- safely co-operate with a partner to plan responses to a variety of tasks and stimuli.

PARTICIPATING AND PERFORMING

- perform appropriate and safe body preparation as warm-up and warm-down activities
- explore safely a variety of tasks set by the teacher and present different responses
- work alone and with others to develop, consolidate, refine and link their repertoire of Gymnastics skills through practice and rehearsal
- remember, select and repeat a range of Gymnastics skills and movements and perform more complex sequences alone and with others
- lift, carry, place and use equipment appropriately and safely.

APPRECIATING AND EVALUATING

- appreciate the importance of good posture and body position in the aesthetic performance of Gymnastics skills and movements
- make simple constructive comments and judgements on their own and others' performances.

Programme of Study requirements

'Pupils should:

- *be enabled, both on the floor and using apparatus, to find more ways of rolling, jumping, swinging, balancing and taking weight on hands, and to adapt, practise and refine these activities.*
- *be guided to perform in a controlled manner, and to understand that the ending of one action can become the beginning of the next.*
- *be given opportunities, both on the floor and using apparatus in response to set tasks, to explore, select, develop, practise and refine a longer series of actions making increasingly complex movement sequences which they are able to repeat.*
- *be enabled to respond to a variety of tasks alone or with a partner, emphasising changing shape, speed and direction through gymnastic actions.'*

Teaching Content Outline

Year: 3 **Unit:** 1

Autumn 1st half term

Title: Revision of travelling

7 x 40 minute lessons

Outline: Review of travelling skills on feet with sub-theme consolidation and refinement. Develop using other body parts and using simple apparatus. Emphasis on developing quality and introduction of sequence building and presentation using floor and apparatus.

Year: 3 **Unit:** 2

Autumn 2nd half term

Title: Introduction to jumping and landing

8 x 40 minute lessons

Outline: Teaching of two feet to two feet jumps and correct landing technique. Introduction of the five basic jumps on feet. Developing sub-themes of direction, space and shape. Conclude with sequence building using learned skills and developments on floor and simple apparatus such as benches.

Year: 3 **Unit:** 3

Spring 1st half term

Title: Developing jumping and landing

7 x 40 minute lessons

Outline: Teaching of the hurdle step. Introduction of jumping using hands and feet. Developing sub-themes of level, size and quality of jumps. Development of hands and feet using apparatus.

Year: 3 **Unit:** 4

Spring 2nd half term

Title: Consolidation of jumping and landing and travelling

6 x 40 minute lessons

Outline: Practice and consolidation of travelling and jumping and landing skills with emphasis on quality of performance using floor and apparatus through the introduction of simple sequence work. Developing sub-themes of direction and shape to give variety to the sequence work.

Year: 4 **Unit:** 5

Autumn 1st half term

Title: Introduction of simple balance skills

7 x 40 minute lessons

Outline: Teaching of basic and simple balance skills on feet, hands and other body parts. Moving in and out of balance encouraging creativity and individual interpretation of tasks when linking balances together.

Year: 4 **Unit:** 6

Spring 1st half term

Title: Developing balance skills

7 x 40 minute lessons

Outline: Incorporation of previously learned simple balance skills into sequence work on floor and apparatus in combination with travelling and jumping and landing skills. Introduction of more complex tasks on apparatus.

Year: 4 **Unit:** 7

Spring 2nd half term

Title: Developing sequence work

6 x 40 minute lessons

Outline: Specific unit concentrating on the creation, practice, development and consolidation of a sequence on floor and then apparatus, made up of a travel, a balance and a jump. Much emphasis should be placed on the movement sub-themes to produce quality work showing control, variety, and breadth in skills performance.

Year: 5 **Unit:** 8

Autumn 1st half term

Title: Introduction of transference of weight theme

7 x 40 minute lessons

Outline: Introduction to the concept of transference of weight and the skills involved. Teaching of the simplest skills in the theme: side roll, salmon roll, simple cartwheel, and simple rocking and swinging.

Year: 5 **Unit:** 9

Autumn 2nd half term

Title: The family of rolls

8 x 40 minute lessons

Outline: Teaching of the forward and backward roll on floor with practice and consolidation of the skills using simple apparatus.

Year: 5 **Unit:** 10

Spring 1st half term

Title: Consolidation of rolling

7 x 40 minute lessons

Outline: Developing combinations and variations of entry and exit in rolls and building sequences in combination with previously learned skills.

Year: 5 **Unit:** 11

Spring 2nd half term

Title: Extending transference of weight skill learning

6 x 40 minute lessons

Outline: Consolidation and development of sequences on floor consisting of a travel, balance, roll and jump. Development of a new skill or variation each week (cartwheel, arab-spring and balance skills). Developing variety and competence in the use of apparatus through the performance of the sequence adapted for apparatus. Complete the unit and year with a performance of individual sequences on floor and apparatus using video recording and audience participation.

Year: 6 **Unit:** 12

Autumn 1st half term

Title: Introduction to partner work

7 x 40 minute lessons

Outline: Revision of individual sequence on floor consisting of a travel, balance, roll and jump. Introduction of partner work in the production of a mutually agreed sequence consisting of Gymnastics skills and movements chosen from the two individual sequences. Emphasis on the quality of skills and movements with variety encouraged by reminding the children about the sub-themes they have become familiar with. Use of simple apparatus incorporated into sequence.

Year: 6 **Unit:** 13

Autumn 2nd half term

Title: Developing partner work with apparatus

8 x 40 minute lessons

Outline: Developing the simple partner work into more advanced; working together to produce linked balances, and rolls. Incorporating the use of larger apparatus and setting specific tasks to develop variety and skills repertoire.

Year: 6 **Unit:** 14

Spring 1st half term

Title: Individual skill consolidation and sequence performance

7 x 40 minute lessons

Outline: Select, develop, practise and refine an individual sequence of Gymnastics skills/movements for presentation on floor and on apparatus of pupils' choice. Working in pairs or threes to assist one another in these processes, together with the use of video to review and refine. Complete the unit with a presentation of the individual sequences.

Year: 6 **Unit:** 15

Title: Partner or small group sequence performance

Spring 2nd half term

6 x 40 minute lessons

Outline: Select, develop, practise and refine a pair or small group sequence of Gymnastics skills/movements for presentation on floor. Working with the use of video to review and refine. Complete the unit with a presentation of the group sequences.

Organisational strategies

The organisation of the pupils is based on a class of 32 children split into six colour groups of five or six, of mixed gender and mixed ability. The groups will be selected and changed as required by the teacher during the Key Stage. Groups and equipment will be organised using apparatus layout cards for each Unit of Work throughout the Scheme (see sample Unit of Work Forward Plan on page 66). These will be devised by the teacher in the early stages of the Key Stage and later by the children. Children will be taught to lift, carry, place, check, use and return the equipment that is used during the lessons in a safe and appropriate manner.

Staff, facilities and equipment required

Lessons will be taught by the class teacher with occasional input from students or visiting teachers to the school. All lessons will be taught in the school hall/gymnasium using mats and apparatus layouts as the curriculum content demands. For each Unit of Work utilising apparatus, a plan of the apparatus layout will be included in the Forward Plan. The minimum apparatus required for the Scheme of Work is listed below.

- 12 large mats (2m x 1.5m)
- 6 benches (with hooks)
- Springboard
- Nest of 3 movement tables
- 2 trestle frames
- 2 agility mats (2m long)
- Buck or vaulting horse
- Sectioned bar box
- Sectioned box
- 2 wooden planks with hooks
- Wooden climbing frame
- 6 ropes (wall mounted)
- 1 safety landing mat

Towards the end of the Key Stage, video recording will be used (if local resources are available) to record the children's work as part of their reviewing and learning processes. A camera, recorder and monitor will be required and the children will do the recording.

Safety precautions

Ensure that appropriate dress is worn and that all jewellery is removed before each lesson. Check that pupils understand the reasons for these simple rules. Establish a code of conduct and safety requirements at the beginning of each unit and remind pupils of them regularly throughout the scheme. Check and record any medical conditions that may affect the activity. Carry out an appropriate evaluation of skills competence and group pupils accordingly during the first lesson of each unit. Ensure that codes of behaviour and safety are clearly understood before the pupils begin the units.

Special needs

(It is likely that a wide range of ability levels will be apparent from the beginning of the first unit. Some children may have special needs that require special provision and it may be necessary to enlist knowledgeable advisory support to help with ideas to cater for children with special needs in the early stages. Nevertheless, the teaching content is designed to cater for all ranges of ability. Individual special needs should be assessed at the beginning of the first Unit of Work and specific provision should be outlined in each Unit of Work Forward Plan.)

Record-keeping and assessment procedures [see also Chapter 10]

Record-keeping with reference to teaching content should include:

- a Scheme of Work with recommendations for future planning and content
- a Forward Plan for each Unit of Work within the Scheme of Work, with a summary and recommendations for future teaching content in subsequent Units
- an ongoing record and formative evaluation of individual lesson content, recorded on Forward Plans and used to inform planning and teaching of subsequent lessons
- where necessary and appropriate, individual lesson plans.

Assessment procedures should include:

- ongoing assessment of class progress in relation to aims and objectives and the PoS requirements throughout the teaching units
- ongoing evaluation of each pupil's progress in relation to Unit of Work aims and lesson objectives, using a Unit of Work record and assessment document throughout the teaching units
- school summative records for individual pupils with reference to end-of-Key-Stage statements updated at the end of each year and at the end of each Key Stage.

End-of-Key-Stage statements

'By the end of the key stage, pupils should be able to:

- *plan, practise, improve and remember more complex sequences of movement.*
- *respond safely, alone and with others, to challenging tasks, taking account of levels of skill and understanding.*
- *evaluate how well they and others perform and behave against criteria suggested by the teacher and suggest ways of improving performance.*
- *sustain energetic activity over appropriate periods of time in a range of physical activities and understand the effects of exercise on the body.'*

Evaluation of scheme

(A record of class progress at the end of each Unit of Work should be made to assist with future planning (as described in Chapter 10) and a summary of the whole scheme should be recorded here.)

Recommendations for future planning

(A statement of any recommendations that become apparent during the teaching should be recorded in order to inform future planning and teaching for other cohorts of children.)

5.3 Sample of Gymnastic Activities Unit of Work Forward Plan

The following section is a sample Forward Plan for Unit 10 (shown on page 63) in the Gymnastic Activities Scheme of Work . A similar blank master document which teachers can use for their own curriculum planning can be found in the Appendix (pages 174–177).

Unit of Work Forward Plan

Area of Activity: Gymnastic Activities

Unit: 10 | **Title:** Consolidation of rolling

Spring 1st half term | 7 x 40 minute lessons | **Day:** Tuesday pm

Class: 5ER **Age:** 9/10 | **No. in class:** 14m, 18f | **Teacher:** E Robertson

Previous knowledge and experience

The children have been taught travelling, jumping and landing, balance and introduced to transference of weight. They should have good locomotion and jumping and landing skills, with simple balance skills. The previous Unit of Work covered forward and backward rolls. Mats and large apparatus have been used previously, though organisation and handling skills need to be reinforced. They have used the group system, with the group/apparatus layout and work card. Well behaved class with good understanding of safety and discipline. Sub-themes of direction, levels, pathways, space have been grasped. Little group co-operation and poor quality of movement.

Aims of the Unit of Work

- to consolidate previously learned skills and understanding of Gymnastics
- to develop skills of weight transference, e.g. forward and backward rolls
- to improve the quality of skills/movement performance
- to introduce sequence building and develop this using apparatus
- to increase awareness of others in the group and safe co-operation on apparatus.

CONTENT OUTLINE

LESSON 1 Introduce class to work to be covered in unit. Check on individual work level and understanding of language and quality of movement skills. Review travelling, jumping and landing and balance skills. Simple sequence on floor using these skills. Apparatus work in groups: individual sequences on apparatus; checking on sub-themes and working on quality development. Mainly discovery learning through question and answer approach with some specific tasks.

LESSON 2 Floorwork: recap sequence from last lesson – emphasise quality. Recap methods of forward and backward rolling. Revise specific rolling methods, including side roll, salmon roll and forward roll. Incorporate a roll into the previously built sequence. Apparatus work: use apparatus in presentation of the sequence, including the roll. Emphasise quality of movement performance, and incorporate changes of direction and level.

LESSON 3 Floorwork: recap types of rolls. Develop the quality of forward rolls and introduce variety of entry and exits and when these can be used. Develop rolling from a position of balance. Introduce simple variations of backward roll. Incorporate children's own ideas into their sequences. Apparatus work: add larger apparatus where appropriate. Develop floor sequences on apparatus with emphasis on quality and changes in level, direction, pathway and speed.

LESSON 4 Floorwork: recap types of rolls. Develop the quality of backward rolls and introduce variety of entry and exits that can be used in all types of rolling. Consolidate rolling from a position of balance. Incorporate children's own ideas into their sequences. Apparatus work: develop sequences on apparatus with emphasis on quality of performance and introduce the 'free use system' for using apparatus.

LESSON 5 Floorwork: recap on sequence from last lesson – emphasise quality and allow specific demonstration of the performance. Highlight aspects of improved performance, variety and creativity. Apparatus work: develop 'free use system' for using apparatus. Performance of sequences on apparatus with emphasis on quality of performance and variety of ideas. If possible, use parent with video camera to record the children's sequences on floor.

LESSON 6 Review highlights of edited video (if available) to show examples of good quality work and originality. Floorwork: allow children to work on the presentation of their floor sequences, having seen the video. Apparatus work: perform enhanced floor sequences on the apparatus and film the work once again. Plan for and practise performance presentation of sequence on apparatus in the final lesson of the unit.

LESSON 7 Review highlights of edited video (if available) to show examples of good quality work and originality using apparatus. Allow children time to practise their sequences, (with guidance), for presentation on floor and apparatus. Presentation of sequences on apparatus, one group at a time, and if possible video the performance for review back in classroom. Edit video for record-keeping and assessment purposes at a later date.

Organisational strategies

Children change in classroom, walk to hall with pumps on and take them off in hall. Class splits into six groups of five or six with group positions during the first lesson, once ability has been assessed in hall. Apparatus work and layout cards to be used and given to group leaders. Hair band and grips box and valuables box will be ready for use. Try to organise a helper/parent for videoing and book video camera and player for sessions (if available).

Facilities and equipment required

Hall/gymnasium.

Apparatus: twelve mats for mat work (two piles of six at each end of the hall), five benches (positioned round hall), two planks, three tiered stacking tables (positioned in hall), springboard, two trestles and sectioned bar box (split and positioned round hall). Video camera, tape and player.

Safety precautions

Dress – t-shirt and shorts or leotard, bare feet or light indoor pumps. No jewellery. Hair tied back. Check hall and apparatus are safe and make apparatus ready. Check on medical problems. Remind class about rules of behaviour and safety, especially with apparatus handling. Take first-aid kit.

Special needs provision

(This section should be used to help plan and record provision for children with special educational needs in Gymnastics. This may include catering for children with physical and mental disabilities, children with emotional difficulties and the physically gifted. Four examples are given below.) →

- One child (Peter) with hearing impairment but can lip read – make sure he can see you and speak clearly. He is also good at copying other children to interpret the task but may need some individual reinforcement.
- One child (Darren) with learning difficulties who can be disruptive but responds well in P.E. if interested and motivated. Responds well to praise but tends to seek attention if firm control is not exercised.
- One child (Joanne) with an artificial leg. Shy about P.E. but is very able and copes with most tasks well. Some encouragement needed but is aware of own capabilities and understands well about safety. Keeps artificial leg on in lessons and wears tracksuit bottoms.
- Two children (Sarah and Leela) are members of a local artistic gymnastics club and have an advanced level of skill. It is essential that they understand what skills are appropriate for school lessons and that they should not try to perform new skills that they are learning at the club. They are excellent demonstrators of simple skills, performed well, and they have good creative ideas which are helpful for other children. Care should be taken not to over-emphasise their talents in a way that might undermine the confidence of the rest of the class.

Equipment and group positions

The plan on the right can be used to make cards showing group apparatus positions, and a group leader may be appointed to supervise the positioning of apparatus by the rest of the group. The names of group members can also be recorded if they are to remain the same for the whole unit.

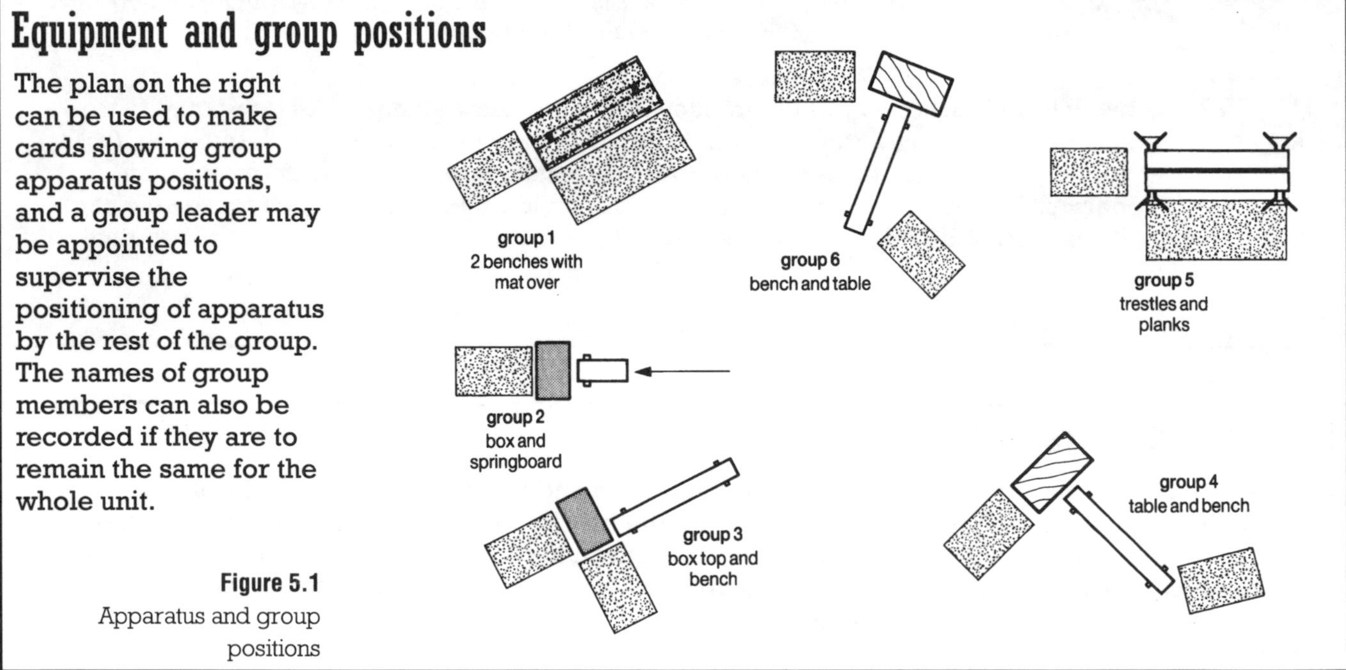

Figure 5.1
Apparatus and group positions

Evaluation of lessons

(The date should be entered beside the lesson number once the lesson has been taught. If individual lesson plans are not used by teachers, a highlighter pen can be used to indicate the work that has been covered in each lesson in case adjustment decisions need to be made. This records what is actually taught relative to what was planned.

Notes should be made in this section each week, with recommendations for future lessons. This is useful for future planning and for record-keeping purposes.)

Summary and recommendations for next unit

(A record of class progress at the end of the Unit of Work should be made to assist with future planning. Individual pupil progress should also be recorded at appropriate times using the method described in Chapter 10.)

5.4 Sample Lesson Plan

A sample plan for Lesson 1 in the above Unit of Work, showing details of tasks and activities, corresponding teaching points and the organisation of children, apparatus and space, has been included on the following pages. Experienced teachers may feel this level of planning is not necessary and that they can work from the lesson outlines in the Forward Plan. Some teachers may find that the children have a better learning experience if they plan individual lessons in the detail shown.

Gymnastic Activities Lesson Plan (1)

Key Stage 2 **Unit of Work 10: Consolidation of rolling**

Lesson number in unit: 1	**Date:** Tuesday 8 February 1994
Time: 2.10 – 2.50pm	**Length of lesson:** 40 mins
Class: 5ER **Age:** 9/10	**Teacher:** E Robertson
No. in class: 14m, 18f	**Venue:** School Hall

Lesson objectives

(S = social, E = emotional, C=cognitive, P = physical)

S: to encourage the pupils to work co-operatively using space and apparatus
E: to provide pupils with an enjoyable and successful learning experience
C: to understand the process of developing a sequence in gymnastics
P: to perform a sequence of movments on the floor and apparatus incorporating a travel, balance and jump with good quality.

Facilities and equipment

Hall/gymnasium
Twelve mats for mat work (two piles of six at each end of the hall)
Five benches (positioned round hall)
Two planks, three tiered stacking tables (positioned in hall)
Springboard
Two trestles
Sectioned bar box and box top (positioned round hall)

Lesson evaluation

Gymnastic Activities Lesson Plan (2)

Phase	Tasks/activities	Teaching points/coaching feedback	Organisation of pupils and apparatus
Preparation	Check hall/apparatus. Check dress, jewellery and hair.	Explain behaviour expected and reasons for safety.	Position mats and apparatus round hall and return to storage positions at end.
Introduction Warm-up (5 mins)	Introduce work to be covered in unit. Travelling round hall using feet. Travelling using any body parts.	Ask questions about previous work covered. Use of space; levels; directions.	Class sitting in a space. Individually about the hall using space.
Floorwork (12 mins)	Sequence of 3 movements: 1 feet, 1 hands and feet and 1 no feet Review different types of jumps Choose a balance on 1 or 2 parts. Sequence of travel, balance and jump.	Question and answer method to explain what a sequence is. Emphasise smooth linkage and flow from one movement to another. Remind about good landings. Control and stillness for 2-3 seconds. Smoothness and control emphasising 'quality'.	Individually about the hall using space. About the room then in own space. About the room.
Apparatus (18 mins)	Split class into 6 groups and sit in group positions as per plan. Working on own apparatus develop/adapt sequence to use the apparatus. Groups move round one apparatus place and continue working on sequence when told. Demonstration of group work to end.	Remind about safety and group co-operation when taking out the apparatus. Good use of direction and pathways of approach Emphasise safe landings off apparatus – control and flow of movement. Explain the safety factors. Look for control and good linking of movements.	Split into mixed gender and mixed ability groups and allocate positions with leader and cards. Leader to supervise apparatus handling and placement. All children working – no queuing. Stop and sit down in group place. Stand and walk in line to next apparatus position. Other children sit off the mats and apparatus.
Conclusion (5 mins)	Return to original group positions and put apparatus back where it came from with leader supervision – when apparatus away find a space and practise a 1 leg balance for control. Standing in a space with good posture. Return class to classroom and change.	Good teamwork as a group – being sensible. Use a good space where your apparatus was. Don't get in anybody's way. Debrief lesson work with question and answer. Check posture and breathing.	Move as before; close supervision if any group not safe and sensible. Assist with the specific positioning of larger apparatus. Line up at door in groups and walk back to class.

5.5 Gymnastic Activities teaching content

The teaching content of the Gymnastic Activities curriculum can be divided into four Skill Themes. Each theme groups together skills that have a common quality of movement. The themes are:

- travelling
- jumping and landing
- balancing
- transference of weight.

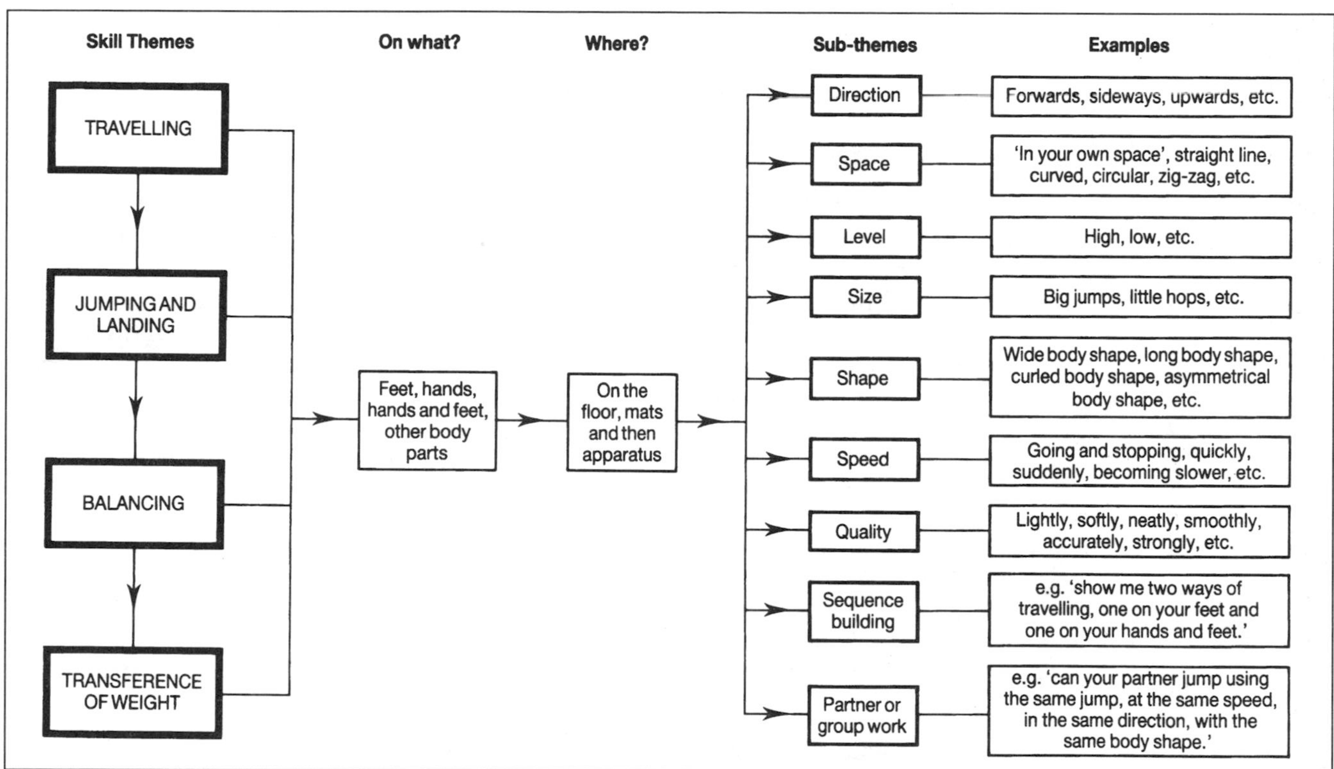

Figure 5.2
Gymnastic Activities Skill Themes

Fundamentally, the teaching content involves the progressive learning and development of a range of Gymnastics skills, both within each of the themes and from one theme to the next. A flow chart illustrating the rationale, progression and content of the themes is shown in figure 5.2. The children's range of skills and their movement vocabulary are increased and developed through the progressive introduction of a variety of dimensions of movement: the 'sub-themes' shown in the flow chart. The following sections provide descriptions of the Gymnastics skill elements of each of the themes. Where it is considered appropriate, the progressions and teaching points associated with the skills have been included to assist teachers towards their safe and effective presentation.

Travelling

The 'travelling' theme is designed as the first theme to be taught and is most suitable for younger children. The content introduces basic movement skills that allow the performer to travel about the gymnasium while developing the concept of body control. These are pre-requisites for progression to more advanced Gymnastics skills. The movement skills included in this theme are:

- walking
- running
- simple jumping

- skipping
- hopping
- sliding
- simple rolling
- swinging.

These skills should be explored progressively by following the pathway indicated in figure 5.2. A suggested method of presenting the teaching content to children is shown in table 5.1 on the following pages. Sections of the content can be used as the basis for lesson planning. The content will provide children with a repertoire of basic movement skills that will allow progressive development through Key Stage 2, building on the skills contained in the 'travelling theme'. The curriculum content should be presented so that pupils have opportunities to respond creatively, and should allow time to practise and consolidate skills. If the content of the 'travelling' theme is not taught at Key Stage 1, it is essential that it constitutes the beginning of the Key Stage 2 Gymnastics curriculum.

The content of this theme introduces children to the basic movement skills, using different body parts, about the floor space, on mats and on apparatus. They learn to control their bodies in the Gymnastics environment and become familiar with the language of gymnastic movement. Movement concepts within 'sub-themes' are developed as an integral part of the theme and this increases the skill repertoire of the children at their own pace. The method of presentation (an appropriate mixture of exploration and direct teaching) allows much scope for creativity and also encourages skill learning at individual ability levels. Apparatus handling skills are developed as the children work through the theme content.

It is important to stress the safety aspect of apparatus use to the children. A variety of apparatus layouts can be used, but try to have the same layout for a series of lessons so that the children know where their apparatus goes. Once the children are more experienced you may be able to allow the children to design, with guidance, their own apparatus layouts. (This is a nice cross-curricular aspect to their P.E. work.)

Many basic skills introduced in this theme are further developed in the other themes and this is indicated where appropriate in the progressions. It is intended that the 'travelling' theme is the first to be covered in a Scheme of Work, followed by the 'jumping and landing' theme, the 'balance' theme and then the 'transference of weight' theme. However, it may be necessary from time to time to 'dip into' the other themes to ensure a skill is being performed safely. Once progression to another theme has occurred it will be necessary to continue to practise the skills learned previously, as these will continue to be used as progression through the Scheme of Work takes place. This is particularly valid when the sub-theme of 'sequence building' is being developed.

Table 5.1 A GUIDE TO TEACHING TRAVELLING SKILLS

Movement task with progressions	Sub tasks (questions to ask the children)	Teaching points that can be given	Associated sub-theme	Where?
Travelling using feet a) Walking (on flat feet, on balls of feet, on heels, with legs straight, with knees bent).	**A mixture of direct teaching and exploration** Can you walk all about the room on your feet? What parts of your feet can you walk on? Can you walk without your heels on the floor? Can you walk with your toes off the floor? Can you walk with your knees bent? Can you take little steps? Big steps? What directions can you go in – forwards, backwards, sideways? Are you looking where you are going?	**Demonstrate where appropriate** Time will need to be spent on using space well. If you have small indidividual mats these can be used to help the children use space. 'Move around your mat', 'move around all the mats', 'puddle game'. Emphasise good posture with flat back, bottom tucked under and tummy pulled in. Emphasise use of language – direction. Are they looking for space and moving into it?	Space Level (high) Level (low) Size Direction	About the room (with very young children begin working 'in own space' before they move about the room).
b) Other ways of travelling, e.g. running, hopping, skipping, jumping. (Jumping is developed in 'Jumping and Landing' theme.)	Show me other ways of moving about the room on your feet! Can you run without touching anyone else or a mat? Can you jump? Can you skip? Can you hop? Can you do it lightly and quietly? (Use individual mats if you have them – move over, round, across, along.)	Allow children to demonstrate their way. Other children will learn by watching. Begin slowly until they can use space well and ensure they can stop on command. Encourage children to move on the 'balls' of their feet. Some young children will find hopping and skipping difficult but will learn with time and practice.	Quality	
c) Linking movements together, e.g. walking then jumping.	Choose two ways to move – can you do the first way and then the second way when I say change?	It may be necessary to stipulate the ways to begin with before giving free choice.	Sequence building	
Travelling using feet and hands Explore ways of travelling: a) Walking.	**Emphasis should be on exploration with direction where necessary through questioning** Show me ways of travelling using your hands and feet! Can you walk? Forwards, backwards, sideways? Can you move your hands first then your feet? What shapes do you make? Can you go with your tummy up? Can you go with your back up? Can you go tummy up, then back up, then tummy up? How did you do it?	If necessary, do 'body part' identification. Ensure they watch where they are going. Like a caterpillar. Stretched then curled – big then small. Twisting and/or turning.	Direction Shape and size Shape	In own space then about the room. (Use little mats if you have them.)
b) Jumping (developed in 'transference of weight' theme).	Can you jump? Can you go in other directions? Can you jump lightly and quietly? Big jumps, little jumps? Can you jump with your feet together, then apart, then together? What animals jump and how?	Encourage children to use the balls of their feet when they are moving. Make sure they use flat hands on floor. Rabbit, frog, kangaroo.	Size Shape Quality and size	
c) Others, e.g. hopping, running.	Try any other way that you can think of/ Can you go in different pathways: curved, zig-zag?	If they choose running make sure it is with control. Explain the language used.	Space	

Table 5.1 cont

Movement task with progressions	Sub-tasks (questions to ask the children)	Teaching points that can be given	Associated sub-theme	Where?
Travelling using other body parts a) Hands and others, e.g. knees, tummy, bottom	What part of your body can you use to move about the room? Change direction? Make pathways? What kinds of movements can you do? Can you slide?	Remind the children about the 'sub-themes' that they have used earlier.	Direction and space	About the room
b) Feet and others, e.g. bottom	Can you move without using your hands? How did you do it? What parts did you use?			
c) Others, e.g. tummy and back (developed in 'transference of weight' theme)	Can you move without using your hands or feet? How did you do it? What do you call the movement?	Rolling sideways, shuffling.		

Mats and apparatus can now be used so that the children learn to travel round, towards and away from, under and over, onto and off, along and across the apparatus using the methods of travelling learned on the floor. Specific tasks can be set by the teacher such as, 'travel without touching the apparatus' or 'use your hands and feet on the floor but only your hands on the mats or apparatus'.
At this stage the children should learn that the floor is the biggest piece of apparatus in the room. Much emphasis should be placed on understanding the language being used. Apparatus such as benches, tables, box tops, planks (at a low level) and trestles can be used. The children can begin to learn how to handle apparatus. Begin with mats and benches, and each week teach them how to handle another piece (see section on apparatus handling and organisation in Chapter 8). Below are some ideas for work that can be set on apparatus.

Movement task with progressions	Sub-tasks (questions to ask the children)	Notes for teachers and teaching points that can be given	Associated sub-theme	Suggested apparatus
Travelling using feet a) Without touching apparatus, e.g. round, towards, away from, under, etc.	Show me ways of travelling about the room on your feet without touching the apparatus; going round, under, etc. Can you travel in different directions? Can you change the way you are moving; e.g. jumping then hopping; skipping then running? Can you move up high/down low?	Encourage good use of space. Make sure the children fulfil the task set. Make sure they watch where they are going. Emphasise control and good quality, i.e. lightly, quietly.	Space Direction Sequence building Quality Level	Mats, benches, tables, box top, trestles and planks. All at very low height.
b) Going over, along, away from, etc, touching with feet only.	When you come to a piece of apparatus use your feet to travel along, onto, off and over the apparatus while moving about the room.	Ensure that the children use the floor space around and between the apparatus effectively.	Space	
	Can you step onto the apparatus and jump off? Show me a way of jumping over or onto a bench or mat. Can you think of another way? Can you do it lightly and quietly?	Observe the children and set tasks that they will be able to fulfil. If they are very young they may not be able to jump over, only onto and off.	Quality	

Table 5.1 cont

Movement task with progressions	Sub tasks (questions to ask the children)	Notes for teachers and teaching points that can be given	Associated sub-theme	Suggested apparatus
Touching with specific parts only	Give direction where necessary.	Choose some children to demonstrate at times.		
a) Travelling about the room using feet (running, hopping, skipping, jumping) and using hands only on the apparatus.	Move round, towards and away from the apparatus in different ways using your feet and use only your hands on the apparatus.	Ensure that children are thinking about what they have done during floorwork and applying it on apparatus.		Mats, benches, tables, box top, trestles and planks. Some at low and some at medium level.
	Have you remembered about different directions, levels?	This should be becoming automatic by now.	Direction	
	Can you put your hands on the apparatus and jump your feet over the apparatus?	Make sure hands are flat on apparatus.		
	Can you use one hand then the other?	Developed in 'transference of weight' theme.		
	Can you travel along, or round the apparatus with your hands on the apparatus and your feet on the floor?			
b) Travelling about the room using hands and feet (walking, jumping, turning, etc) and using hands only on the apparatus.	Similar sub-tasks as above and remind children about sub-themes of direction, levels, using space well, etc. You may want to specify the method of travel on floor if children need to practise a skill, then change it or then allow a free choice. Depends on the age and ability.	Ask children if they remember the different ways of moving using hands and feet. Allow class to watch groups of children working. They will get ideas and teaching points can be emphasised.		Planks and some benches can be hooked into trestles, tables and wall bars if secure.
c) Other combinations.	How can you move about the room using your feet on the floor and your hands and feet on the apparatus? Can you move about the room and the apparatus without using your feet? What body parts do you use? What kind of movements can you use?	Give children ideas of what to watch for when observing others working. Use question and answer technique to encourage children to think about what they and others are doing, e.g. 'what movements can you see?', 'did you see anyone moving backwards?', 'what body shapes can you see when they move?'	Quality	
	How do you get onto and off the apparatus? Can you move without using your hands or your feet?		Direction Shape	

Jumping and landing

This is designed as the second theme to be taught. The content develops simple jumping skills learned in the 'travelling' theme, by progressing to the correct techniques of the five basic jumps on feet, and explores the variety of methods of jumping using hands and feet on floor, mats and apparatus.

THE FIVE BASIC JUMPS

Figure 5.3
Two feet to two feet

Figure 5.4
Two feet to one foot

Figure 5.5
One foot to two feet

Figure 5.6
One foot to the same foot

Figure 5.7
One foot to the other foot – a stag leap

These jumps and their many combinations can be explored progressively through the sub-themes. For example, jumping on hands and feet to form a sequence of four jumps about the room, moving forwards and backwards while changing the shape of the body. It is not possible to list all the potential combinations of movements, but if you use figure 5.2 as a basis for development the pupils will acquire a wide repertoire of quality Gymnastics skills that can be developed towards advanced skills that they will learn at a later stage.

Some examples of jumping skills with developments using the sub-themes are:

- Two feet to two feet, figure 5.8 (a), (b) and (c).

Figure 5.8
(a) in second position, with half turn making a tuck shape

(b) in first position, with quarter turn making a star shape backwards

(c) off a box top, making a piked shape

- Two feet to one foot then the other foot (Figure 5.9) – a hurdle step lunge (which is used in many floor skills that use feet and hands).

Figure 5.9
a hurdle step lunge

Some more examples where a recognised skill is identified by a name are listed below.

Figure 5.10
a hurdle step onto a bench with a stetch jump off

- The vault hurdle step: a short run into a jump onto two feet (which can be performed onto a bench), which can be followed by a variety of jumps.

- The hurdle step can be linked in sequence with a jump onto hands and feet and developed into:

Figure 5.11(a)
a squat on, jump off vault performed on a bench

Figure 5.11(b)
a squat on, jump off vault performed on a box top

Figure 5.11(c)
a squat on, jump off vault performed on a springboard and sectioned box

Safe, progressive development during Key Stage 2 and Key Stage 3 towards vaulting and tumbling skills depends on the early acquisition and consolidation of jumping and landing skills.

Balancing

The content of this theme is concerned less with movement in space and more with stationary skills that show the body in still and balanced positions. It is not suggested that balance skills should always be taught in isolation from the skills in the other themes. However, the skills within this theme are sufficiently important and distinct within the Gymnastics curriculum to merit classification within their own theme, and progressive teaching of these skills should occur. They can be presented as a contrast to the skills and movement qualities acquired in the 'travelling' and 'jumping and landing' themes.

Study of figure 5.2 shows that balancing can use many parts of the body as a base. Children can be encouraged to develop creativity in exploring the many possibilities for showing balance by the teacher asking them to select combinations of body parts. To help with this, terminology such as *'points'* or small parts (feet, hands, knees, and elbows) and *'patches'* or large parts (shoulders, back, stomach, etc) can be used when setting tasks or activities for the children to explore. Care should always be taken to ensure that vulnerable parts of the anatomy are not subjected to stress that could cause short- or long-term injury. As a specific example, headstands are not recommended. If in doubt, leave it out.

Some examples of recognised balance positions and skills are:

- On a patch or large part.

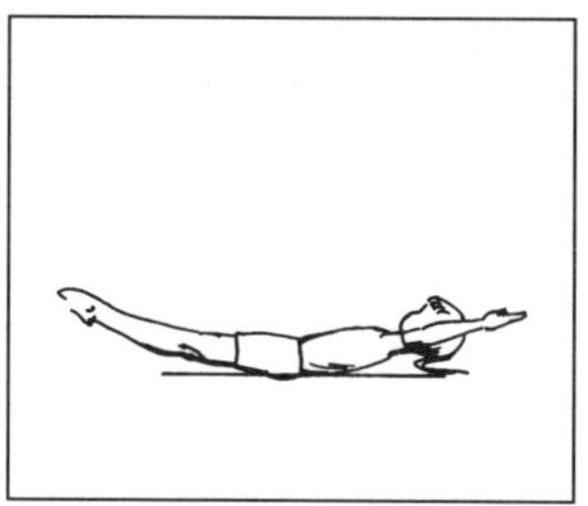

Figure 5.12
A dish shape

Figure 5.13
An arch shape

Figure 5.14
Piked V-sit

Figure 5.15
A shoulder stand

Figure 5.16
Knee and foot scale

- On one point.

Figure 5.17
Side scale

Figure 5.18
Arabesque

Figure 5.19
Y balance

- On more than one point.

Figure 5.20
Piked straddle stand

Figure 5.21
Japanese handstand

Figure 5.22
A 'bunny' handstand

Figure 5.23
Front support

Figure 5.24
Back support

Figure 5.25
Side support

There are many variations that can be explored, acquired and practised by working progressively through the flow chart in figure 5.2. An example of some variations of the shoulder stand are:

- The shoulder stand.

d

Figure 5.26
Variations of the shoulder stand (a) straddled (b) tucked (c) in splits (d) one leg bent, one leg straight (e) on a bench (with the above variations) (f) balancing on a partner, etc.

HANDSTAND

Children experience a great deal of satisfaction from achieving success in the performance of a handstand, and it is important that it is taught safely. It is an example of a more advanced balance skill and it may be useful to show the progressions that should be used to teach this skill.

Pre-requisites: Hold a dish shape and an arched shape lying on the floor. Be comfortable in an inverted position and take whole body weight on straight arms, i.e. a 'bunny' handstand.

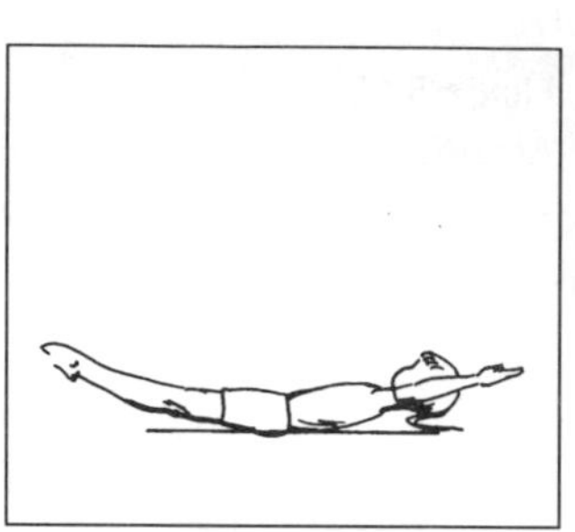

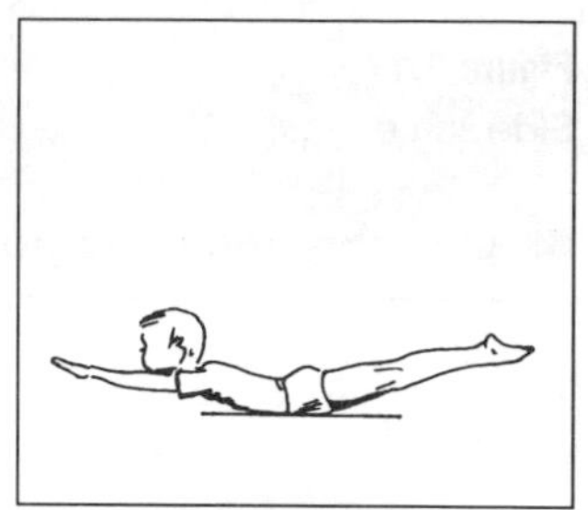

Figure 5.27 Handstand

(a) a dish shape (b) an arch shape (c) a 'bunny' handstand

Progressions	Teaching points
1. Lie on back in straight shape.	arms above head; push your back against floor
2. Lie on tummy in straight shape.	tighten all your muscles and stretch into a long shape
3. Practise 'bunny' jumps with straight arms, arms shoulder width apart.	do it gently and under control; keep looking at your hands
4. Perform 'bunny' handstand with support from a partner.	partner supports round hips; don't let them fall over
5. Jump to a 'bunny' handstand without support from a partner.	only do it when you feel controlled – and do it slowly
6. Perform a 'bunny' handstand with support from two partners and straighten your legs.	keep your arms straight and look at your hands straighten your legs slowly
7. Step into handstand with support from two partners and step down again. (Partners support round hips and legs.)	reach forward with your hands; hands shoulder width apart; keep your body straight and look at your hands
8. Step into handstand with one partner supporting round thighs and step down again	see if you can keep your legs straight and balance; reach up tall and stretch your shoulders
9. Practise on a mat doing a handstand against the wall – tummy against the wall (for advanced children only).	try to get your hands and chest as close to the wall as possible; come down slowly and carefully

Supporting technique To support the 'bunny' handstand, kneel to the side of where the gymnast is going to put his/her hands down. Put one hand round the back and the other on the hip closest to you. Be ready to push the gymnast back in the direction she or he came from. To support the handstand, stand to the side and just in front of where the child is going to put his/her hands down. Be ready early and support round the hips and thighs as she or he comes up. Be ready to push back in the direction she or he came from. Once she or he is well controlled you can support round the thighs. Make sure legs don't come over too far and be ready to push him/her gently back onto his/her feet.

Figure 5.28
Handstand progressions and supports

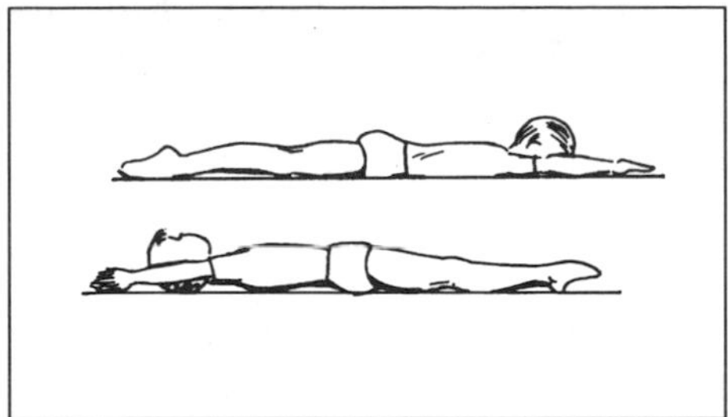
Progressions 1 and 2

Progression 3

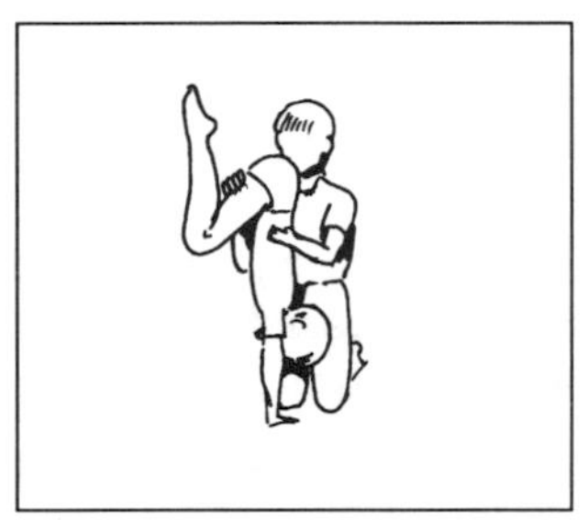
Progression 4

Progression 5

Progession 8

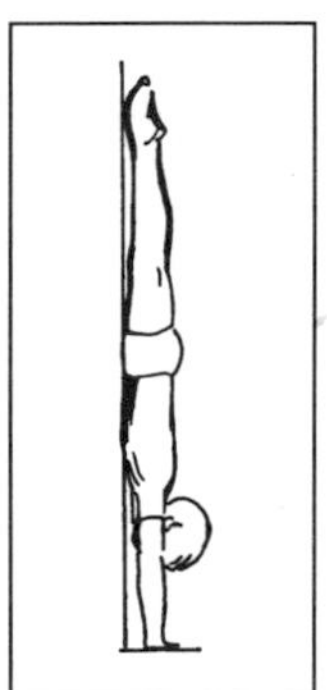
Progression 9

The content is appropriate for Key Stage 1 and 2 pupils, and the more advanced skills can be developed through a child's Gymnastics experience. Once balance skills have been acquired and practised, simple work on moving in and out of balances and linking balances together to make sequences is a natural development of the theme. Children will also create balances of their own in response to open-ended tasks set by the teacher. Taken to a higher level these can lead to the Gymnastics form of Sports Acrobatics.

Transference of weight

The content of this theme is concerned with movements or skills that involve literally transferring weight from one part of the body to another. Some of these actions are simple, e.g. rocking and bunny hopping, and are likely to have been explored in the 'travelling' theme. However, development of these basic actions through this theme will lead towards what must be considered more advanced Gymnastics skills.

The basic Gymnastics skills within this theme that could be taught to primary children are shown on the following pages. Because of the nature of these skills they are more difficult to perform. If they are to be taught successfully and safely it is essential that the correct progressions and associated teaching points are understood. To assist with this, a description of the correct progressions for teaching the more advanced skills is presented.

Some children may not be capable of achieving all the progressions that have been included (perhaps because they lack the necessary body strength or they have special educational needs in Physical Education). This should be assessed not as a failure but as an achievement of the child's individual level of potential in that skill. Other children will be able to work through the progressions very quickly and with ease. All children should be encouraged to perform the progressions with good quality of movement (pointed toes, extended ankles, straight legs, body in tension, etc), showing good starting and finishing positions.

To assist teachers to recognise when children are ready to progress to each skill a list of pre-requisites is provided for each. Many of these pre-requisites are skills and body positions which have been shown earlier. If the children cannot perform these it is not safe to teach the more advanced skill and time should first be spent teaching the pre-requisites. Correct supporting techniques for each skill are also described where these are necessary for safe practice. It is perfectly acceptable to teach the children to support one another working in pairs and threes, but it is vital that they understand their responsibility. A demonstration by the teacher of the correct and safe supporting technique is often very helpful. Diagrams are provided where this is thought useful.

SALMON ROLL

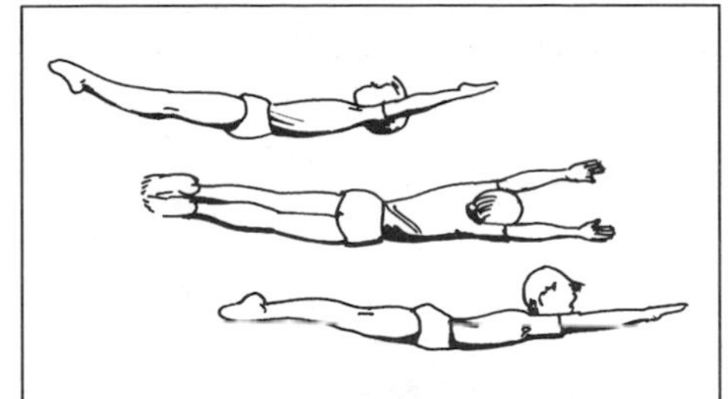

Figure 5.29
Salmon roll

Pre-requisites: Hold a dish shape and an arched shape lying on the floor.

Progressions	Teaching points
1. Show and hold a dish shape lying on the floor on the back.	tight tummy and bottom muscles; arms extended above head
2. Show and hold an arched shape in the prone position on the front.	tight bottom and leg muscles; extend at the hips; arms extended through shoulders
3. Lying on the side, change the body shape from a dish shape to an arched shape three times.	as above
4. From a straight position on the floor move to the dish shape, and at the same time roll onto the front arriving in an arched position.	keep body in tension and make a smooth change from one shape to another; swing the arms to help change position

SIDE ROLL

Figure 5.30
Side roll

Pre-requisites: Be comfortable in straddle sit with straight legs and hold a piked, straddled shoulder stand.

Progressions	Teaching points
1. Sitting in straddle sit, fold forward to place chest/stomach onto the thigh.	keep the legs straight and try to fold from the waist
2. Lying on the back, straddle legs and, holding onto the legs behind the knees, rock from side to side.	try to round the shoulders and roll smoothly from side to side
3. From straddle sit fold forward as in 1 above, sweep the trunk in a circular motion rolling sideways onto the shoulder, across the back, onto the other shoulder and return to straddle sit facing the other way.	keep the rolling action smooth by pulling on the back of the knees with the arms bent

Supporting technique To support the side roll stand behind the gymnast. Assistance to roll can be given by gently helping with the fold forward, and assisting gymnast to initiate the sideways movement by pushing on the back and then the legs.

FORWARD ROLL

Figure 5.31
Forward roll

Pre-requisites: Be comfortable in an inverted position, i.e. in straddle stand, hands on the ground between the feet and looking through the legs; hold a tucked sitting position; hold a good front support position; take whole body weight on straight arms in a 'bunny' handstand.

Progressions	Teaching points
1. Rocking back and forward on back.	round back; chin on chest; 'hug' knees
2. Shoulder stand.	arms above head on ground; tight tummy; push toes to ceiling
3. Rock back to shoulder stand.	
4. Shoulder stand rock forward to squat stand.	start roll by swinging with straight legs; swing arms forward and reach forward
5. From standing, bend knees to squat, arms out in front, place hands on floor and jump to bent leg handstand (a'bunny' handstand).	good standing posture, bend knees and keep back round; place hands shoulder width apart; keep arms straight; keep looking at ground in front of hands
6. From front support position, partner lifts the legs at the knees and assists the performer to roll onto the shoulders under control towards the shoulder stand position.	check strong front support; tuck head in with chin on chest; slowly lift legs as gymnast bends arms to place shoulders onto the ground
7. Link together stages 5, 6 and 4 in that order with the assistance of a partner	ensure correct posture and control throughout; partner assists responsibly
8. Perform the entire skill, ending the roll in a standing posture.	head up; good body positions and posture throughout

Supporting technique Support can be given at various stages, and since the skill is relatively slow, moving support is not difficult. When supporting the forward roll always stand or kneel at the side of the gymnast. Make sure that you stand close enough so that you are working with bent arms. If you are at arm's length you do not have control and are unlikely to be able to assist if something goes wrong.

Figure 5.32
Forward roll progression

Progression 1

Progression 2

Progression 3

Progression 4

Progression 5

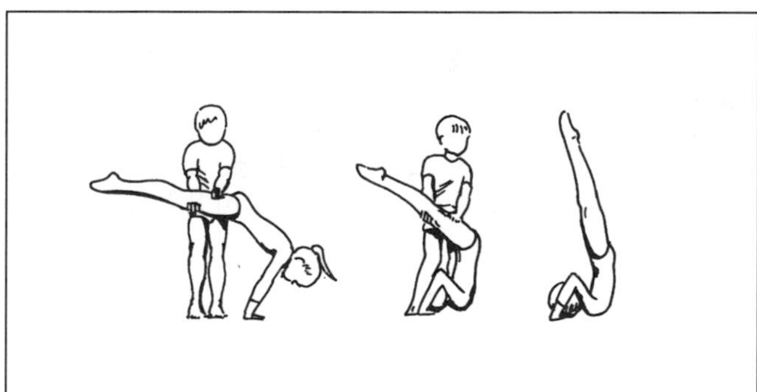
Progression 6

BACKWARD ROLL

Figure 5.33
Backward roll

Pre-requisites: Be comfortable in an inverted position, i.e. 'bunny' handstand; hold a tucked sitting position; hold a good front support position and do a press-up (this is needed for the push phase and is therefore very important); take whole body weight on straight arms.

Progressions	Teaching points
1. Rocking back and forward on back.	round back; chin on chest; 'hug' knees
2. Tucked shoulder stand.	arms bent and palms flat on ground behind the shoulders; tight tummy; round back and legs bent at knee
3. From sitting, rock back to tucked shoulder stand under control, with hands on ground by ears, three times.	roll slowly to stay under control; keep chin on chest; hands flat on ground; elbows pointing to ceiling
4. From standing, bend knees to squat, arms bent to place hands by ears, roll back to tucked shoulder stand under control.	good standing posture, bend knees and keep back round; place hands shoulder width apart; keep arms straight; keep looking at ground
5. As above down a slope (springboard), with partner assisting to lift the hips and gently place the feet on the floor.	push strongly with the hands to lift the hips; keep the back round and the head tucked in
6. As above without the slope and finish in a good standing posture.	ensure correct posture and control throughout; partner assists responsibly
7. Perform the entire skill and end the roll in a standing posture.	head up; good body positions and posture throughout

Supporting technique The most useful supporting technique for the backward roll ensures that the head is tucked in during stage 6 above. The supporter should place the hand on the back of the neck to make sure that the head is kept tucked in as the gymnast rolls backwards. Assistance can also be given by lifting the hips from the side as the roll over occurs in stage 5.

Figure 5.34

Backward roll progressions and supporting techniques

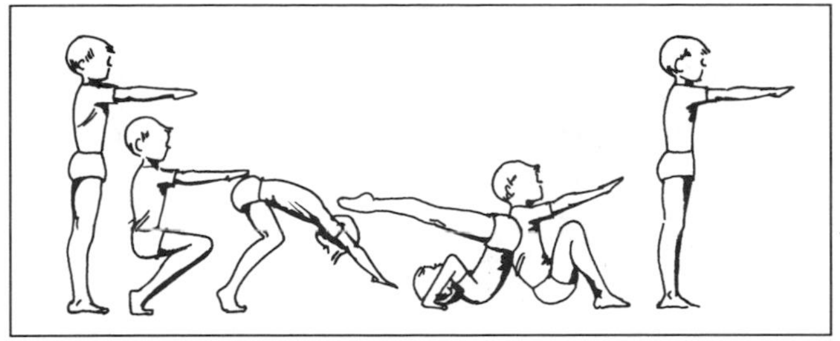

Progression 1

Progression 2

Progression 3

Progression 4

Progression 5

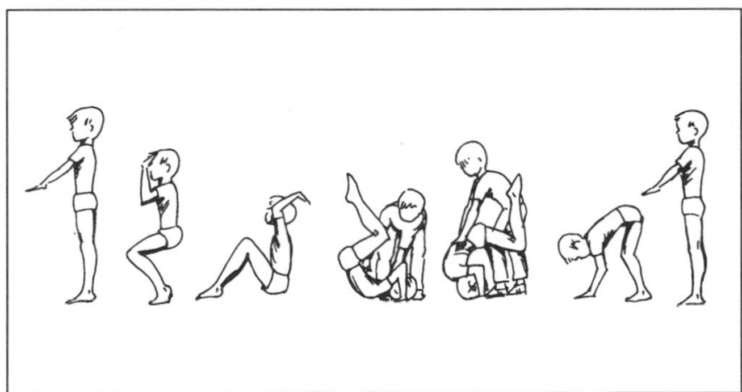

Progression 7 with support technique

CARTWHEEL

Figure 5.35
Cartwheel

Pre-requisites: Hold a straddle stand with the back flat and the body tight; take whole body weight on straight arms in 'bunny' handstand.

Progressions	Teaching points
1 Perform a 'bunny jump' moving the feet sideways.	keep arms straight and back flat; look at the hands throughout
2. Perform a mini-cartwheel using a 'pond' with the sequence foot–hand–hand–foot.	try to put hands and feet in a straight line
3. Jump across a bench: two hands on the bench, take-off from one foot and land on the far side of the bench with the other foot.	push strongly off the ground with the front leg and swing the back leg over the bench; kick legs higher as confidence grows
4. Cartwheel over a box top or down a springboard using the sequence foot–hand–hand–foot with support.	place one hand then the other; start with a good lunge position with front knee bent to help the push; keep body straight
5. As above but extend the legs through the split handstand.	start pushing hard with the arms; finish in a good standing posture
6. Progress to cartwheeling on the floor, with support, then without support.	work with a little speed to help keep the body straight

Supporting technique To support the cartwheel, stand at the back of the gymnast. As she steps into the cartwheel, place your nearest hand onto the gymnast's leading hip; as the cartwheel rotates towards the straddled handstand place your other hand on the other hip and allow your arms to cross as you assist the gymnast to stand. You must stand close to the gymnast, put the first hand on the hip early, and move with her during the cartwheel.

Figure 5.36
Cartwheel progressions and supporting technique

Progression 1

Progression 2

Progression 3

Progression 4

Progression 5

Progression 6

ARAB SPRING

Figure 5.37
Arab spring (or round-off): a cartwheel with quarter turn and legs coming together

Pre-requisites: A hurdle step (see page 77, Figure 5.9); a good cartwheel with a straight body.

Progressions	Teaching points
1. Cartwheel on the floor, starting facing forward and ending facing backwards with feet together.	working with a little speed helps keep the body straight; land one foot then bring theother foot in to meet
2. Cartwheel with quarter turn to fall flat on to a safety mat.	keep a tight, straight body shape; good lunge position into the cartwheel and make the turn with the whole body
3. Cartwheel off a small platform to finish facing the platform.	
4. Perform a 'donkey kick' off a box top to stand, first with support then without.	with the legs bent and hips and shoulders extended, snap the feet to the floor and thrust off the hands
5. As above, but join the feet together early in handstand and thrust off with the hands to snap to a standing position facing the platform.	concentrate on the correct positioning of the hands and feet, and keeping the body straight in the snap-up position to stand
6. Combine stages 4 and 5 together down a springboard or on the floor.	concentrate on keepingbody tension and pushing with the legs to gain momentum and speed
7. Practise the whole skill along a line marked on the floor, finishing the skill with a stretch jump at the end.	

Supporting technique The arab spring requires support in the later stages of the skill as the most difficult part is the 'snap-up' at the end. This is best supported from the handstand phase onwards using the nearest hand on the chest and the other on the back. Make sure the gymnast does not fall backwards at the end. Supporting practice is possible during the 'donkey kick' stage. This also prevents over-rotation which can cause the gymnast to fall backwards.

Figure 5.38
Progression and supporting technique

Progression 1

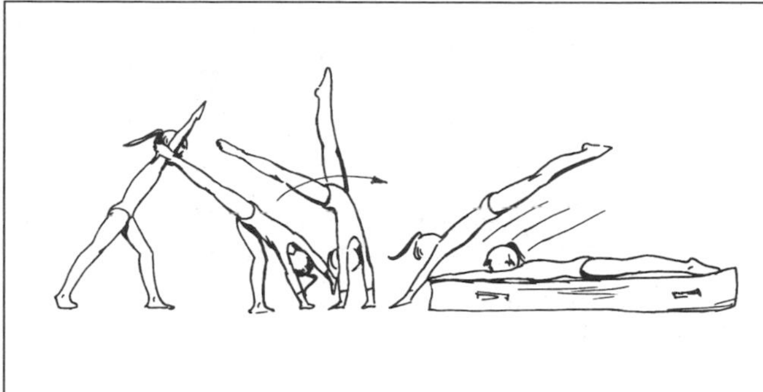

Progression 2

Progression 3

Progression 4

Progression 5

Progression 6

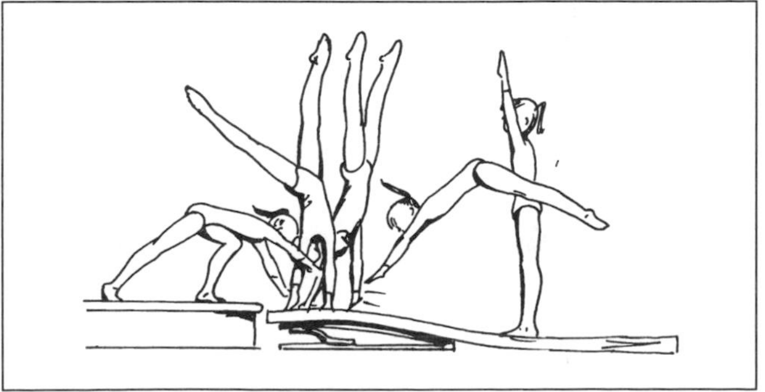

Progression 7

There are a great many variations to these skills which can be explored using figure 5.2, for example, by changing the starting and finishing positions of the skills, changing the body shapes made during the movements, varying the speed in performance and linking a number of skills together into sequences. Once these skills and their variations have been mastered (which will take some time) pupils will have a very sound basis to Gymnastics skill and ability.

Summary

Progressive development through all four themes can constitute the basis of the content of a Gymnastics Scheme of Work. Careful selection and planning of the curriculum content, if taught appropriately, will allow the Programme of Study requirements to be met and will greatly contribute towards the attainment of a number of the statutory end-of-Key-Stage statements.

5.6 Structure of lessons

For all children, a structured approach to the teaching of Gymnastic Activities is required for maximum value to be achieved from lessons. A structure for consideration of a 40-minute lesson is suggested below.

OPENING ACTIVITY AND WARM-UP

This section takes the form of a simple introductory task that is part of the 'main theme'. If the children are responsible and it is safe, the task can be set in the classroom and the children can begin practising as soon as they arrive in the hall. It is useful to make the task a development of, or direct extract from, the previous week's lesson. It should also be a warm-up activity which stimulates cardio-vascular circulation and develops flexibility. This section will last for anything from five to ten minutes.

SKILL LEARNING AND DEVELOPMENT

Floorwork This is the core of the lesson during which the tasks set will be related to the current skill theme. Development of these tasks will occur through practice, exploration, selection, consolidation and refinement, and should include development through the sub-themes. This is more likely to be achieved through a question and answer technique providing problem-solving opportunities, with direction and encouragement from the teacher. This section will last from ten to fifteen minutes and should conclude with positioning of apparatus for the next part of the lesson.

Apparatus work This is a direct extension of the work covered during floorwork and should be relevant to the current theme. Apparatus work can take the form of either of the two methods described in Chapter 3. This section will last from ten to fifteen minutes, which will include returning apparatus to storage positions.

CLOSING ACTIVITY

This part of the lesson should include an activity designed to maintain and develop body strength, and should end with a useful settling down activity to prepare the children to return to the classroom. It should last for not more than five minutes.

5.7 End-of-Key-Stage statements

The above teaching content, when presented progressively using a range of teaching styles throughout Key Stages 1 and 2, will more than satisfy the

Gymnastic Activities Programme of Study and will lead towards the attainment of a number of the end-of-Key-Stage statements as set out on page 65.

5.8 National governing bodies for Gymnastics

British Amateur Gymnastics Association, Technical Department, Ford Hall, Lilleshall Hall National Sports Centre, Near Newport, Shropshire. Telephone 0952 677137.

The British Schools Gymnastics Association, Talbot Cottage, Forest Road, Binfield, Woking, Berks. RG11 5SG. Telephone 0344 423041.

GYMNASTICS AWARD SCHEMES

The Kit-e-Kat Award Scheme is a performance award scheme designed at six levels and suitable for primary schoolchildren. Information and packs are available from the BAGA.

General Gymnastics Teachers Coaching Award Class 5 is a coaching award specially designed for primary teachers and allows holders to run a school gymnastics club.

Dance

6.1 Introduction

DANCE

'It is an art form and as such is an essential part of a balanced Physical Education programme. As well as the development of the artistic and aesthetic elements, dance is also concerned with acquiring control, co-ordination and versatility in the use of the body, and helps to maintain flexibility and develop strength.'
(DES 1991, page 75)

The Physical Education National Curriculum (NC) Statutory Orders require that Dance be taught as one of the six areas of activity within a balanced programme of Physical Education at Key Stage 2 (seven to eleven years). The NCC further recommends that Dance be taught throughout all four years within the Key Stage. This chapter outlines suggested content that could be taught in order to deliver the NC general and Dance Programmes of Study for Key Stage 2.

Without doubt, initial planning and preparation to teach Dance can be quite demanding of time and energy, but the end result is immensely rewarding and well worth the effort. Once ideas and resources (music tapes and a range of other stimuli) have been acquired, they can be used many times, since good teaching uses the children's own ideas and each child and class will bring fresh new ideas to every lesson. By presenting stimulating ideas and tasks, the teacher can provide a wealth of creative opportunities for children through Dance. A balance between direct teaching and guided exploration will help children to express themselves in a way few other activities will allow.

6.2 Dance Scheme of Work

The following pages present a suggested Dance Scheme of Work for Key Stage 2, based on the model for whole curriculum planning suggested in Chapter 2. Section 6.5 provides further information about teaching content in Dance. A blank Scheme of Work document is provided in the Appendix (pages 170–173).

Dance Scheme of Work

Key Stage: 2

Area of activity: Dance

Cohort: 1994-95

Units of Work (length of unit x length of lessons)

	Autumn	Spring	Summer
Year 3	7+8 x40 mins	7+6 x40 mins	
Year 4	7+8 x40 mins	7+6 x40 mins	
Year 5		7+6 x40 mins	
Year 6	7+8 x40 mins	7+6 x40 mins	

Process aims

The Scheme of Work will work towards enabling pupils to carry out the following:

PLANNING AND COMPOSING

- plan appropriate responses to Dance tasks set by the teacher in response to a range of stimuli
- individually compose Dance sequences to fulfil open-ended tasks showing creativity and individual interpretation of a range of stimuli
- co-operate with a partner to plan responses to a variety of tasks and stimuli
- plan, refine and adapt Dance performances alone and with others.

PARTICIPATING AND PERFORMING

- perform appropriate and safe body preparation as warm-up and warm-down activities
- explore a variety of tasks set by the teacher and present different responses
- work alone and with others to develop, consolidate, refine and link their repertoire of Dance steps and movements through practice and rehearsal
- remember, select and repeat a range of Dance steps and movements and perform more complex body actions alone and with others.

APPRECIATING AND EVALUATING

- appreciate the importance of good posture and body position in the aesthetic performance of Dance steps and movements
- make simple constructive comments and judgements on their own and others' performances.
- make dances with clear beginnings, middles and ends involving improvising, exploring, selecting and refining content, and sometimes incorporating work from other aspects of the curriculum, in particular music, art and drama.

Programme of Study requirements

'Pupils should:

- *make dances with clear beginnings, middles and ends involving improvising, exploring, selecting and refining content, and sometimes incorporating work from other aspects of the curriculum, in particular music, art and drama.*
- *be given opportunities to increase the range and complexity of body actions, including step patterns and use of body parts.*
- *be guided to enrich their movements by varying shape, size, direction, level, speed, tension and continuity.*
- *in response to a range of stimuli, express feelings, moods and ideas and create simple characters and narratives in movement.*
- *describe and interpret the different elements of a dance.'*

Teaching Content Outline

Year: 3 **Unit:** 1

Title: 'Learning letters and forming words' (basic body actions)

Autumn 1st half term

7 x 40 minute lessons

Outline: Revision of basic body actions used in Dance, such as travelling, jumping, rolling, turning and twisting and gesturing. Actions will be explored that involve body parts being used in isolation, e.g. the head or the shoulders, and together, e.g. knees and elbows moving symmetrically. The teaching will encourage the children to develop an understanding of *where* they are moving (using changes in level or direction of movement and varying pathways) and *how* they are moving (by introducting variations in the speed, quality and energy/tension of their movements). This should be done by presenting the children with a variety of ideas, using expressive words and pictures, and sounds, using percussion and various pieces of music.

Year: 3 **Unit:** 2

Title: Making sentences (action phrases)

Autumn 2nd half term

8 x 40 minute lessons

Outline: This unit is primarily concerned with linking basic body actions together into what are known as 'action phrases' in dance terminology. (This could be compared to linking simple movements together to perform recognised complete skills in Gymnastics.) The content of the lessons will concentrate on the techniques of linking selected body actions together into 'action phrases' which may or may not convey some meaning. Emphasis should be placed on how to select the actions to be linked and the body parts to be used. As in the first unit, the children should be encouraged to be aware of *where* they are performing, and of their movement quality in terms of *how* they are moving.

Year: 3 **Unit:** 3

Title: 'Telling a story' (basic dance composition)

Spring 1st half term

7 x 40 minute lessons

Outline: This unit will develop the 'action phrases' into simple dance compositions, so that the children begin to recognise their basic components – beginnings, middles and ends. The content of the lessons will concentrate on techniques of selecting appropriate phrases and linking them together to create some degree of meaning. The children should develop their dance vocabulary towards the expression of simple emotions such as sadness and happiness, and will work in groups composing a whole class dance.

Year: 3 **Unit:** 4

Title: 'Country dancing'

Spring 2nd half term

6 x 40 minute lessons

Outline: This unit will introduce simple dance steps, such as *slipping*, *skip change of step* and *pas de basque*, and patterns, such as *casting off*, *leading a partner* and *four hands round and back*, which are used in country dancing. The children should learn a small range of simple country dances that involve partners and small groups. Simple explanations will be given to help the children understand the origins of the dances learned.

Year: 4 **Unit:** 5

Title: 'Reviewing the story'

Autumn 1st half term

7 x 40 minute lessons

Outline: This unit will recap the basic body actions and skills in dance composition that were learned in Y3, and will involve the development of phrases and small compositions that come from the children's own movements and ideas. The purpose of this unit is to allow the children to explore, select, refine and practise their dance experiences. Emphasis will be placed on further enriching their vocabulary through awareness of *where* they are moving (direction, levels and pathways), and *how* they are moving (speed, shape, size and tension).

Year: 4 **Unit:** 6

Title: 'Developing the characters'

Autumn 2nd half term

8 x 40 minute lessons

Outline: Character representation will be introduced to the children using the circus as a theme. The variety of characters found in a circus (clowns, jugglers, strong (wo)men, flying trapeze artists, tumblers, stunt (wo)men etc) will be used to develop an understanding of how movement, gesture and expression can be used to portray recognisable characteristics. Music, writing and pictures will be used to stimulate the children to select and explore whole body movements, gestures and expressions to convey particular characteristics which to them represent circus performers. The unit will begin with a lesson that introduces the children to characterisation through basic body actions and gesture using body parts. Subsequent lessons should allow the children to explore particular characterisation, and the unit will conclude with the performance of a whole class dance in which individuals and groups of children portray the range of characters found in their circus.

Year: 4 **Unit:** 7

Title: Responding to stimuli

Spring 1st half term

7 x 40 minute lessons

Outline: The development of the use of stimuli will form the focus for this Unit of Work. Children's dance vocabulary and performance should be extended, using their own ideas stimulated by the presentation of everyday objects such as pieces of cloth, a sponge, or a crisp packet, as well as words, sculpture and music.

Year: 4 **Unit:** 8

Title: Expressing moods and feelings

Spring 2nd half term

6 x 40 minute lessons

Outline: The 'theme' around which this unit will develop will be one selected from current affairs. The children will be asked to reflect on their thoughts and feelings about particular current issues or major news stories of the moment (such as war, the Greenhouse Effect, animals threatened with extinction) which they feel strongly about. They will be asked to try to show how they feel through dance. From the images and feelings, ideas for group dances will be selected that the children can adapt, refine and practise individually, in small groups and as a whole class.

Year: 5 **Unit:** 9

Title: 'Spring cleaning'

Spring 1st half term

7 x 40 minute lessons

Outline: The theme of 'spring cleaning' with the images and actions involved will be used to introduce the class to dance composition, drawing on the skills, vocabulary and understanding developed over the previous two years. The class will work on telling a story through movement, developing the narrative and characters as the story unfolds.

Year: 5 **Unit:** 10

Title: Folk dance

Spring 2nd half term

6 x 40 minute lessons

Outline: This unit will look at a selection of national and folk dances to broaden the children's rhythmic experience and increase their repertoire of step and spatial patterns. The stories behind the dances should be explained and the steps and formations taught. Dances for pairs, fours, eights and large groups should be taught, such as *March of the Mods*, *Canadian Barn Dance*, *Bluebell Polka*, *Virginia Reel*, and *The Siege of Carrick.*

Year: 6 **Unit:** 11

Title: Inter-personal relationships explored through dance

Autumn 1st half term

7 x 40 minute lessons

Outline: This unit will use a 'sports' theme to focus on the expression of relationships through dance movement and composition. Teaching will involve the exploration of the variety of human interactions encountered in individual, partner and team sports and the difference between types of sports such as contact sports, invasive and non-invasive team games and 'individuals against the elements' sports. The children should be given freedom to develop their own ideas and compositions within this theme, and to choose their own working groups. Mini-presentations of their dances to the rest of the class will be used to stimulate discussion and interpretation and to develop the children's descriptive skills.

Year: 6 **Unit:** 12

Title: Dance presentation

Autumn 2nd half term

8 x 40 minute lessons

Outline: This unit will specifically work towards a class dance performance as part of the school's Christmas festivities. The various roles of those involved in the planning and preparation for a performance (writers, directors, choreographers, performers, make-up, costume and scenery designers, lighting and sound technicians, etc) could be filled by members of the class where the children feel this is appropriate. In the early stages of the unit the children will be encouraged to think about how their compositions from the previous unit can be refined and developed to come together as a whole class dance. Decisions and judgements will need to be made by the class about a whole range of issues relating to both the dance performance and the practicalities of the presentation.

Year: 6 **Unit:** 13

Title: Dance around the world

Spring 1st half term

7 x 40 minute lessons

Outline: The exploration of a range of Dance styles from a selection of countries around the world will be the focus of this unit. The unit will be introduced using a video as stimulus such as Michael Jackson's *It Doesn't Matter if You're Black or White.* Each lesson will look at a particular country's style of national, historical or contemporary dance in order to extend the children's dance vocabulary, rhythm, imagination and experience. Percussion and music, and traditional and contemporary cultural images, should be used as stimuli for the children to create their own dance representations.

Year: 6 **Unit:** 14

Title: Modern dance styles – jazz dance

Spring 2nd half term

6 x 40 minute lessons

Outline: This unit will develop the Dance vocabulary through jazz dance. Michael Jackson's video *Thriller* or a similar stimulus will be used to demonstrate jazz dance style. The class should learn the basic jazz dance steps and body actions in the first half of the unit. Later lessons should work towards a whole class jazz composition to a story and/or a piece of music they have selected.

Organisational strategies

The organisation of the pupils is based on a class of 32 children. Working groups will be selected and changed by the teacher or may be self selecting as required by the teaching content throughout the Key Stage.

Staff, facilities and equipment required

Lessons should be taught by the class teacher with occasional input from students or visiting teachers to the school. All lessons will be taught in the school hall/gymnasium using stimuli and or props as the curriculum content demands. A cassette player will be used to play music and this, together with percussion instruments, will be kept in the school's music resource store. For each unit of work utilising music or other stimuli, a list of the specific requirements will be included in the Forward Plan. A selection of pieces of music and other stimuli suggested for the Scheme of Work is listed below. →

Warm-up music *Ghostbusters* theme tune; *Popcorn* (Gershan/Kingsley); current chart hits; *In the Mood* (Glenn Miller).

The circus *Barnum on Ice* (Coleman); *The Hammer* (Panorama Band); *Pink Panther* (Mancini); *Cool* from *West Side Story* (Bernstein); *Trisch-Trasch Polka* (Strauss); *The Well of the Souls* (Williams); *Colonel Hathi's March* (Disney's *Jungle Book*).

Spring cleaning *The Entertainer* (Scott Joplin); *Fossils* (Saint-Saens); *My Favourite Things* (Alpert); *Half Holiday* (Wakeman).

Sports theme *Chariots of Fire* (Vangelis); *Ski Sunday Theme Tune* (New Dance Orchestra); *Rugby Special Theme Tune* (BBC Theme Tunes); *Fanfare for the Common Man* (Copland); *Offside* (Stoller); *Training* (*Rocky 4* tune).

Dance around the world *It Doesn't Matter if You're Black or White* (Michael Jackson) and video.

Country Dance *Country Dancing* (GDB Records – a compilation of ten country dances for all ages).

National folk dance *March of the Mods*, *Canadian Barn Dance*, *Bluebell Polka*, *Virginia Reel*, and *The Siege of Carrick* – a range of music is available at any good record shop for these dances.

Jazz dance *Thriller* (Michael Jackson) and video.

Flashcards 'What?', 'Where?', 'How?', and 'Why?' cards.

Art and language Samples of children's own work; poem *Playing at Circuses* (E.J.M. Woodland); *Poems for Movement* (E.J.M. Woodland). Pictures, photographs, posters, sculpture and drawings.

Towards the end of the Key Stage, the children's work could be recorded on video as part of their reviewing and learning processes. A camera, recorder and monitor will be required and the children should do the recording.

Safety precautions

Ensure that appropriate dress is worn and that all jewellery is removed before each lesson. Check that pupils understand the reasons for these simple rules. Establish a code of conduct and safety requirements at the beginning of each unit and remind pupils of them regularly throughout the scheme. Check and record any medical conditions that may affect the activity. Carry out an appropriate evaluation of skills competence and group pupils accordingly during the first lesson of each unit. Ensure that codes of behaviour and safety are clearly understood before the pupils begin the units.

Special needs

(It is likely that a wide range of ability levels will be apparent from the beginning of the first unit. Some children may have special needs that require special provision and it may be necessary to enlist knowledgeable advisory support to help with ideas to cater for children with special needs in the early stages. Nevertheless, the teaching content is designed to cater for all ranges of ability. Individual special needs should be assessed at the beginning of the first Unit of Work and specific provision should be outlined in each Unit of Work Forward Plan.)

Record-keeping and assessment procedures [see also Chapter 10]

Record-keeping with reference to teaching content should include:

- a Scheme of Work with recommendations for future planning and content
- a Forward Plan for each Unit of Work within the Scheme of Work, with a summary and recommendations for future teaching content in subsequent Units
- an ongoing record and formative evaluation of individual lesson content, recorded on Forward Plans and used to inform planning and teaching of subsequent lessons
- where necessary and appropriate, individual lesson plans.

→

Assessment procedures should include:

- ongoing assessment of class progress in relation to aims and objectives and the PoS requirements throughout the teaching units
- ongoing evaluation of each pupil's progress in relation to Unit of Work aims and lesson objectives, using a Unit of Work record and assessment document throughout the teaching units
- school summative records for individual pupils with reference to end-of-Key-Stage statements updated at the end of each year and at the end of each Key Stage.

End-of-key-stage statements

'By the end of the key stage, pupils should be able to:

- *plan, practise, improve and remember more complex sequences of movement.*
- *respond safely, alone and with others, to challenging tasks, taking account of levels of skill and understanding.*
- *evaluate how well they and others perform and behave against criteria suggested by the teacher, and suggest ways of improving performance.*
- *sustain energetic activity over appropriate periods of time in a range of physical activities and understand the effects of exercise on the body.'*

Evaluation of scheme

(A record of class progress at the end of each Unit of Work should be made to assist with future planning (as described in Chapter 10) and a summary of the whole scheme should be recorded here.)

Recommendations for future planning

(A statement of any recommendations that become apparent during the teaching should be recorded in order to inform future planning and teaching for other cohorts of children.)

6.3 Sample of Dance Unit of Work Forward Plan

The following section is a sample Forward Plan for Unit 1 (shown on page 96) in the Dance Scheme of Work. A similar blank master document which teachers can use for their own curriculum planning can be found in the Appendix (pages 174–177).

Unit of Work Forward Plan

Area of Activity: Dance

Unit: 1 | **Title:** Learning letters and making words (basic body actions)

Autumn 1st half term | 7 x 40 minute lessons | **Day:** Tuesday pm

Class: 3PP **Age:** 7/8 | **No. in class:** 16m, 16f | **Teacher:** P Parker

Previous knowledge and experience

A range of Dance lessons developing basic body actions have been taught at Key Stage 1 and the children have worked with simple rhythm using percussion and music.

Aims of the Unit of Work

- to revise basic body actions such as travelling, jumping, rolling, turning, twisting and gesturing
- to explore body parts being used in isolation and together (symmetrically and asymmetrically)
- to develop children's understanding of *where* they are moving (using changes in levels, direction and pathways)
- to develop children's understanding of *how* they are moving by introductions of variations in speed, quality and tension
- to present the children with a range of stimuli including ideas, words, pictures, sounds and music.

CONTENT OUTLINE

LESSON 1 (TRAVELLING)	Introduction: Warm-up to music that includes running, jumping, shaking, twisting and turning, and body isolations. *Ghostbusters* theme tune; *Popcorn* (Gershan/Kingsley); something from Michael Jackson or the charts. Response to stimuli: using 'What?' flashcard children are asked to concentrate on what their body is doing. Ask for examples, e.g. jumping, twisting. How many ways can you think of travelling? How many ways of jumping? Can you find a simple way of rolling? Development: join together a travel, a jump and a roll! Music: *Barnum on Ice* (Coleman); *The Hammer* (Panorama Band); *Pink Panther* (Mancini).
LESSON 2 (TURNING AND TWISTING)	Introduction as Lesson 1. Response to stimuli: recap last lesson's 'travel, jump and roll'. Look at *pausing and stillness.* The children travel round using all the space and *freeze* on command. Each time they should try to hold a different position. Introduce different ways of turning and twisting, allowing the children to explore. Encourage children to make different shapes with the body as they twist and turn. Development: extend the travel, jump and roll, by adding a pause, turn, twist and stretch. Introduce the idea of symmetry/asymmetry. Music: *Pink Panther* (Mancini).
LESSON 3 (GESTURING)	Introduction as Lesson 1. Response to stimuli: choose a class theme (e.g. holidays, moods, wedding) and discuss images of these with the children. Each child should pose for an imaginary photograph for the theme, then join with a partner and choose a different pose together. Finally they can join with another pair and explore group poses that they can make together. Development: begin in the individual pose, then travel, jump, roll, meet with partner and hold the pair pose together. Turn, stretch, twist and meet with the other pair for the 'group' photograph. Music: *Barnum on Ice* (Coleman) – introduce sounds and pictures related to the class theme, such as sounds of the seaside or wedding bells.
LESSON 4 (WHERE? LEVELS, UP HIGH, DOWN LOW, ETC)	Introduction as Lesson 1. Response to stimuli: use a 'Where?' flashcard with levels to stimulate the children to think about travelling in different ways at different levels. Allow them to explore and demonstrate their ideas. Development: review the 'phrase' from the previous lesson, asking the children to introduce changes of level into their small sequence/phrase. Allow the children to practise and polish their individual, pair and group phrases. Music: *Barnum on Ice* (Coleman).
LESSON 5 (WHERE? PATHWAYS AND DIRECTION)	Introduction as Lesson 1. Response to stimuli: use a 'Where?' flashcard with direction and pathways to stimulate the children to think about travelling in different directions and using different pathways. Allow them to explore their ideas, giving them examples (run round in a circle backwards, jump sideways making a zig-zag pathway). Ask them to travel in a pathway *'writing'* the first letter of their name. Can they change direction when the pathway changes? Development: recap the dance at the end of the last lesson. Can they change the dance by changing their direction and their pathway? Music: *Barnum on Ice* (Coleman).

LESSON 6 (HOW?)	Introduction as Lesson 1. Response to stimuli: recap the dance from last lesson. Use a 'How?' flashcard and ask the children to describe how they moved (e.g. fast/slowly, lightly/strongly, happily/sadly). The children should have the opportunity to discuss and explore changes in speed, tension/energy changes and gestures and movements showing expression. Development: working together in their groups, the children can decide how they want their dance from previous lessons to look. They should have the opportunity to practise and explore their ideas and then add them to their original dance. Music: speed – *Barnum on Ice* (Coleman); tension – *Cool* from *West Side Story* (Bernstein); happy/light and flowing – *Trisch-Trasch Polka* (Strauss); slow/sad – *The Well of the Souls* (Williams).
LESSON 7 (THE GROUP DANCE)	Introduction as Lesson 1. Response to stimuli: recap dance from last lesson. Ask the children in their groups to think about a starting position and pose and a finishing position. They should then practise and polish their dance in preparation for showing it to the rest of the class. Development: each group should demonstrate its dance and the others should comment on why they liked it, referring to *what* movements were used, *where* it was performed and *how* it was performed. The groups are free to choose any piece of music that has been used in previous lessons to help as a stimulus for their dance.

Organisational strategies

Children change in classroom, walk to hall with pumps on and take them off in hall. Hair band and grips box and valuables box will be available. The pairs and groups will be self-selecting.

Facilities and equipment required

Hall/gymnasium.

Cassette recorder and flashcards. Encourage children to bring pictures relating to the themes the day before the lesson. Have the pieces of music on labelled individual cassettes for speed of location.

Safety precautions

Dress – t-shirt and shorts or leotard, and bare feet. No jewellery. Hair tied back. Check that the hall is safe. Check on medical problems. Remind class about rules of behaviour and safety. Take first-aid kit.

Special needs provision

(This section should be used to help plan and record provision for children with special educational needs in Dance. This may include catering for children with physical and mental disabilities, children with behavioural and emotional difficulties and the physically gifted. Three examples are given below.)

- One child (Peter) with hearing impairment but can lip read. He is also good at observing other children to interpret the task, but may need some individual reinforcement. Has obvious problems with rhythm and musical interpretation, but can feel rhythm if allowed to touch the speaker of the cassette player.
- One child (Darren) with learning difficulties who can be disruptive but responds well in P.E. if interested and motivated. Responds well to praise but tends to seek attention if firm control is not exercised.
- One child (Joanne) with an artificial leg. Shy about P.E. but is very able and copes with most tasks well. Some encouragement needed but is aware of own capabilities and understands well about safety. Keeps artificial leg on in lessons and wears tracksuit bottoms.

Evaluation of lessons

(The date should be entered beside the lesson number once the lesson has been taught. If individual lesson plans are not used by teachers, a highlighter pen can be used to indicate the work that has been covered in each lesson in case adjustment decisions need to be made. This records what is actually taught relative to what was planned.

Notes should be made in this section each week, with recommendations for future lessons. This is useful for future planning and for record-keeping purposes.)

Summary and recommendations for next unit

(A record of class progress at the end of the Unit of Work should be made to assist with future planning. Individual pupil progress should also be recorded at appropriate times using the method described in Chapter 10.)

6.4 Sample Lesson Plan

A sample plan for Lesson 1 in the above Unit of Work, showing details of activities, useful teaching points, use of stimuli and the organisation of children and space, has been included on the following pages. Experienced teachers may feel this level of planning is not necessary and that they can work from the lesson outlines in the Forward Plan. Many teachers, however, may find that the children have a better learning experience if they plan individual lessons in the detail shown.

Dance Lesson Plan (1)

Key Stage 2 Unit of Work 1: Learning letters and making words

Lesson number in unit: 1

Date: Tuesday 14th September 1994

Time: 2.10 – 2.50pm

Length of lesson: 40 mins

Class: 3PP **Age:** 7/8

Teacher: P Parker

No. in class: 16m, 16f

Venue: School Hall

Lesson objectives

(S = social, E = emotional, C = cognitive, P = physical)

S: to encourage the pupils to work co-operatively to use the space available
E: to encourage pupils to value their own ideas
C:to begin to learn and remember the warm-up routine
P: to enable pupils to perform simple body actions and begin to link them together in time to the music.

Facilities and equipment

Hall/gymnasium
Cassette player
Cassette with pre-recorded music: *Popcorn* (Gershen/Kingsley) and *Pink Panther* (Mancini)
'What?' flashcard

Lesson evaluation

Dance Lesson Plan (2)

Phase	Tasks/activities	Teaching points/coaching feedback	Organisation of pupils and apparatus
Preparation	Check hall is safe and clean. Check dress, jewellery and hair.	Explain behaviour expected and reasons for safety.	Prepare cassette recorder and make cassettes ready.
Introduction	Introduce work to be covered in Dance lessons and this unit in particular.		Class sitting in a space.
Warm-up (5 mins)	Clap the rhythm of the music *Head* ■ turn and look left, then right x 8 ■ tilt head to left and right x 8	Stand feet slightly apart and toes pointing forwards. In time with the music standing with knees bent. Eyes always looking forwards.	The warm-up described here will be repeated during lessons 2 to 7 so that the children learn the sequence and so that there is continuity across the unit lessons. It also enhances their vocabulary of dance movements and provides an opportunity for consolidation of their dance repertoire. Pupils copy the teacher who stands at the front of the class. Children in own spaces with at least an arm's stretch all round them.
	Shoulders ■ shrug alternately up and down x 8 ■ both up and down together x 4 ■ round forwards, backwards alternately x 8 ■ round together x 4 ■ alternately but together x 8	Knees slightly bent, head up. Work to the rhythm of the music.	
	Arms ■ swing forwards, backwards individually x 4 ■ both arms together x 4 ■ shake arms to side, then to other x 4	Nice straight arms and brush your ears. 4 times each side 2 times each side 1 time each side	
	Legs ■ bend knees then stretch up x 8 ■ above with arm swing up and down x 8 ■ stretch up to ceiling for 4 counts and curl over for 4 counts then unroll for 4 counts	Knees go over toes, back straight.	
	Whole body ■ stand facing front and swing arms to left for 4 then to right for 4 ■ bounce 2 feet together x 8 ■ small jumps 2 feet together x 8 ■ 8 higher bounces ■ walk forwards for 8 and back for 8 ■ run forwards for 8 and back for 8 ■ side step to right for 8 then to left for 8 ■ 4 sidesteps and 4 counts to do a full turn ■ in your space stretch up and hold for 8 ■ curl up and relax for 8	Cushion landing by bending knees slightly. Nice and light on your toes – 'spring!' On toes, hold tight, squeeze your muscles Slowly curl up and bend knees slightly with head looking at knees.	
	■ go to knees curled for count of 4 ■ go to lying and roll onto back for 8 counts	Slow and peaceful to calm pupils. Relax and lie quietly for count of 8.	

Dance Lesson Plan (3)

Phase	Tasks/activities	Teaching points/coaching feedback	Organisation of pupils and apparatus
Response to stimuli (23 mins)	Present the 'What?' flashcard and ask what it says. Explain that the lesson is concentrating upon body actions, i.e. *what* the body is doing and *what* it can do.	Don't say too much and allow the response to come from the children's ideas.	Class sit around the teacher as focal point.
	Ask for examples of body actions (e.g. walking, running, jumping, rolling, turning, crawling, sliding). 'I will put some music on and I want you to explore all these different ways of moving that we have talked about.'	If the children seem stuck for ideas point them to the warm-up and ask them to think of *what* they did in that. Encourage the children to keep changing their movements and exploring their ideas.	Moving around using all the space provided, being careful not to touch or bump into anyone else.
	Pick out some original ideas and ask the children to demonstrate to the class.	Choose someone who is jumping as a lead in to the next stage.	
	Jumping ■ Let's look at jumping – show me how many ways you can think of jumping. ■ Explain and demonstrate 5 basic jumps. ■ Let the children try these jumps.	Allow the children to explore their own ideas about ways of jumping. Try to encourage the children to move in time with the music and remind them that they are 'dancing'. This may help to ensure they understand the distinction between Dance and Gymnastics.	Moving about the space.
	Rolling ■ Now ask the children to suggest different ways of rolling. ■ Pick out good ideas and ask for demonstrations.	Try to discourage formal Gymnastics rolling such as forward and backward rolls.	
Development (12 mins)	■ Choose your favourite travelling idea! ■ Travel for 4 beats in the music (i.e. walk left, right, left, right). ■ Add onto your travel idea your favourite jump then your favourite roll. ■ Dance the whole piece through together – travel, travel, travel, travel, jump and roll! ■ Pick out children to demonstrate.	You may need to make this more simple for the children to begin with and count out the music with them, giving an example and going through it stage by stage. Also give them time to practise each part with the music once they have chosen their idea. Some children will need help in putting the whole thing together and constant praise and encouragement is needed.	
Summary	Sit the children down and ask them what the lesson has been concentrating upon. Summarise what they have explored and what they have come up with.	Give the children positive feedback about what they have done and how well they have done it. End on a positive note and suggest something encouraging as an introduction for next week's lesson.	
	Standing in a space with good posture. Return class to classroom and change.	Standing quietly and calmly. Check their posture and calm breathing.	In their own space. Line up at door in groups and walk back to class.

6.5 Dance teaching content

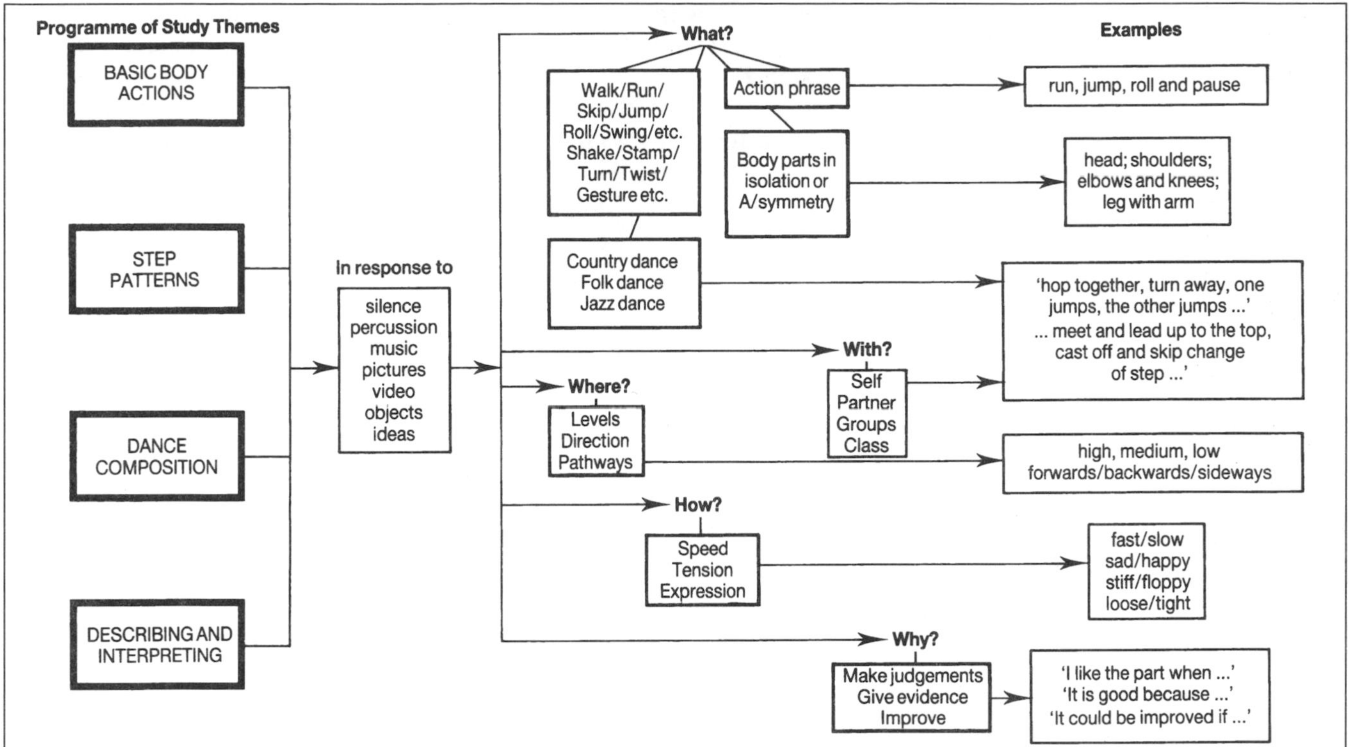

Figure 6.1
Dance Skill Themes

The Dance teaching content for Key Stage 2 can be presented diagrammatically as shown in figure 6.1. Four 'skill themes' have been identified from the Dance Programme of Study: *basic body actions, step patterns, dance composition*, and *describing and interpreting dance*. These skills can be developed in response to a range of stimuli and dance experiences that enhance the children's understanding of *what* movements they are capable of, *how* they can perform these movements, *where* they can move on the floor and in space and *who* they can work with. If the teaching content is presented in this way, the children develop a clear understanding of their dance skills, vocabulary and creativity. With experience, the children learn to make informed judgements about *why* a particular movement looks good or bad and how to improve their presentation of dance compositions.

The Scheme of Work on pages 95–100 is an example of Key Stage 2 teaching that presents the Dance curriculum as illustrated in figure 6.1. The scheme can be divided into four distinctive **strands.** These are:

- learning to tell stories
- developing the stories
- composing and performing dance
- other styles of dance.

These are developed through the Scheme of Work both in order to meet the requirements of the Programme of Study *and* to provide enjoyable and stimulating Dance experiences that children and teachers will find immensely fulfilling.

Strand 1 – Learning to tell stories

An understanding of the content of this strand can be facilitated by comparing it with the development of story-writing skills. The first stage is 'learning letters and forming words'. The children are taught a range of body actions, gestures and step patterns through the presentation of a variety of ideas, using expressive words and pictures; and sounds, using percussion and various pieces of music. Examples of some basic body actions are given in figure 6.1 such as walk, run, skip, jump, turn, twist and curl, but this is not an exhaustive list. Children will extend their personal vocabulary indefinitely through interpretation of the tasks, activities and stimuli presented to them in Dance lessons. Teachers can use the children's own interpretations and ideas as a resource for group and whole class teaching material. Using a *'How?'* card like the one shown in figure 6.3 will help the children think about variations in speed, quality and energy/tension in their movements.

WHAT? **(Body Action)** bend/twist/stretch/step/turn/jump/travel/gesture	**HOW?** **(Dynamics)** speed/tension/expression
■ copy/repeat exactly (as shown by the teacher) ■ repeat on other body side ■ symmetry/asymmetry ■ together at the same time (unison) ■ one after the other (canon) ■ vary the body shape	■ repeat at same speed ■ increase/decrease speed ■ change energy/tension – strong/light ■ change fluency – jerky/smooth ■ change mood – happy/sad
DEVELOPMENT OF DANCE IDEAS	
WHERE? **(Space)** levels/pathways/directions	**WITH?** **(Relationships)** self/partner/group/class
■ repeat same spatial design ■ change front/focus ■ change direction ■ change level ■ change size ■ vary pathway ■ awareness of floor and air patterns ■ awareness of plane	■ change the number of people dancing – solo, duo, trio, etc ■ use unison/canon ■ 'question/answer' through movement ■ contrasting actions

Figure 6.2
Development of dance ideas

Figure 6.3
A 'flashcard' stimulus

Similarly, a 'Where?' flashcard can encourage changes in level, direction of movement and floor and air patterns. A simple example is useful to illustrate the variety of movement possible using this technique. Figure 6.4 shows how a simple jump can be performed in a number of ways, by varying *where* it is performed and *how* it is performed. The descriptive word used to stimulate each variation is shown alongside.

Figure 6.4 (a) jump (b) high (c) lightly (d) asymmetrically

Figure 6.2 should help teachers to devise lesson ideas that will develop variety in children's movement repertoire. The lesson content outlines in the sample Forward Plan describe ideas for progressive development in the early stages of this strand.

The second stage of this strand equates with 'putting words together into sentences'. The equivalent to a 'sentence' in dance is known as an **action phrase**, that is a series of smoothly linked and fluid body actions which bear some relationship to one another. Emphasis should be placed on how to select the actions to be linked and the body parts to be used. The teacher can set specific tasks that will require the children to perform action phrases in response. An example of this would be a task in which the children link together a jump, a travel and a curl. An action phrase that fulfils this task is shown in figure 6.5.

Figure 6.5
An action phrase showing a jump, a travel and a curl linked together

The third stage of the strand introduces basic composition, so that the dance begins to have a structure which 'tells a story'. A starting position and a finishing position are added to the action phrase, so that it becomes a basic dance composition with a beginning, a middle and an end. Figure 6.6 shows the original phrase as a simple dance composition.

Figure 6.6
A basic dance composition

This can be further developed by asking the children to perform their composition as if, for example, they were very happy (as represented in figure 6.7) or very sad.

Figure 6.7
A 'happy' action phrase (a jump in celebration, a walk with arms behind back and whistling a tune, followed by a contented curl in a sitting position hugging knees and grinning widely)

The progression shown above is an isolated example of how three basic body actions can be transformed into an aesthetically pleasing and expressive dance composition. Once the children have been through this learning process a number of times they will have acquired a sound dance vocabulary which is the essential basis for 'telling interesting stories'. Allowing the children to work from a wide range of stimuli (see Unit 7 in the Scheme of Work) will ensure that they experience a variety of movement styles as a result of exploration of their own ideas.

Strand 2 – Developing the stories

This strand stretches the children's Dance vocabulary and expressive repertoire by introducing simple characterisation and the portrayal of emotions, using appropriately selected story themes. For example, in the 'circus' theme suggested in Unit 6 the action phrase in figure 6.7 can be developed by asking the children to represent a circus character, such as a clown, performing antics on a tight-rope. The action phrase might then look like that shown in figure 6.8.

Figure 6.8
A 'clown' action phrase

The variety of characters found in a circus (clowns, jugglers, strong (wo)men, flying trapeze artists, tumblers, stunt (wo)men, etc) is ideal for extending the children's understanding of how movement, gesture and expression may be used to portray recognisable characteristics. Music, writing and pictures can be used to stimulate the children to select and explore whole body movements, gestures and expressions to convey particular characteristics to represent circus performers. Below is an example of a poem that will inspire dance in young children.

PLAYING AT CIRCUSES

I'm a little pony,
Trotting round the ring,
I paw the ground, and shake my head
To make my bright bells ding.
Now I am an Elephant,
My steps are big and slow.
I swing my trunk and nod my head
Slowly to and fro.

Look at me, a laughing clown,
And see the tricks I do;
I clap my hands above my head
And bend my long legs too.
But now I feel so tired
That I must sit awhile.
I fold my arms and keep quite still
And smile a happy smile.

E.J.M. Woodland

Thus, the story theme provides the stimulation for ideas which are portrayed in the children's dance compositions. However, it should be noted that it is not essential, or even always desirable, for the compositions to be literal dance dramatisations. They may be abstract, where the theme is simply the initial stimulus and the children dance for the sake of dance, rather than always to tell a story.

Teaching and learning should build upon the children's own ideas by developing their action phrases and simple dance compositions using a selection of the possibilities listed below.

- join with a partner and teach each other your compositions
- perform one of your dances:
  one after the other (in canon)
  both at the same time (in unison)
- both do partner A's dance followed by partner B's dance
- compose a new dance using a phrase from each plus a new phrase
- each pair join with another pair to make a group of four and combine dances to make a small group composition

The teacher can guide the development of the children's dance experience by leading and/or assisting with whole class dance compositions. Below are some examples of progressions that will bring this about.

- allow the children to practise individually, in pairs and in small groups
- observe the action phrases or dances that look good
- ask the children to demonstrate these
- allow the class to pick action phrases they would like in their dance
- split the class into groups and sections as required
- teach the chosen action phrases to the groups or the whole class
- make up a phrase for the whole class to learn
- decide on a starting position to open the dance and a finishing position to close the dance
- put the dance together as a whole into a balanced composition

An example of a composition using the circus theme is shown in figures 6.9–6.13.

Figure 6.9
Open the dance with the starting position

Figure 6.10
The whole class phrase

Figure 6.11
The ringmaster, then all the clowns, then all the tight-rope artists, then the clowns on the tight-rope, the ringmaster again, then the tumblers and the jugglers

Figure 6.12
The whole class phrase again with the ringmaster

Figure 6.13
Finally, close the dance with the finishing position

Another method of expanding the children's Dance experience is deliberately to select a story theme that will stimulate strong emotions and vivid images (Unit 8 in the Scheme of Work). From these images and feelings, ideas for Dance can be explored, selected, adapted, refined and practised individually, in small groups and as a whole class through the processes described above.

Strand 3 – Understanding dance composition and performance

This strand is concerned with developing the children's understanding of dance composition and performance. Mini-presentations to the rest of the class can be used to stimulate discussion and interpretation and development of the children's descriptive skills. The strand should specifically encourage the children to think about how their compositions can be refined and developed to come together in a whole class dance which will be performed live to an audience. (This could take place during the school Christmas Festival or simply be performed in front of another class.) With guidance from the teacher, the class should make informed decisions and judgements about a whole range of issues relating to both the technicalities of the dance performance and the practicalities of the presentation. The various roles of those involved in planning and preparing for a performance (writers, directors, choreographers, performers, make-up, costume and scenery designers, lighting and sound technicians, etc) may be filled by members of the class where this is felt to be appropriate and practical. In so doing, the children's judgemental skills will sharpen and their knowledge about what makes a good or better performance, and how to improve the presentation of dance compositions, will be improved (the 'why?' consideration shown in figure 6.1 on page 107).

Strand 4 – Other styles of dance

Within this strand the children's experience of Dance is extended using a range of different Dance styles. Examples used in the Scheme of Work include country dance, national and folk dance, and jazz dance. One unit also explores a range of Dance styles from around the world.

This selection of Dance styles will broaden the children's rhythmical experience and increase their repertoire of step and spatial patterns. Their historical and cultural understanding of the place of Dance in society can be enhanced if the significance of the steps and formations and the stories behind the dances are explained when they are taught. The significance of costume, staging, audience participation and make-up can also be discussed. The teaching material can also provide a useful contrast in style, which helps to deliver a balanced Dance experience, helping to cater for the tastes of children who find pure creative Dance less attractive.

Summary

Progressive development through all four strands will provide an enriching and valuable Dance experience for all children. If the curriculum content is carefully planned and enthusiastically delivered, with an emphasis on developing the children's own ideas, and if progression through the four strands gives consideration to a balance of styles, the Programme of Study requirements will be met and the Dance curriculum will greatly contribute towards the attainment of a number of the statutory end-of-Key-Stage statements.

6.6 Structure of lessons

A structured approach to the teaching of Dance is essential for the full development of each child's performance, knowledge, understanding and experience, and is fundamental to effective teaching.

INTRODUCTION

This section takes the form of a series of activities which warm and mobilise the body's joints and muscles, using both whole body actions, such as swinging and gentle stretching, and actions using individual body parts. These may or may not be related to the main part of the lesson once the children have acquired a basic movement vocabulary.

RESPONSE TO STIMULI

This section involves the learning and development of body actions through both direct teaching and exploration in response to tasks and Dance stimuli. The children should be encouraged to share ideas, make observations and discuss these, so that they gradually increase their movement skills and vocabulary.

DEVELOPMENT OF IDEAS

This section works towards composing, practising and presenting dances. The children should be guided to select, refine and polish the elements of a dance composition leading to a finished performance.

CLOSING ACTIVITY

This section should include a variety of elements:

- calming and cooling-down activities
- sharing, observing, reflecting, discussing and appreciating the work performed by other members of the class or group
- discussing what has been achieved and what further progressions, ideas or outcomes might be considered for a subsequent lesson.

6.7 End-of-Key-Stage statements

The above teaching content, when presented progressively using a range of teaching styles throughout Key Stage 2, will more than satisfy the Dance Programme of Study and will contribute towards the attainment of a number of the end-of-Key-Stage statements as set out on page 100.

6.8 Useful organisations concerned with Dance

The Arts Council (Dance Department), 14 Great Peter Street, London, SW1P 3NQ. Telephone 071 973 6489.

National Resource Centre for Dance, University of Surrey, Guildford, GU2 5XH. Telephone 0483 509316.

The Council for Dance Education and Training, 5 Tavistock Place, London, WC1H 9SS.

Arts Education for a Multicultural Society (AEMS), 24 Highbury Grove, London, N5 2AE. Telephone 071 359 7122.

Athletic Activities

7.1 Introduction

ATHLETIC ACTIVITIES

'Athletic Activities concern the pursuit of the fulfilment of individual potential . . .' and . . . 'build on children's natural capacities to run, jump and throw. They promote all-round physical development – speed, strength, stamina and flexibility.'
(DES 1991, page 75)

The Physical Education National Curriculum (NC) Statutory Orders require that Athletic Activities be taught as one of the six areas of activity within a balanced programme of Physical Education at Key Stage 2 (seven to eleven years).

In order to satisfy these requirements, it is suggested that Athletic Activities be taught during the summer term of each of the four years of Key Stage 2. This chapter outlines a suggested Scheme of Work that could be taught in order to deliver the National Curriculum general and Athletic Activities Programme of Study requirements. More detailed information about teaching content in Athletic Activities is contained in section 7.5 of this chapter.

7.2 Athletic Activities Scheme of Work

Scheme of Work

Key Stage: 2 | **Area of activity:** Athletic Activities | **Cohort:** 1994-95

Units of Work (length of unit x length of lessons)

	Autumn	Spring	Summer
Year 3			6+6 x 40 mins
Year 4			6+6 x 40 mins
Year 5			6+6 x 40 mins
Year 6			6 x 40 mins

Process aims

The Scheme of Work will work towards enabling the pupils to carry out the following:

PLANNING AND COMPOSING

- plan safe body warm-up and warm-down activities for a range of athletic activities
- co-operate with a partner and in a small group to plan a small competition.

PARTICIPATING AND PERFORMING

- perform safe warm-up and warm-down activities
- work alone and with others to develop, consolidate and refine their Athletics skills through practice

➔

- lift, carry, place and use equipment appropriately and safely
- perform and develop basic actions in running, throwing and jumping
- practise measuring and comparing their performance in running, jumping and throwing
- participate in competitive Athletics situations against themselves and others.

APPRECIATING AND EVALUATING

- appreciate the importance of good posture and body position in the performance of Athletics skills and events
- make simple constructive comments and judgements on their own and others' performance.

Programme of Study requirements

'Pupils should:

- *practise and develop basic actions in running (over short and longer distances and in relays), throwing and jumping.*
- *be given opportunities for and guidance in measuring, comparing and improving their own performance.*
- *experience competitions, including those they make up themselves.'*

Teaching Content Outline

Year: 3 **Unit:** 1

Title: Introduction to running, jumping and throwing actions

Summer 1st half term

6 x 40 minute lessons

Outline: This unit introduces the pupils to the activities involved in this part of the P.E. curriculum and provides a taster of each of the three main activities: running, throwing and jumping. Two lessons will be spent on each, drawing primarily on the pupils' natural body actions. Introduce pupils to the actions and events of Athletic Activities, and how these will be taught to them in school. The children will experience a range of basic running actions through activities which require variations of pace/speed, such as jogging, half pace, three quarter pace and sprinting. Children will be encouraged to observe the simple effects of these types of running on the body. Throwing practice and games will be used to introduce the basic throwing actions involved in underarm and overarm throwing. Simple jumping activities for distance and height will be used to develop an understanding of these basic movement skills. The pupils will be involved in the process of observing and comparing their own performances and those of a partner.

Year: 3 **Unit:** 2

Title: Development of running actions and events

Summer 2nd half term

6 x 40 minute lessons

Outline: This unit develops basic running actions and introduces the pupils to the difference between sprinting (fast running), middle-distance (mid-pace running) and long-distance (jogging) athletic events. The action of the legs (length and speed of stride), the arm swing and position and how to breathe when running will be taught. The children will practise a range of basic running actions with variations of pace/speed. Practice and activities will involve observing, measuring and comparing their own performances and those of a partner, and trying to improve their personal best. Children will be encouraged to observe the effects of these types of running on their body, and simple explanations will be provided. Group/team competition will be introduced, using relay style running games.

Year: 4 **Unit:** 3

Title: Developing throwing actions from Games into athletic actions

Summer 1st half term

6 x 40 minute lessons

Outline: This unit develops basic throwing actions and introduces the pupils to the difference between throwing for accuracy and throwing for distance. It develops from the Games units taught throughout the previous year. Throwing for distance with an overarm throwing action, using the shoulder pass/javelin technique, will be developed and practised using a variety of bean bags and small balls. The children will learn the stages of the standing overarm throwing action – correct stance, preparation backswing, ready position, arm swing, body action and follow-through. Introduce the use of a short run-up to enhance performance to those children able to respond. Throwing heavier objects, such as cricket and rounders balls, will be practised. Other athletic throwing actions, i.e. pushing and slinging, will also be introduced, demonstrated and practised, using medium-sized balls and quoits and adapted apparatus. The processes of observing, measuring and trying to improve children's personal best performance will be integral to the teaching content.

Year: 4 **Unit:** 4

Title: Developing jumping actions into athletic actions

Summer 2nd half term

6 x 40 minute lessons

Outline: Introduction of basic jumping for distance and jumping for height. The standing broad jump and high jump techniques, and simple hop, step and jump techniques leading towards the triple jump will all be introduced. This will lead on to three and five stride approaches in the long jump and the high jump as an introduction to the more formal recognised Athletics jumping events.

Year: 5 **Unit:** 5

Title: Extending running actions and events

Summer 1st half term

6 x 40 minute lessons

Outline: This unit extends the basic running actions, introduces simple but effective starting techniques for sprinting, teaches the action used in hurdling events, and introduces the pupils to aspects of health-related fitness using the difference between sprinting, middle-distance and long-distance athletic events. Correct techniques and styles will be reinforced and the pupils will have the opportunity to measure and record simple fitness indicators, such as pulse and breathing rates, when practising and performing the different events. Simple training techniques to improve performance will also be explained. Group/team competition will be developed, and the children will learn simple baton-changing techniques which require them to work together to assist each other. The unit will conclude with a mini-competitive event which should allow children to select their event(s) and the type of competition they would like. The children should assist with the organisation of the event, and act as officials and recorders, as part of the learning process.

Year: 5 **Unit:** 6

Title: Extending throwing and jumping actions and events

Summer 2nd half term

6 x 40 minute lessons

Outline: This unit extends the basic throwing and jumping actions. The approach, take-off and flight phase techniques for high jump, long jump and triple jump will be taught. Pupils will practise correct techniques and styles, and will have the opportunity to measure and record practice and performance of the different events. Simple training techniques to improve performance will also be explained. The unit should conclude with a mini-team competition which will require groups of mixed ability children to work together to assist each other when competing as a team rather than as individuals. As in the previous unit, the children will assist with the organisation of the event, and act as officials and recorders, as part of the learning process.

Year: 6 **Unit:** 7

Title: Developing simple training programmes

Summer 2nd half term

6 x 40 minute lessons

Outline: The children will each select one running, one throwing and one jumping event. Working in pairs and co-operative groups, the children will record their best performances in the chosen events during the first lesson of the unit. Drawing on the knowledge and understanding they have gained during previous Units of Work and with guidance from the teacher the children will develop their own programme of work for the remainder of the unit. They will be given a number of guidelines to use, and targets that they should meet, in preparation for the last lesson in the unit. During the last lesson the children should re-record their performance and comparisons can then be made. A simple award scheme for primary school Athletics will be used to give children targets and comparisons to work with in addition to their own personal best performance.

Organisational strategies

The organisation of the pupils is based on a class of 32 children split into four colour groups of eight, of mixed gender and mixed ability. Much of the teaching content will utilise the four colour-coded baskets of Games equipment described in Chapter 3. Any additional specialist Athletics equipment needed for each lesson will be organised into four sets, and each group of children will be given responsibility for a number of pieces of equipment. The children will be taught to collect, carry correctly and return the equipment that will be used during the lessons.

Staff, facilities and equipment required

Lessons will be taught by the class teacher with occasional input from students and visiting teachers or specialists to the school. Where possible, Athletics lessons will be taught outdoors, using the grass and playground areas as the curriculum content demands. A wet weather alternative in the school hall should be available if required; teachers should attempt to teach the same curriculum using adapted practices.

The equipment required in addition to the colour-coded baskets is listed below.

High jump stands, rope and bar	4 x 30m measuring string
Long jump rake (if sandpit is available)	4 x 10m measuring string
1 x 40m tape measure	4 stop watches
Skittles and ropes to form hurdles	

The children will be trained to lift and carry heavier Athletics equipment such as hurdles and high jump stands and to rake and maintain the sand in the landing areas.

Safety precautions

Ensure that appropriate dress is worn and that all jewellery is removed before each lesson. Check that pupils understand the reasons for these simple rules. Establish a code of conduct and safety requirements at the beginning of each unit and remind pupils of them regularly throughout the scheme. Check and record any medical conditions that may affect the activity. Carry out an evaluation of skills competence and group pupils accordingly during the first lesson of each unit. Ensure that codes of behaviour and safety are clearly understood before the pupils begin the units.

Special needs

(It is likely that a wide range of ability levels will be apparent from the beginning of the first unit. Some children may have special needs that require particular help at the beginning of the course and it may be necessary to enlist a knowledgeable parent or advisory support to help with special needs in the early stages. Nevertheless, the teaching content is designed to cater for all ranges of ability. Individual special needs should be assessed at the beginning of the first Unit of Work.)

Record-keeping and assessment procedures [see also Chapter 10]

Record-keeping with reference to teaching content should include:

- a Scheme of Work with recommendations for future planning and content
- a Forward Plan for each Unit of Work within the Scheme of Work, with a summary and recommendations for future teaching content in subsequent Units
- an ongoing record and formative evaluation of individual lesson content, recorded on Forward Plans and used to inform planning and teaching of subsequent lessons
- where necessary and appropriate, individual lesson plans based on the content outline in the Forward Plan with an evaluation and recommendations for the next lesson.

Assessment procedures should include:

- ongoing evaluation of class progress in relation to aims and objectives throughout the teaching units
- ongoing observation and recording of each pupil's progress, in relation to the aims and pupil targets throughout each of the Units of Work
- school summative records for individual pupils with reference to end-of-Key-Stage statements updated at the end of each year and at the end of each key stage.

End-of-Key-Stage statements

'By the end of the key stage, pupils should be able to:

- *respond safely, alone and with others, to challenging tasks, taking account of levels of skill and understanding.*
- *evaluate how well they and others perform and behave against criteria suggested by the teacher, and suggest ways of improving performance.*
- *sustain energetic activity over appropriate periods of time in a range of activities and understand the effects of exercise on the body.'*

Evaluation of scheme

(A record of class progress at the end of each Unit of Work should be made to assist with future planning (as described in Chapter 10) and a summary of the whole scheme should be recorded here.)

Recommendations for future planning

(A statement of any recommendations that become apparent during the teaching should be recorded in order to inform future planning and teaching for other cohorts of children.)

7.3 Sample of Athletic Activities Unit of Work Forward Plan

The following section is a sample Forward Plan for Unit 1 (shown on page 116) in the Athletic Activities Scheme of Work. A similar blank master document which teachers can use for their own curriculum planning can be found in the Appendix (pages 174–178).

Unit of Work Forward Plan

Area of Activity: Athletic Activities

Unit: 1

Title: Introduction to running, jumping and throwing actions

Summer 1st half term

6 x 40 minute lessons

Day: Tuesday pm

Class: 3ER **Age:** 7/8

No. in class: 15m, 17f

Teacher: E Robertson

Previous knowledge and experience

The children have taken part in basic Athletic Activities within Key Stage 1 and have experienced basic running, jumping and throwing actions in Games and Gymnastics and through small informal competitive situations in lessons. Little formal teaching of specific athletic techniques has been done.

Aims of the Unit of Work

- to introduce pupils to the actions and events of Athletic Activities
- to experience a range of basic running actions used in jogging, half pace, three quarter pace and sprinting
- to introduce the basic throwing actions involved in underarm and overarm throwing
- to introduce jumping activities for distance and height
- to observe the simple effects of these types of activities on the body, and for pupils to compare their own performance with that of a partner.

CONTENT OUTLINE

LESSON 1 Introduce class to work to be covered in Scheme of Work. Explain the actions and events of Athletic Activities, and how these will be taught in school. Explain the different types of running events and the actions used in long-distance and middle-distance running and sprinting. Following a warm-up, the children should practise running at jogging pace, half pace and three quarter pace. While they are practising, ask them to observe the different effects of these types of running on their body.

LESSON 2 The children should be taught the basic arm and leg actions for sprinting and experience a range of basic sprinting activities, including individual sprints over a range of distances. Small relay activities should be taught, together with the simple baton-changing practices. Children should compare the simple effects of these types of running on the body with those observed in Lesson 1. The children should use stop watches to measure and record their performances.

LESSON 3 Throwing practices and games should be used to introduce the basic actions of underarm and overarm throwing. Tennis balls, cricket balls and quoits should be used to develop the overarm and slinging techniques used for distance throwing in Athletics events. Accuracy over distance should also be practised, with the children working in pairs. The children should also be taught techniques to measure and record their performance. Safety considerations in throwing events should be specifically indicated so that children understand how to practise safely.

LESSON 4 This lesson should be a direct expansion of Lesson 4, with time allowed for children to practise and improve their techniques. A comparison with their performance in the previous lesson should be made. The children should work in small groups, throwing over previously marked distances, to allow them to estimate then measure the distances thrown.

LESSON 5 This lesson should introduce the children to basic actions of jumping for distance. The technique for the standing long jump should be explained and demonstrated. A short run-up should then be introduced, using a one foot take-off and an arm swinging action, and a good landing position.

LESSON 6 A basic high jumping action using the scissors technique should be introduced, using a piece of elastic held by two children. The emphasis should be on developing and practising the correct action rather than attempting to achieve a great height in the jump.

Organisational strategies

Children change in the classroom and are split into groups at the beginning of each lesson. Small groups of four, five or six should be used to allow maximum practice activity to take place. Emphasise the correct and safe techniques for carrying and using equipment throughout. Emphasise good warm-up and body preparation throughout the unit.

Facilities and equipment required

The grass area in the school field.

Apparatus: 4 coloured baskets of equipment; elastic ropes; wooden batons; measuring tapes and stop watches. Each group will also have a card for recording measurements.

Safety precautions

Dress – t-shirt and shorts, jogging suit or tracksuit and outdoor pumps. No jewellery. Hair tied back. Check working area and equipment is safe and made ready. Check on medical problems. Remind class about rules of behaviour and safety, especially with equipment handling. Take first-aid kit.

Special needs provision

(This section should be used to help plan and record provision for children with special educational needs in Athletic Activities. This may include catering for children with physical and mental disabilities, children with emotional difficulties and the physically gifted.)

Activities positions

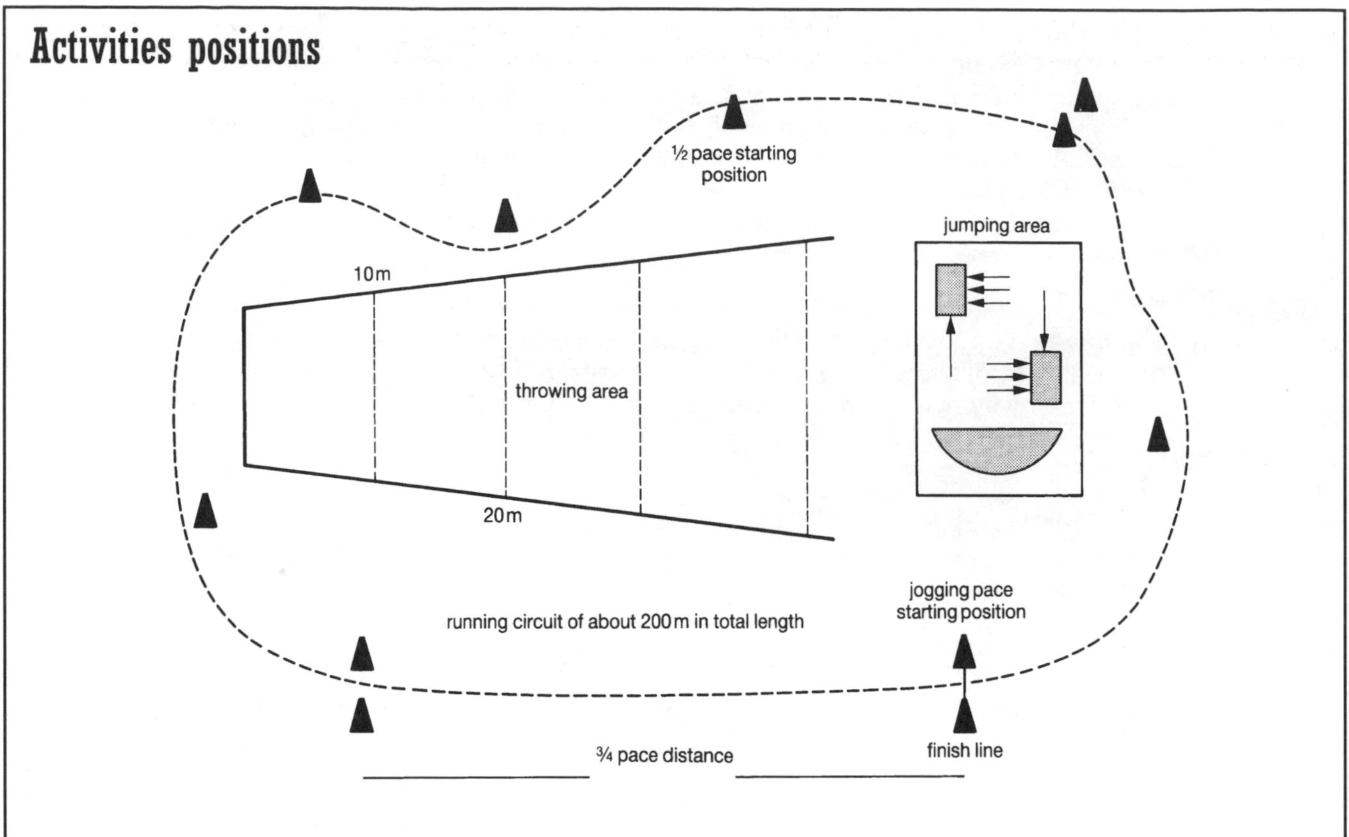

Figure 7.1
Athletic Activities plan

Evaluation of lessons

(The date should be entered beside the lesson number once the lesson has been taught. If individual lesson plans are not used by teachers, a highlighter pen can be used to indicate the work that has been covered in each lesson in case adjustment decisions need to be made. This records what is actually taught relative to what was planned.

Notes should be made in this section each week, with recommendations for future lessons. This is useful for future planning and for record-keeping purposes.)

Summary and recommendations for next unit

(A record of class progress at the end of the Unit of Work should be made to assist with future planning. Individual pupil progress should also be recorded at appropriate times using the method described in Chapter 10.)

7.4 Sample Lesson Plan

A sample plan for Lesson 1 in the above Unit of Work, showing details of tasks and activities, corresponding teaching points and the organisation of children, equipment and space, has been included on the following pages.

Athletic Activities Lesson Plan (1)

Key Stage 2 **Unit of Work 1: Introduction to running, jumping and throwing actions**

Lesson number in unit: 1	**Date:** Tuesday 19th April 1995
Time: 2.10 – 2.50pm	**Length of lesson:** 40 mins
Class: 3ER **Age:** 7/8	**Teacher:** E Robertson
No. in class: 15m, 17f	**Venue:** School field

Lesson objectives

(S = social, E = emotional, C = cognitive, P = physical)

S: to work in small groups and show an understanding of the range of ability within the class
E: to provide pupils with an enjoyable and successful learning experience
C: to enable the children to observe the effects of different types of running on their body
P: to experience running at a range of paces, especially jogging and three quarter pace.

Facilities and equipment

School field with marked-out areas for running over a range between 40m and 200m
Hall/gymnasium if wet weather
Stop watch and whistle

Lesson evaluation

Athletic Activities Lesson Plan (2)

Phase	Tasks/activities	Teaching points/coaching feedback	Organisation of pupils and apparatus
Preparation	Check field and equipment baskets. Check dress, jewellery and hair. Allocate group leaders to carry baskets.	Explain behaviour expected and reasons for safety. Remind class that care should always be taken when carrying equipment for Athletic Activities. Briefly explain what Athletic Activities include at KS2.	Change in classroom and line up at door when clothes are tidy. Group leaders to go and collect baskets and position them in allocated places on the field.
Introduction	Introduce work to be covered in unit.		
Warm-up (5 mins)	Free skipping practice using ropes from the basket. Stretching exercises to stretch leg tissue. Sitting astride – reach over towards toes. In crouch position extend 1 leg behind and try to put heel on the ground. Kneel down with legs together and gently stretch backwards with hands beside hips on ground. Gentle arm swinging exercises standing.	Encourage movement while skipping as well as stationary. Make sure you have a good space. Stretch slowly – don't bounce! Keep the back leg straight. Make sure ankles and knees are together.	Line up at basket and take out a skipping rope and practise in a space. Work in a good space.
Skill learning and development	Explain the different pace running actions of jogging, half pace and three quarter pace. Jogging pace running in small groups. Allow a rest to recover. Half pace running in small groups over half the distance. Allow a rest to recover. Three quarter pace running in small groups over a short distance. Allow a rest to recover. (Observe the children and if they are managing the pace of work repeat each exercise so they can learn from a second attempt, especially the shorter distances.)	Explain the differences and emphasise the need to 'pace' themselves. Try to develop a relaxed rhythm in your running – nice and slowly to begin with – it's not a race. What effect has it had on your body? What happens when you rest? Keep trying to pace yourself. What effect has it had on your body this time? Don't start off too fast. Concentrate on running to the finishing line. Try to make your arms and legs go a bit faster. Remember to keep breathing and to relax.	Get the children to set up the circuit using the marked out area. Set children running in groups round the circuit at timed intervals of 10 seconds between groups. Explain the distance they have to run. Set the groups running one at a time. Ask those watching to observe the actions and the pace others run at.
Conclusion	Gently jog round the circuit and collect the markers. Line up at basket and make sure it's tidy. Debrief the lesson as they change.	Try to relax and breathe deeply. Emphasise the importance of taking care of the equipment when carrying it.	Allow the children to jog at their own pace. Put equipment away, return to the classroom quietly and calmly, get changed. Have a wash if desired.

7.5 Athletic Activities teaching content

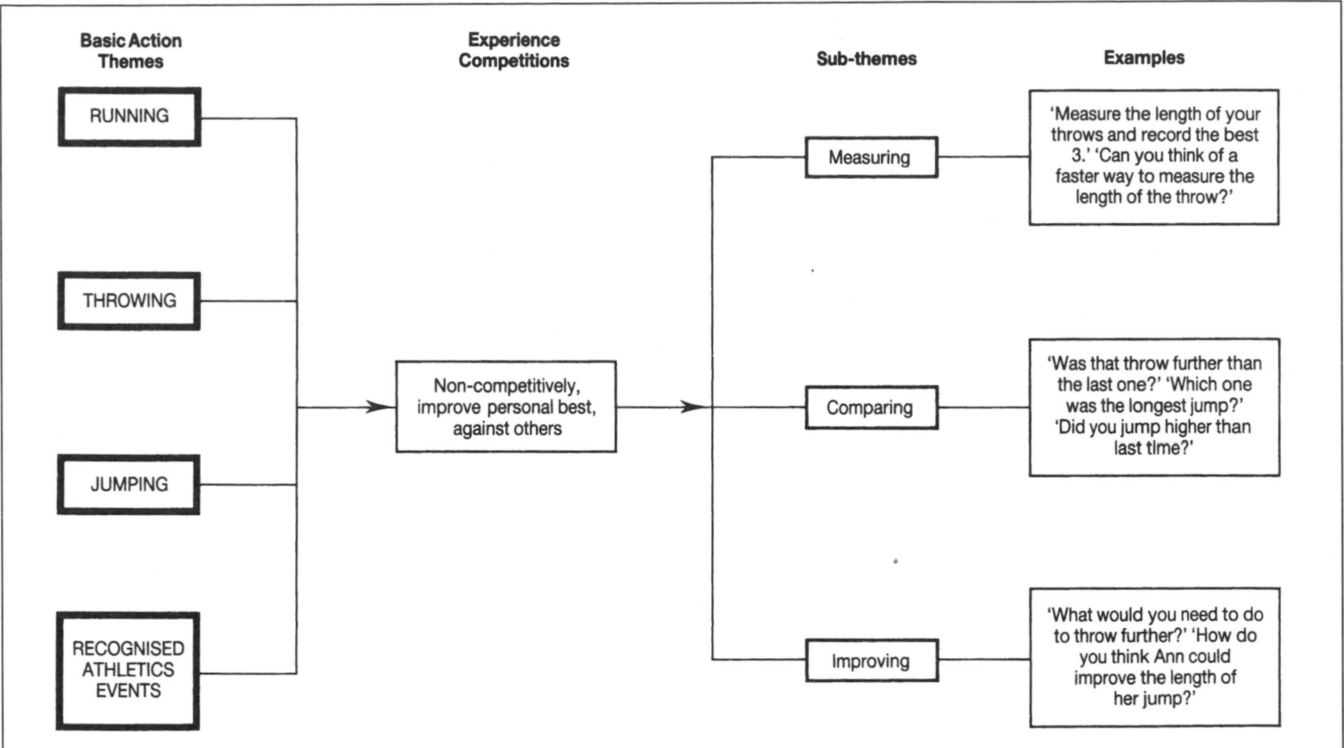

Figure 7.2
Athletic Activities Action Themes

The National Curriculum requires that pupils should develop basic athletic actions, and be given opportunities to measure, compare and improve their performances and to experience competition. In order to achieve this, the teaching content of the Athletic Activities curriculum may be organised into four basic 'action themes'. These are:

- running
- throwing
- jumping
- recognised Athletics events.

Fundamentally, the teaching content involves the progressive learning and development of the skills within the themes in a variety of competitive situations, incorporating the processes of measuring, comparing and improving. A flow chart illustrating the content and progression is shown in figure 7.2.

The basic techniques described in this section will provide a sound base for future participation and learning in Athletic Activities. Descriptions of the basic actions have been kept as simple as possible, and diagrams have been used to illustrate the physical performance of the major skills and techniques. The diagrams have been drawn to reflect accurate arm, leg and body positions during the performance and may therefore be taken as an indication of the results that children should aim to achieve. The processes of measuring, comparing and improving should form an integral part of learning throughout the presentation of the curriculum.

Running

The first basic action theme to be taught in Athletics is running. Running is a natural action, and in the early stages little technical information and few teaching points are necessary. Teachers should emphasise activity and practice, allowing the children to perform many repetitions of the activities set. In the first instance, the emphasis should be on running at two thirds speed over short distances such as 40 metres. The learning focus should be on a relaxed action, fast arms and legs and a natural head and body position.

As speed and distance increase, children should be taught to run through the finishing line/tape, and some children may need to be taught efficiency in running style by emphasising that arm and leg actions should be in line. All running should be from a standing start, using the starting commands of 'on your marks–set–go'.

Figure 7.3
The basic running technique with arm and leg actions in line

Hurdling over high barriers is not an event for normal class teaching, but much enjoyment and learning can be achieved by using cones or skittles with sticks or skipping ropes at appropriate heights. The emphasis should be on running and rhythm; the barriers should be placed at suitable distances to enable the pupils to take three strides between them.

Figure 7.4
The basic hurdling technique over two hurdles (made using skittles and skipping ropes), with three strides between the hurdles

Running over longer distances can be done using a small circuit which children can lay out themselves, like that shown below. The children should develop a comfortable jogging action which is relaxed, with regular breathing. They can also develop an understanding of pace work by learning to judge how far they can run at a variety of speeds.

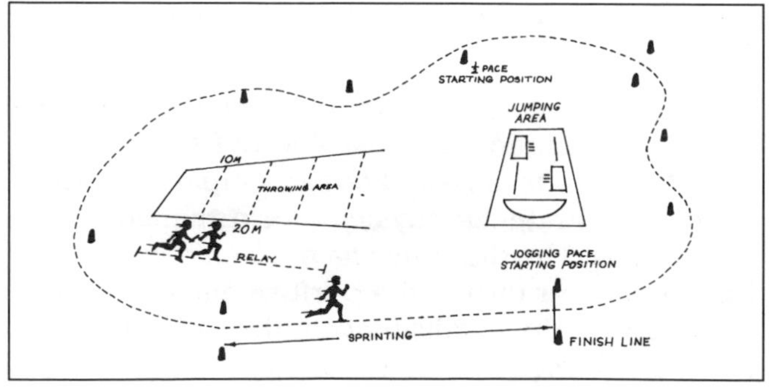

Figure 7.5
A circuit with markers and distances for a variety of paces indicated between markers

Team running is also an enjoyable activity. Shuttle relays, using the exchange of a piece of equipment such as a bean bag or a quoit can be followed by baton changing and simple relay passing techniques such as the upsweep method of baton exchange.

Figure 7.6
The upsweep technique of baton changing

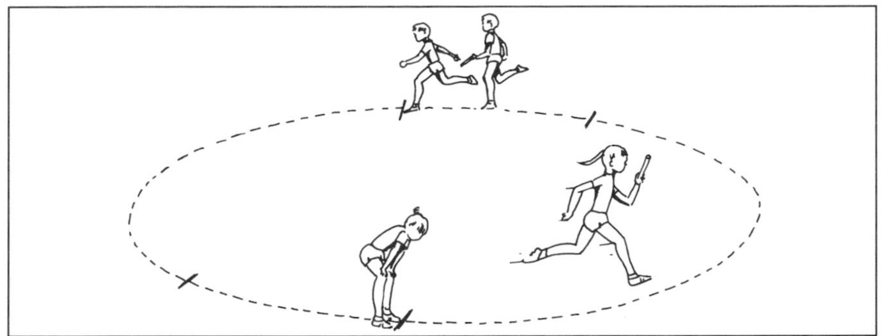

Figure 7.7
Children running in relay activities

Throwing

Basic throwing actions are also taught as part of the Games Scheme of Work. In Athletic Activities these throwing actions can be extended towards athletic events firstly by extending the range of equipment used, to include heavier objects such as cricket and rounders balls and quoits, and secondly by introducing throwing for distance and accuracy and throwing to a partner and over measured distances.

The pushing action, as in shot-putting, and rotating/slinging action, as in discus throwing, can be presented towards the end of the key stage with highly modified equipment.

Figure 7.8
The pushing action with a modified shot

Figure 7.9
The rotating/slinging action with a quoit

Jumping

The basic action theme of jumping should link up with and then extend the jumping and landing theme in Gymnastics. The children should be taught how to achieve a safe and controlled landing before speed, length or height are allowed in the jumps.

The standing long jump, triple jump and high jump actions should be taught first.

Figure 7.10
Standing long jump action

Figure 7.11
Hop, skip and jump actions

Figure 7.12
Standing scissors high jump action

Once the jumping action and the correct, safe and controlled landing in each event have been acquired, the children can learn and practise a three-stride approach (run-up), then increase this to five, seven and then nine strides. The development of a good approach technique leads towards learning the scissors action in the high jump, whilst in the long jump children should concentrate on a controlled run-up and vigorous take-off.

Figure 7.13
A controlled run-up and vigorous take-off in the long jump, using a five-stride approach

Figure 7.14
A controlled approach and scissors action in high jump

Recognised Athletics events

After the initial stages have been introduced and developed the latter part of Key Stage 2 should see the emergence of recognised formal Athletics events. This will involve the children in understanding and learning the rules, keeping records of their performances and measuring time/length, much of which should be peer based.

7.6 Structure of lessons

For all children, a structured approach to the teaching of Athletic Activities is required for maximum benefit to be gained from the teaching content. A suggested structure for the lessons is given below.

INTRODUCTION

This section will include the warm-up, limbering and stretching exercises and will then link the previous lesson into the current one.

SKILL LEARNING

This section is where new skills are introduced and taught, either through whole class teaching methods or to smaller groups on a more informal basis.

DEVELOPMENT

In this section the work introduced in the earlier part of the lesson, together with previously taught activities, can be practised and improved. Performance against time and distance can be measured, as can performance against other 'teams' from the class.

CONCLUSION

This will include a warm-down period, the putting away of equipment and apparatus and a preview of the next lesson.

7.7 End-of-Key-Stage statements

The above teaching content, when presented progressively using a range of teaching styles throughout Key Stage 1 and 2, will more than satisfy the Athletic Activities Programme of Study and will lead towards the attainment of a number of the end-of-Key-Stage statements as set out on page 119.

7.8 The national governing body for Athletics

The Amateur Athletics Association, 225a Bristol Road, Edgbaston, Birmingham.

ATHLETICS AWARD SCHEMES

Five Star Award Scheme: National Administrator, 290 Beacon Road, Loughborough, Leicestershire, LE11 2RD.

English Schools Award Scheme: Secretary, 26 Newburgh Green, New Malden, KT3 5HS.

Thistle Award Scheme: Caledonia House, South Gyle, Edinburgh, EH12 9DQ.

Outdoor and Adventurous Activities

8.1 Introduction

OUTDOOR AND ADVENTUROUS ACTIVITIES

'Outdoor and Adventurous Activities involve physical activity in different contexts which require the application of basic physical skills in such a way that they enhance motor skill development. There are long-term benefits in terms of the development of endurance and physiological training which are complemented by mental challenges where the focus can be competitive or non-competitive. The activities enable pupils to experience a degree of challenge and risk which can develop the confidence to travel and manage the body in potentially hazardous environments where pupils can choose their own level of participation and adventure threshold.'
(DES 1991, page 76)

The Physical Education National Curriculum (NC) Statutory Orders require that Outdoor and Adventurous Activities be taught as one of the six areas of activity within a balanced programme of Physical Education at Key Stage 2.

At first sight the Programme of Study requirements may appear rather daunting. However, there are a number of activities that require no specialist knowledge on the part of the teacher but which will directly contribute to the Programme of Study requirements.

It is perfectly acceptable to teach many of these activities using a cross-curricular approach, combining them with other subjects such as Geography, Mathematics, Science, Technology and Art. However, provision should be made for recording and evaluating the teaching and learning in relation to the specific Outdoor and Adventurous Activities Programme of Study requirements. Teachers will be more than capable of making links with other areas of the curriculum where they exist, and no attempt has been made in this chapter to cross-reference activities with other subjects.

Some teachers, on the other hand, may be more confident using a subject-specific approach to planning this area of the curriculum. Consequently, a Scheme of Work specifically designed to meet the Programme of Study requirements is presented below as part of the whole curriculum planning model presented in Chapter 2. It is suggested that six units of Outdoor and Adventurous Activities be taught during the four years of Key Stage 2.

Whichever method is adopted, teachers should approach planning with confidence, drawing on their existing knowledge in other areas of the curriculum. When participating in Outdoor Activities, every precaution should be taken to ensure that any activity is safe. Adventurous outdoor pursuits involving inherent risk should only be taught by appropriately qualified and responsible personnel, ensuring the correct ratio of adults to children, and taking all possible safety precautions. If in doubt, schools should err on the side of caution and seek advice and guidance from local authority advisors, governing bodies, the Sports Council or a national outdoor centre. (Some useful addresses and telephone numbers are supplied at the end of this chapter.)

More detailed ideas for teaching content are contained in section 8.5 of this chapter. A blank Scheme of Work document is provided in the Appendix (pages 170–173).

8.2 Outdoor and Adventurous Activities Scheme of Work

Scheme of Work

Key Stage: 2

Area of activity: Outdoor & Adventurous Activities

Cohort: 1994-95

Units of Work (length of unit x length of lessons)

	Autumn	Spring	Summer
Year 3	7x40 mins		
Year 4	7x40 mins		
Year 5			6+6 x40 mins
Year 6			6+6 x40 mins

Process aims

The Scheme of Work will work towards enabling the pupils to carry out the following:

PLANNING AND COMPOSING

- safely co-operate with a partner and in small groups to plan an appropriate outdoor activity
- plan appropriate strategies to solve problems set by the teacher.

PARTICIPATING AND PERFORMING

- explore safely a variety of tasks set by the teacher and present different responses
- select, prepare, carry, check and use equipment appropriately and safely
- perform and develop basic skills in navigation, campcraft and climbing
- be aware of and record environmental phenomena and outdoor experiences.

APPRECIATING AND EVALUATING

- appreciate the need for safety in the performance of outdoor and adventurous activities
- appreciate and develop a respect for the outdoor environment and other participants in outdoor activities.

Programme of Study requirements

'Pupils should:

- *be taught the principles of safety in the outdoors and develop the ability to assess and respond to challenges in a variety of contexts and conditions.*
- *experience outdoor and adventurous activities in different environments (such as school grounds and premises, parks, woodlands or sea shore) that involve planning, navigation, working in small groups, recording and evaluating.*
- *be taught the skills necessary for the activity undertaken with due regard for safety, including the correct use of appropriate equipment.'*

Teaching Content Outline

Year: 3 **Unit:** 1

Title: Working with the local outdoor environment

Autumn 1st half term

7 x 40 minute lessons

Outline: Introduction to the local outdoor environment through awareness raising activities which take place out of doors. Developing visual and auditory observation skills outdoors; understanding the local environment through study of simple maps and plans of the school surroundings; observing and recording environmental conditions such as temperature, rainfall and sunshine; observing and recording local flora and fauna; planning a walk in the outdoors, including the selection of appropriate clothing. The teacher and children will plan these activities together and the children should learn how to record the main features of the activities.

Year: 4 **Unit:** 2

Title: Introduction to navigation skills and orienteering

Autumn 1st half term

7 x 40 minute lessons

Outline: Introduction to navigation skills and equipment. Mapwork including gaining an understanding of scales, and of the conventions of colour and symbols to represent man-made and natural features. Simple location exercises on known areas such as school buildings, fields and the playground, and mapping the route from home to school, to apply the skills learned. Compass work introducing bearings and using grid references. These navigation skills should be developed with simple orienteering activities in the school grounds or local park/woodlands.

Year: 5 **Unit:** 3

Title: Teamwork, trust and survival skills

Summer 1st half term

6 x 40 minute lessons

Outline: This unit will take place in the school hall/gymnasium and in a nearby outdoor setting (woodland or park). The children will take part in a range of problem solving activities, set by the teacher, that require them to plan and co-operate in teams. Planning safe responses in a variety of contexts will be built into the activities. Examples of activities will include *rescuing an injured team mate*, and *the sighted leading the blind.* Evaluating their own responses to the tasks set will form an integral part of the teaching.

Year: 5 **Unit:** 4

Title: Orienteering

Summer 2nd half term

6 x 40 minute lessons

Outline: This unit will concentrate on a range of individual and team orienteering activities in competitive and non-competitive situations.

Year: 6 **Unit:** 5

Title: Campcraft and equipment selection and care

Summer 1st half term

6 x 40 minute lessons

Outline: The content of this unit is based on planning a mini 24-hour outdoor expedition. Planning the expedition route, selecting the necessary equipment (e.g. clothing, rucksacks, food, stoves, tents), location of the overnight camp (in the school grounds or a local camping facility). Skills of tent pitching and striking, lighting camping stoves and cooking with them, evaluating the variety and choice of food, and packing and carrying rucksacks. It is hoped that the children will be able to conclude the unit by carrying out the expedition they have planned with help from volunteers (parents and/or teachers). If this is not possible, the unit will conclude with a local navigational walk (with children carrying survival equipment) to take place during an afternoon at the end of the unit.

Year: 6 **Unit:** 6

Title: Introduction to rock climbing

Summer 2nd half term

6 x 80 minute lessons

Outline: This unit should take place at a local facility which has a climbing wall, under the supervision of an appropriately qualified instructor. Simple pitch rock climbing, and introduction of the use of ropes and associated safety equipment and skills. Safety in the outdoors will be emphasised throughout. Information about access to local community organised outdoor activities will also be provided. If possible, the children will also take part in this activity in an outdoor setting during a residential experience at the end of the school year.

Organisational strategies

The organisation of the pupils is based on a class of 32 children. Groups and equipment will be organised using a mixture of self-selecting and teacher-directed strategies as required by the lesson content. Children will be taught to select, care for, carry, check, use and return the equipment that will be used during the lessons in a safe and appropriate manner.

Staff, facilities and equipment required

Lessons will be taught by the class teacher with occasional input from students or visiting teachers to the school. Unit 5 will require assistance from volunteer parents, teachers or other responsible adults for the overnight camp to take place. The last unit in the scheme should be led by a qualified and experienced climbing skills expert. The school hall/gymnasium, the school grounds and the local park and woodlands will be used where the teaching content demands. Lessons will be introduced in the classroom, where appropriate preparation work will be covered. For each unit of work, which requires specialist equipment and apparatus, a list and plan of the apparatus layout will be included in the Forward Plan. The equipment and apparatus required for the Scheme of Work are listed below.

Navigation equipment

- Plans of the classroom and school buildings
- Maps of the school grounds and local surrounding area
- 8 sets of compass, ruler, string and map-board with plastic cover
- Orienteering markers and cards

Campcraft equipment Tents, rucksacks and sleeping bags, lightweight camping stoves and a selection of cooking equipment and utensils. A selection and variety of food appropriate for camping will be available. In addition, the children will be asked to supply items of personal clothing, equipment and emergency rations for the range of activities to be taught.

Gymnasium equipment

- 12 large mats (2m x 1.5m)
- 6 benches (with hooks)
- Nest of 3 movement tables
- 2 trestle frames
- 6 ropes (wall mounted)
- Sectioned bar box
- Sectioned box
- 2 wooden planks with hooks
- Wooden climbing frame

Other useful equipment will include books containing reference material for navigation skills, weather conditions and flora and fauna.

Safety precautions

All pupils will be appropriately dressed for the activity and environmental conditions and this will be checked before leaving school premises. Parents will be advised by letter, one week in advance, of any specialist activities which require additional personal clothing or equipment, such as those →

described in Unit 5. An emphasis on safety and the management of risk factors in Outdoor and Adventurous Activities will be an integral part of the teaching content of the Scheme of Work. Medical problems will be checked and taken into consideration throughout. The class will be taught rules of behaviour and safe conduct, especially in relation to activities which have a potential risk factor associated with them.

Special needs

(It is likely that a wide range of ability levels will be apparent from the beginning of the first unit. Some children may have special needs that require special provision and it may be necessary to enlist knowledgeable advisory support to help with ideas to cater for children with special needs in the early stages. Nevertheless, the teaching content is designed to cater for all ranges of ability. Individual special needs should be assessed at the beginning of the first Unit of Work and specific provisions should be outlined in each Unit of Work Forward Plan.)

Record-keeping and assessment procedures [see also Chapter 10]

Record-keeping with reference to teaching content should include:

- a Scheme of Work with recommendations for future planning and content
- a Forward Plan for each Unit of Work within the scheme with a summary and recommendations for future teaching content in subsequent Units
- for more experienced and specialist teachers, an ongoing record and formative evaluation of individual lesson content used to inform the planning and teaching of subsequent lessons
- where necessary and appropriate individual lesson plans based on the content outline in the Forward Plan with an evaluation and recommendations for the next lesson.

Assessment procedures should include:

- ongoing evaluation of class progress in relation to aims and objectives throughout the teaching units
- ongoing observation and recording of each pupil's progress, in relation to the aims and pupil targets throughout each of the Units of Work
- school summative records for individual pupils with reference to end-of-Key-Stage statements updated at the end of each year and at the end of each key stage.

End-of-key-stage statements

'By the end of the key stage, pupils should be able to show that they can:

- *perform effectively in activities requiring quick decision making.*
- *respond safely, alone and with others, to challenging tasks, taking account of levels of skill and understanding.*
- *evaluate how well they and others perform and behave against criteria suggested by the teacher and suggest ways of improving performance.*
- *sustain energetic activity over appropriate periods of time in a range of physical activities and understand the effects of exercise on the body.'*

Evaluation of scheme

(A record of class progress at the end of each Unit of Work should be made to assist with future planning (as described in Chapter 10) and a summary of the whole scheme should be recorded here.)

Recommendations for future planning

(A statement of any recommendations that become apparent during the teaching should be recorded in order to inform future planning and teaching for other cohorts of children.)

8.3 Sample of Outdoor and Adventurous Activities Unit of Work Forward Plan

The following section is a sample Forward Plan for Unit 2 (shown on page 133) in the Outdoor and Adventurous Activities Scheme of Work. A similar blank master document which teachers can use for their own curriculum planning can be found in the Appendix (pages 174–177).

Unit of Work Forward Plan

Area of Activity: Outdoor and Adventurous Activities

Unit: 2	**Title:** Introduction to navigation skills and orienteering	
Autumn 1st half term	7 x 40 minute lessons	**Day:** Tuesday pm
Class: 4ES **Age:** 8/9	**No. in class:** 18m, 14f	**Teacher:** E Smith

Previous knowledge and experience

In the previous unit the children have been introduced to the local outdoor environment through awareness raising activities which take place out of doors. They have been taught visual and auditory observation skills and developed an understanding of the local environment through study of simple maps and plans of the school surroundings. They have planned and participated in a walk in the outdoors and have observed and recorded environmental conditions and local flora and fauna.

Aims of the Unit of Work

- to introduce the children to simple navigation skills and equipment
- to develop an understanding of maps and plans including scales and conventions of colour and symbols to represent man-made and natural features
- to be able to map the route from home to school
- to be able to use a compass, taking and using bearings and grid references
- to take part in simple location and orienteering exercises in the local environment.

CONTENT OUTLINE

LESSON 1 Introduce class to work to be covered in unit. Introduce plans and maps to the class and explain their use and how they are made. Explain the use of scales and of symbols and colour to represent features, using a simple map of the school grounds. Working in groups, the children should make a simple plan of the classroom, locating and marking, using recognisable symbols, the position of main features such as windows, doors, the teacher's desk, where they sit, the store cupboard, the computer, etc.

LESSON 2 Using a map of the local area ask the children to locate a number of features using the map symbols and then calculate their distance from the school using the map scale. Determine the shortest route that they could take from home to school if they were walking.

LESSON 3 Use a simple diagrammatic map of the school fields or local parkland to navigate a route from the classroom to a specified feature and back. Children should record on their map, using appropriate symbols, a number of features along the route.

LESSON 4 Introduce the class to grid references (four and six figure) and how to take a bearing using a compass. Working in groups using a local large scale map, the children should describe and record a number of features for which they have been given grid references. Working in reverse, the children should be given the description and symbol for particular features and should then find the features on the map and give the grid reference. These should be both theoretical and practical activities.

LESSON 5 This lesson will involve practically based activities in the school grounds. Children should work in groups with compasses, taking bearings and finding locations marked on their maps.

LESSON 6 This lesson will involve the children in a simple orienteering activity in the school grounds, utilising the map work that they have learned in earlier lessons. The activity and the scoring system to be used should be explained to the children when they have been split into groups. Unusual or interesting items (arrows, crosses, plaques, stones etc) should be positioned at pre-determined locations marked on their map, and the children should work together in teams of four to find and record the items at each location before returning to the classroom to have their cards scored. Each group will have only one map, so they must work together as a team.

LESSON 7 This lesson will develop the orienteering activity carried out in the previous lesson but should take place in the local park. Volunteer parents should be recruited to assist the teacher with the supervision of the exercise.

Organisational strategies

Work is introduced in the classroom, where children are taught and briefed about the outdoor activities in the unit. Where possible, the timing of the lessons will be flexible to take advantage of good weather conditions for the outdoor activities. Children change in the classroom for the orienteering activities, and showers are available if necessary. Appropriate groupings to be determined at the beginning of each lesson or activity.

Facilities and equipment required

Facilities include the school buildings and grounds and the local park. Plasticised plans of the school grounds and large scale maps (1:5000) of the local area surrounding the school. One compass per group.

Safety precautions

Remind the class about rules of safety and behaviour, particularly about showing consideration for the environment they are working in and other users.

Special needs provision

(This section should be used to help plan and record provision for children with special educational needs in Outdoor and Adventurous Activities. This may include catering for children with physical and mental disabilities, children with emotional difficulties and the physically gifted. Three examples are given below.

- One child (Peter) with hearing impairment but can lip read – make sure he can see you and speak clearly. He is also good at observing other children to interpret the task but may need some individual reinforcement.
- One child (Darren) with learning difficulties who can be disruptive but responds well in P.E. if interested and motivated. Responds well to praise but tends to seek attention if firm control is not exercised.
- One child (Joanne) with an artificial leg. Shy about P.E. but is very able and copes with most tasks well. Some encouragement needed but is aware of her own capabilities and understands well about safety. Keeps artificial leg on in lessons and wears tracksuit bottoms.)

Evaluation of lessons

(The date should be entered beside the lesson number once the lesson has been taught. If individual lesson plans are not used by teachers then a highlighter pen can be used to indicate the work that has been covered in each lesson in case adjustment decisions need to be made. This records what is actually taught relative to what was planned.

Notes should be made in this section each week with recommendations for future lessons. This is useful for future planning and for record-keeping purposes.)

Summary and recommendations for next unit

(A record of class progress at the end of the Unit of Work should be made to assist with future planning. Individual pupil progress should also be recorded at appropriate times using the method described in Chapter 10.)

8.4 Sample Lesson Plan

A sample plan for Lesson 6 in the above Unit of Work, showing details of tasks and activities, corresponding teaching points and the organisation of children, apparatus and space, has been included on the following pages. Experienced teachers may feel this level of planning is not necessary and that they can work from the lesson outlined in the Forward Plan. Some teachers may find that the children have a better learning experience if they plan individual lessons in the detail shown.

Outdoor and Adventurous Activities Lesson Plan (1)

Key Stage 2 **Unit of Work 2: Introduction to navigating skills and orienteering**

Lesson number in unit: 6

Time: 2.10 – 2.50pm

Class: 4ES **Age:** 8/9

No. in class: 18m, 14f

Date: Tuesday 11th October 1994

Length of lesson: 40 mins

Teacher: E Smith

Venue: School building and grounds

Lesson objectives

(S = social, E = emotional, C = cognitive, P = physical)

S: to co-operate as a group in carrying out the activity
E: to complete the activity with a measure of success
C: to plan a route round the course and evaluate its success
P: to pace running speed over the distance of the course.

Facilities and equipment

8 copies of the map of the school grounds used for orienteering type activities. Interesting items at each location marked on the map (positioned by responsible Year 6 children at the end of the lunch break)
Chart to record the scores and groups as they return from the course

Lesson evaluation

Outdoor and Adventurous Activities Lesson Plan (2)

Phase	Tasks/activities	Teaching points/coaching feedback	Organisation of pupils and equipment
Preparation	Prepare the maps of the school grounds and organise two Y6 children to act as course layers.	Stress the importance to the course layers of placing the items at the correct locations marked on the map.	Consult with the children and check that they know the physical location of the marked positions on the map.
Introduction	Introduce the activity and explain the criteria that the groups will work within.	The time they take to change is included in the activity; 1 point is awarded for every correctly located item; the time taken is recorded for the whole group to return to the classroom and get dressed; the winning group is the one with the most points *and* the shortest time.	Split children into 8 groups of 4 and hand out the maps and the cards and pencils to record the items they locate.
Activity	Begin the activity with the children getting changed, and as soon as the whole group reports ready to teacher, set the group off with a record of its starting time. As children return and all members of group are dressed they are given their time and their score card is marked.	Suggest that they plan their route before they set off; their clothes must be tidy and will be checked before they are allowed to start; suggest that they pace themselves over the course.	Stress that they should not disturb any other classes in the school by making too much noise. Walk round and observe the groups working so that appropriate feedback can be given. Children record on the wall chart their own score and the time they have taken to complete the course.
Evaluation and Debrief	Debrief the activity, drawing out points and allowing discussion about the activity. Give feedback on results for each group. Briefly explain what they will do in the next lesson.	Did they plan the route? Did they change their plan? Was their planning successful? How could they improve their plan/time? How well did they pace themselves? Did the group stay together or did it split up? Be encouraging and positive where appropriate.	Children sitting in their groups and discussing with the teacher and each other.

8.5 Outdoor and Adventurous Activities teaching content

The aim of the Outdoor and Adventurous Activities curriculum in the primary school is to provide children with the basic skills and understanding to equip them to make informed choices in later life about their participation in activities in the outdoors which have varying degrees of adventure and risk associated with them. It does not require them to take part in a full range of adventurous outdoor pursuits, such as canoeing, skiing or mountaineering, during curriculum time. Children should, however, experience a range of activities in the outdoors designed to develop their skills, their ability to plan their participation, and an appreciation and respect for the environment in which they are working.

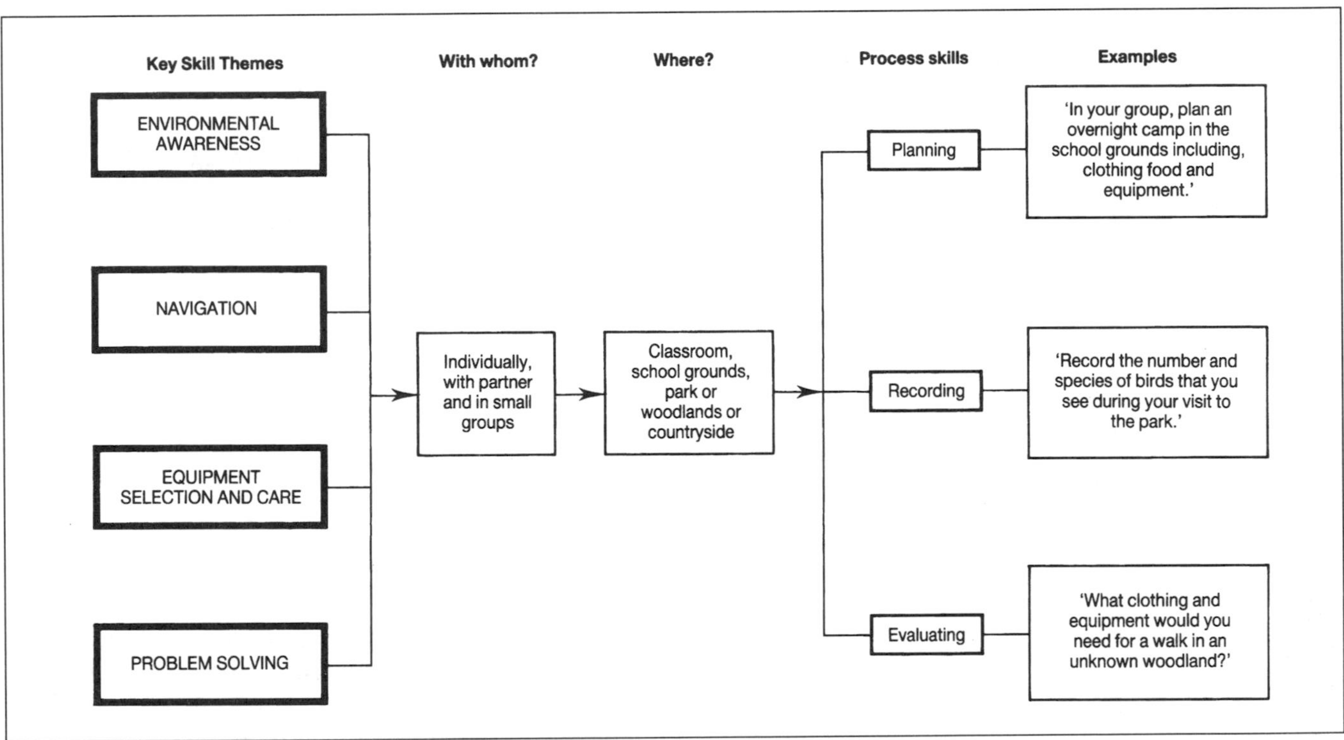

Figure 8.1
Outdoor and Adventurous Activities Skill Themes

The skills which children should be taught can be divided into four areas. These are:

- environmental awareness
- navigation
- problem-solving
- equipment selection and care.

An integral part of the teaching of these skills should be to develop the children's ability to plan, record and evaluate their participation in activities in the outdoors.

A flow chart illustrating this curriculum content is shown in figure 8.1. The Scheme of Work presented in section 8.2 illustrates how this content may be planned and delivered over the four years of Key Stage 2. The following sections provide some ideas for activities that teachers can use when planning and teaching this area of the curriculum.

Environmental awareness

Children's awareness of the outdoor environment can be developed through both practical and theoretical awareness raising activities in the classroom, the school grounds and any local park, woodland, sea shore or countryside. Some examples of both theoretical and practical activities are listed below.

Responding to environmental conditions In this activity the children are asked to choose, from lists supplied by the teacher, clothing and footwear that they think would be correct for a variety of weather conditions and environmental locations. Examples of these could be:

- a sunny day at the beach
- a walk in the park in the rain
- a cold windy day on a mountain.

They could write down what they would choose to wear and what activities they think would be safe and appropriate for the conditions and location, and then discuss why they think other clothing and activities would not be suitable.

Learning to observe These are activities to develop children's visual and auditory observation skills outdoors. One activity might teach them to use their peripheral vision by asking them to describe to a partner everything that they can see while looking at a specific object in front of them. Another example would be to ask one child to describe everything that she or he can hear; one partner writes this down, while another uses a tape recorder to record all the sounds that occur. The two records can then be compared back in the classroom.

Our local weather These activities involve observing and recording environmental conditions such as temperature, rainfall and sunshine. Recording can be ongoing over specified periods of time, ranging from hours, weeks or months to a whole year if seasonal changes are to be observed. The teacher should develop the children's ability to make links and draw conclusions about suitable outdoor activities from the results of the observations.

Local flora and fauna This activity will develop the children's understanding of and respect for the natural environment and its other uses, human, animal and plant. The class can be split into small groups, each of which is set a task to observe and record some aspect of animal, bird or plant life in a local outdoor location. Identifying (and perhaps drawing) types of trees, flowers, birds and animals and observing their habitat and behaviour are interesting and stimulating activities that will raise their awareness of the environment.

Going for a walk This activity provides an opportunity for children to be involved in planning an outdoor experience. They can make judgements and take decisions on aspects such as the length of time it will take them; the route they should take and any hazards they must negotiate (such as a main road to cross or a stream they must bridge); the weather conditions and consequently what they should wear; what footwear would be most comfortable; whether they need any equipment or food with them and if so what, and how it would best be carried (a rucksack?); and who they should inform about where they are going and when they will be back. Parallels can easily be drawn by the teacher between this experience and planning and participating in a more adventurous activity, such as a walk in the hills.

The teacher and children should plan these activities together, with the children learning how to record the main features of the activities.

Navigation

Through this area of the curriculum, children will acquire the ability to identify their physical location and learn how to find a safe route from one point to another. These skills can be acquired and practised in a relatively safe environment, but they become vital when children are participating in adventurous activities in what can sometimes become hazardous environmental conditions.

Navigation skills can be learned using plans, maps, compasses and simple measuring devices. A knowledge of how to interpret scales, colours and symbols on maps is necessary to identify man-made and natural features and to be able to recognise potential hazards. Simple location exercises in and around the school buildings, fields and playground, including mapping the route from home to school, allow the skills learned to be applied in practical activities out of doors. Compass work should include taking and following bearings to locate features using four and six-figure grid references.

A specific example of an exercise is to ask children to recognise and identify the hazards on the route shown on the map in figure 8.2. Questions that could be asked are:

- What is the shortest route by path from school to the sports centre? How far is it?
- What kinds of trees grow in the wooded area?
- What is the map reference at the point where the road crosses the stream?
- How far is it round the ponds by road?

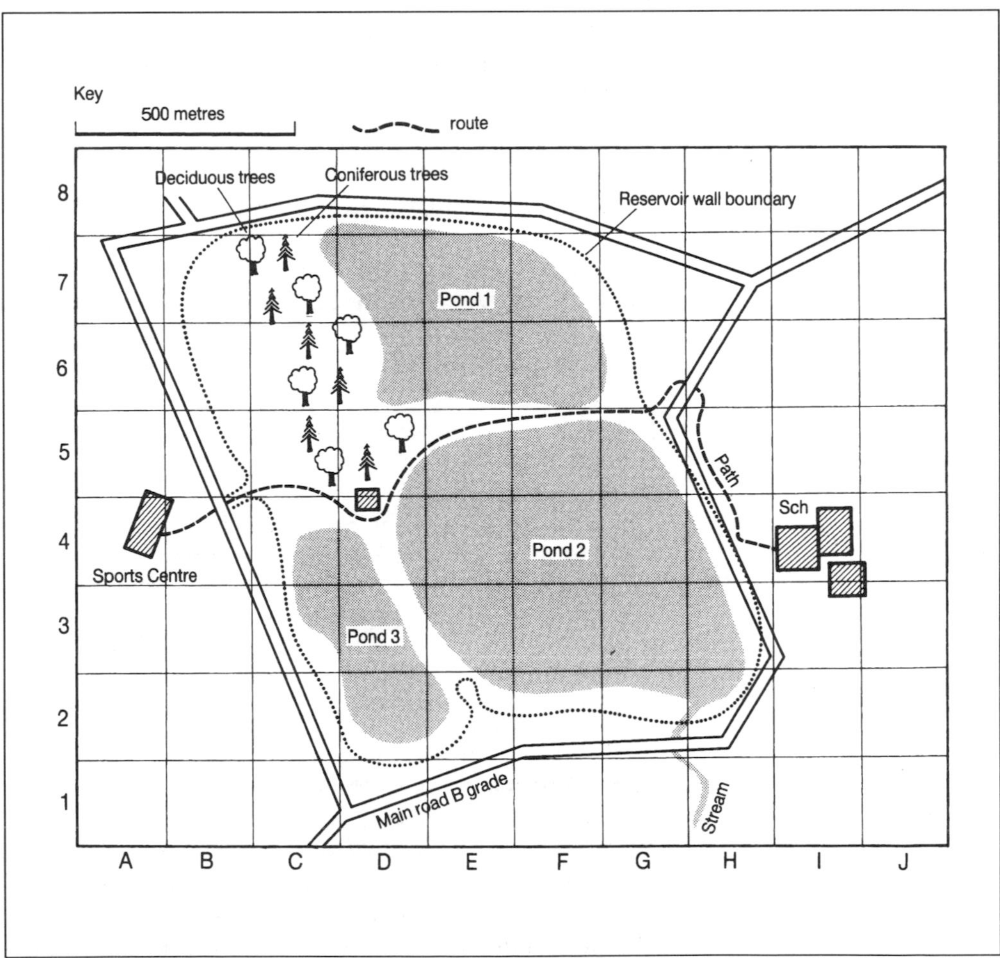

Figure 8.2

Simple orienteering activities in the school grounds or local park/woodlands will allow these navigation skills to be developed through an enjoyable and practical activity that is both physically and mentally demanding. Using permanent, observable characteristics at given locations (such as a plate on a park bench or a word on a signpost) eliminate the need for time-consuming course preparation. Large scale maps of the local park or the area surrounding the school can usually be obtained from the local tourist information centre, the local authority planning or parks department, or from Ordnance Survey, although the latter can be quite expensive.

Equipment selection and care

Selecting the correct equipment and its care are vital skills for safety in Outdoor and Adventurous Activities. Taking part in the activities listed below will begin to teach children the principles and practicalities of selecting and caring for basic outdoor equipment.

Packing and carrying rucksacks This activity can involve selecting, rejecting and packing a range of equipment needed for an outdoor expedition. The children can be taught about the features of a good, well-packed rucksack (size, weight, comfort of straps, weather resistance, distribution of load, etc) and the importance of packing emergency resources (such as spare clothing, emergency rations, water, first-aid kit, survival blanket, whistle, torch, etc).

Figure 8.3
A rucksack

Pitching and striking tents As well as learning how to erect and strike tents, the children should learn to recognise the features of a safe pitch and what precautions they should take in inclement weather. If possible, they could also learn how to make and take shelter using natural features and materials.

Lighting and cooking with camping stoves This activity can be used to teach children about the safe use of camping stoves and to alert them to the potential hazards, to themselves and the environment, of the careless use of matches and combustible materials. They can also be introduced to the basics of nutrition through the variety and choice of food that is available for camping.

The above practical activities and others like them can be taught initially with information and guidance being provided by the teacher and then by involving the children in problem-solving activities.

Problem-solving

This area of the curriculum is concerned with developing the children's ability to respond to physical challenges and problems in a safe and appropriate manner and to co-operate together as part of a team. Activities can take place in the school hall/gymnasium and in a nearby outdoor setting (woodland or park). Three examples of suitable activities are described below, but there are many more which teachers or children may devise for themselves. Safety must always take priority in these activities and care should be taken to ensure that children understand this when setting tasks. Caution should always be exercised when setting groups to compete against one another and against time, especially when equipment or bodies are raised above ground level. The physical skills needed to complete the activities, such as lifting and carrying equipment, should always be taught first.

Negotiating the obstacles This is a simple activity in which a team must negotiate a series of obstacles while remaining in contact with one another.

Rescuing an injured team-mate In this activity the children work in groups and are required to rescue an 'injured team-mate' who cannot walk, while negotiating a number of obstacles positioned between them and 'safety'. A dummy or substitute (such as a large cardboard box or bin liner filled with lightweight material) should be used to represent the casualty. The activity can take place in a gymnasium, using standard equipment such as benches, mats, ropes and wall bars, or in a local adventure playground. The group has five minutes at the beginning of the activity to plan the best method of carrying the casualty to safety and must then carry out this plan.

The sighted leading the blind This activity can be carried out in pairs or in groups. One child is blindfolded and his or her partner or group must lead him/her through a course set by the teacher. A typical task could require the 'sighted' child to lead the 'blind' child along a route chalked on the floor to a designated destination, negotiating obstacles, which the blind child must not touch, on the way. The sighted child may give verbal commands but may not touch his/her partner. A variation could eliminate the use of verbal commands and only allow pre-determined signals (such as hand claps) to provide the instructions for turning right or left or moving forwards. The children themselves should determine their signalling strategy.

There are many more problem-solving and teamwork activities that can include related areas of the curriculum such as 'navigation' and 'equipment selection and care'. Erecting a tent blindfold in a group, with instructions from one sighted member, is a good activity to develop teamwork, leadership and co-operation and communication skills. Navigation activities where groups must find and collect pieces of equipment following clues or map references are also enjoyable. The children should always be taught to evaluate their planning and their responses to the tasks so that they learn to make informed judgements about likely outcomes and learn from their experiences.

Adventurous Activities and a residential experience

Unit 6 in the Scheme of Work in section 8.2 involves climbing at a local sports centre. There are a number of community facilities, such as sports centres, swimming pools, universities, local reservoirs, or dry ski slopes, which can provide useful sources of expertise and equipment, allowing schools access to adventurous activities such as canoeing, climbing, windsurfing and skiing. These could take place as extra-curriculum activities if time and resources make it impossible to incorporate them into in-school curriculum time.

Many schools provide a residential experience for children towards the end of Key Stage 2. As well as providing the setting to practise what they have already learned, this is an excellent opportunity for children to experience an adventurous activity such as canoeing, hillwalking or climbing if expertise and facilities are available close to the residential centre. It is well worth the additional effort and planning when the children have an enjoyable, exciting, safe and memorable experience.

8.6 Structure of lessons

The diverse nature of the activities taught in this area of the curriculum does not make for one set lesson format. Teachers should use their own knowledge and common sense to determine the most appropriate lesson structure to use. Nevertheless, a structure has been suggested below which will suit a number of activities.

INTRODUCTION

This section can take place either in the classroom or 'on site' and introduces the children to the activity or task that will form the main part of the lesson. If the main activity is physically demanding (as in the case of orienteering), this section should also have the function of providing a physical warm-up. The introduction can be extended to provide children with planning and discussion time before they begin the activity.

SKILLS AND ACTIVITIES

This is the core of the lesson, during which skills can be practised, and the tasks and activities set by the teacher should be carried out by the children. It should involve the children in recording aspects of the activity upon which they have been briefed.

ACTIVITY EVALUATION AND DEBRIEF

This part of the lesson should allow the children time to discuss and evaluate their experiences and responses and to complete their recordings. It also provides the teacher with the opportunity to develop the children's ability to make links and draw conclusions from their observations about safety and suitable outdoor activities.

8.7 End-of-Key-Stage statements

The above teaching content will contribute towards the attainment of a number of the end-of-Key-Stage statements as set out on page 135.

8.8 Useful organisations and national outdoor centres

Council for Environmental Education, University of Reading, London Road, Reading, Berks. RG1 5AQ. Telephone 0734 756061.

National Association for Outdoor Education, Waterloo Cottage, Llanegryn, Ywywyn, Gwynedd, LL36 9SW.

Duke of Edinburgh's Awards Scheme, 5 Prince of Wales Terrace, Kensington, London, W8 5PG.

Glenmore Lodge Outdoor Training Centre, Aviemore, Inverness-shire, PH22 1QU. Telephone 047 986256.

Plas Y Brenin National Centre for Outdoor Activities, Capel Curig, Gwynedd, LL24 0ET. Telephone 06904 214.

Holme Pierrepont National Watersports Centre, Adbolton Lane, Holme Pierrepont, Nottingham, NG12 2LU. Telephone 0602 821212.

The Northern Ireland Mountain Centre, Tollymore, Bryansford, County Down, Northern Ireland. Telephone 03967 22158.

Swimming

9.1 Introduction

SWIMMING

'Swimming is a crucial survival skill and an essential pre-requisite for participation in a whole range of activities in and around water. Swimming is also the activity with the most consistent participation across age groups for both women and men, and which provides the best all-round exercise in terms of enhanced flexibility, strength, speed and stamina.'
(DES 1991, pages 77 and 78)

The Physical Education National Curriculum (NC) Statutory Orders require that Swimming be taught as one of the six areas of activity within a balanced programme of Physical Education at Key Stage 2 (seven to eleven years). It is recommended that children experience Swimming and water-related activities at both Key Stages 1 and 2, but if this is not possible then a minimum experience at Key Stage 2 is essential to ensure that the very specific end-of-Key-Stage statement relating to Swimming is attained. If Swimming is taught at Key Stage 1, the first part of the Programme of Study should be taught during that key stage. If it is not, the entire content of the Programme of Study should be covered during Key Stage 2.

Many Local Education Authorities have their own comprehensive guidelines to which schools should adhere. Swimming and water-related activities should only be taught by specifically qualified teachers or instructors so that the obvious safety considerations are not compromised. For this reason this chapter does not contain any technical information about the teaching of swimming, but concentrates on the presentation of a suggested Scheme of Work which schools can use as guidance when negotiating the curriculum that their pupils will experience in Swimming lessons.

9.2 Swimming Scheme of Work

It should be emphasised that the content of the Scheme of Work is progressive, and obviously not all children will progress at the same rate. The children should therefore work in ability groups, and the teaching content will need to be presented according to individual and/or group development. This means that the content of the scheme should be used only as a guide, and adapted as required by the individuals responsible for curriculum delivery. For this reason careful records should be kept of each pupil's progress. Some additional guidance relating to pre-programme organisation, teaching content and progression is given in sections 9.3 and 9.4.

SWIMMING

Scheme of Work

Key Stage: 2 | **Area of activity:** Swimming | **Cohort:** 1994-95

Units of Work (length of unit x length of lessons)

	Autumn	Spring	Summer
Year 3			6+6 x 30 mins
Year 4	7 x 30 mins		6+6 x 30 mins
Year 5	7+8 x 30 mins		
Year 6			6 x 30 mins

Process aims

At Key Stage 2 the following aims are specific to swimming:

PLANNING AND COMPOSING

- to develop a proper balance between confidence and caution in and near water
- to develop familiarity with the medium in safe and controlled conditions.

PARTICIPATING AND PERFORMING

- to learn water skills, games and swimming strokes
- to learn survival skills appropriate to their confidence
- to learn the principles of water safety and assess the nature of water hazards.

APPRECIATING AND EVALUATING

- to understand that swimming skills can be used for survival, recreation and competition, and that they can support other water-based activities
- for pupils to learn to appreciate and evaluate their own skills
- to develop appropriate social attitudes and behaviour before, during and after Swimming lessons.

Programme of Study requirements

'Pupils should:

- *be taught the codes of hygiene and courtesy for using swimming pools.*
- *be given opportunities to develop confidence in water; be taught how to rest in water, how to float and how to adopt support positions.*
- *be taught a variety of means of propulsion using either arms or legs or both, and develop effective and efficient swimming strokes on front and back.*
- *be taught the principles and skills of water safety and assess the nature, visibility and location of water hazards in a variety of conditions.*
- *be taught survival skills appropriate to their competence in water and be encouraged to evaluate their own abilities and limitations.*
- *be encouraged to assess their swimming and water skills efficiency against a range of criteria.*
- *explore the elements of movement in the water through simple games.*
- *be made aware of the role of swimming and water safety skills in supporting other water-based activities and activities near water.'*

Teaching Content Outline

Year: 3 **Unit:** 1

Title: Introduction to water activities and confidence building

Summer 1st half term

6 x 30 minute lessons

Outline: Introduction to water-based activities, concentrating on building confidence in the water. Introduction of basic safety and hygiene in and around the pool. Activities should include: safe entry to the water; getting the feet off the bottom and regaining the standing position while holding the rail; developing confidence to put the face in the water and submerge the body; breathing techniques; using buoyancy aids and floats, floating positions and gliding positions; simple propulsion techniques using the legs and arms.

Year: 3 **Unit:** 2

Title: Introduction to basic stroke technique

Summer 2nd half term

6 x 30 minute lessons

Outline: Introduction to swimming stroke actions using floats and buoyancy aids. Teaching of appropriate leg, arm and whole stroke actions as skill and confidence develop. Selected targets/awards for the children to work towards to provide realistic incentives and help build confidence.

Year: 4 **Unit:** 3

Title: Developing swimming stroke techniques

Autumn 1st half term

7 x 30 minute lessons

Outline: A direct extension of the previous unit, allowing practice and consolidation of swimming stroke techniques to develop confidence. Swimming on the back and front should be covered with children working in ability groups at their own appropriate level.

Year: 4 **Unit:** 4

Title: Introduction to survival and rescue skills

Summer 1st half term

6 x 30 minute lessons

Outline: Concentrating on teaching survival swimming techniques. Activities should include: safe entry to shallow and deep water; treading water; swimming under water and collecting objects from the pool bottom; rescue techniques using objects to throw and reach; removing clothing in the water; efficient techniques for distance swimming; understanding the nature of hazards in and around water; what to do and how to get help in an emergency situation.

Year: 4 **Unit:** 5

Title: Developing swimming stroke techniques (2)

Summer 2nd half term

6 x 30 minute lessons

Outline: Further stroke development and, where appropriate, the introduction of new swimming strokes. Children should work in ability groups and should be taught correct techniques for front crawl, breast stroke and backstroke where appropriate.

Year: 5 **Unit:** 6

Title: Advanced stroke technique and water entry

Autumn 1st half term

7 x 30 minute lessons

Outline: This is a continuation of the previous unit and should introduce competitive swimming and water entry techniques.

Year: 5 **Unit:** 7

Title: Health and fitness through water-based activities

Autumn 2nd half term

8 x 30 minute lessons

Outline: Introduction to the principles and practices of swimming training programmes and water-based activities and their effects on health and fitness. Children should experience swimnastics and swim-mobility activities, as well as practices for swimming over a variety of distances and speeds.

Year: 6 **Unit:** 8

Title: Water-based games and competitive swimming

Summer 1st half term

6 x 30 minute lessons

Outline: Concentration on team games and competitive activities in water. Activities should include: games to develop strength and stamina; problem-solving and survival and rescue games; water-polo type games. The children should work in teams with an appropriate use of a healthy competitive element.

Organisational strategies

Facilities, equipment and transport should be booked in advance and parents and children should be notified of the arrangements for the Swimming curriculum. A response slip should be used, requesting that the school be informed of any medical or health contra-indicators which are likely to affect participation. Supervision of changing arrangements and pupil movement about the facility will be the responsibility of the class teacher, in order to ensure good standards of safety, courtesy and hygiene. All pupils should be made aware of codes of behaviour and should know that they must never enter the water until told to do so by the person responsible for them during lessons.

The children should be assessed by the Swimming teacher(s) and grouped according to ability so that they can work at an appropriate level. Groupings will be re-assessed at intervals so that children continue to progress at their own rate.

Staff, facilities and equipment required

Lessons should be taught by appropriately qualified swimming teacher(s)/instructor(s) with occasional input from students and visiting teachers or specialists to the school. The equipment required for lessons will be available at the pool and used at the discretion of the qualified teachers.

Safety precautions

Ensure that appropriate dress is worn and that all jewellery is removed before each lesson. Check that pupils understand the reasons for these simple rules. Establish a code of conduct, safety requirements and emergency procedures at the beginning of each unit and remind pupils of them regularly throughout the scheme. Check and record any medical conditions that may affect the activity. Carry out an appropriate evaluation of skills competence and group pupils accordingly during the first lesson of each unit. Ensure that codes of behaviour and safety are clearly understood before the pupils begin the units.

Special needs

(It is likely that a wide range of ability levels will be apparent from the beginning of the first unit. Some children may have special needs that require particular help at the beginning of the course and it may be necessary to enlist a knowledgeable parent or advisory support to assist with special needs in the early stages. Nevertheless, the teaching content is designed to cater for all ranges of ability. Individual special needs should be assessed at the beginning of the first Unit of Work.)

Record-keeping and assessment procedures [see also Chapter 10]

Record-keeping with reference to teaching content should include:

- A Scheme of Work with recommendations for future planning and content
- A Forward Plan for each Unit of Work within the Scheme of Work, with a summary and recommendations for future teaching content in subsequent Units
- Lesson Plans based on the content outline in the Forward Plan, with an evaluation of each lesson and recommendations for the next lesson.

Assessment procedures should include:

- ongoing evaluation of each pupil's progress in relation to aims and objectives throughout the teaching unit, using a Unit of Work record and pupil assessment documents
- departmental records of individual pupil's progress in the form of Physical Education profiles that will be updated at the end of each Unit of Work each year, and each Key Stage (mainly formative and diagnostic)
- school summative records for individual pupils with reference to end-of-Key-Stage statements updated at the end of each year and at the end of each Key Stage.

End-of-Key-Stage statements

'By the end of the key stage, pupils should be able to:

- *respond safely, alone and with others, to challenging tasks taking account of levels of skill and understanding.*
- *swim unaided at least 25 metres and demonstrate an understanding of water safety.*
- *evaluate how well they and others perform and behave against criteria suggested by the teacher, and suggest ways of improving performance.*
- *sustain energetic activity over appropriate periods of time in a range of physical activities and understand the effects of exercise on the body.'*

Evaluation of scheme

(A record of class progress at the end of each Unit of Work should be made to assist with future planning (as described in Chapter 10) and a summary of the whole scheme should be recorded here.)

Recommendations for future planning

(A statement of any recommendations that become apparent during the teaching should be recorded in order to inform future planning and teaching for other cohorts of children.)

9.3 Pre-programme organisation

The aims of the Scheme of Work (page 148) may be achieved through successful communication and planning, which should be negotiated together with the teacher(s)/instructor(s) who will deliver the curriculum content. The following points should be considered in the pre-programme organisation.

Advanced communication with parents should give, in writing, the arrangements made for the school Swimming curriculum. Essential information about dates, times, venues and swimwear required, and advice about showering procedures should be provided. A response slip should be used asking that the school be informed of any medical or health contra-indicators which are likely to affect participation. It is also worth considering making a request for parental assistance with the Swimming programme in the same communication.

Schools should book facilities and instructors/teachers well in advance and facilities and pool depths should be checked. If transport is needed, it should be arranged carefully, with detailed attention to dates, times and stopping places. If a public pool is used it may be advantageous to timetable the Swimming sessions so that pupils can report direct to the facility at the start of the morning. Travel on foot should be adequately supervised by the number of adults required for the safe movement of schoolchildren on public roads. Close supervision of changing arrangements and pupil movement about the facility will assist in developing good standards of safety, courtesy and hygiene. All pupils should be made aware of codes of behaviour and should know that they must never enter the water until told to do so by the person responsible for them during lessons.

9.4 Swimming teaching content

At Key Stage 2 the teaching content of the Swimming curriculum can be divided into three main Skill Themes:

- confidence building
- watermanship and survival skills
- stroke technique and development.

Figure 9.1 presents a diagrammatic representation of the teaching content. The first aspect that should be covered is confidence building. Skills and activities should include:

- controlled entry into water of appropriate depth, walking or using other forms of travelling alongside the rail or rope
- floating with buoyancy aids if needed, and learning prone and supine support positions if the water is shallow
- learning to regain feet from prone, supine or random positions in the water with the aid of a standing partner
- playing games which involve races (walking, running, hopping); chasing; throwing and catching
- submerging (e.g. picking up objects, counting fingers, handstands); team and single games.

Once the above skills and activities have been mastered and confidence is established, a progressive introduction of points of watermanship and stroke technique is then desirable. The skills and activities that should be covered within the area of watermanship are:

- water skills related to breathing, submerging, swimming short distances under water, resurfacing, turning, rolling and spinning
- survival skills, such as treading water
- safe feet-first entry into water; exit from water by steps and climbing the pool side.

The skills and activities that should be covered within the area of stroke technique and development should include:

- the principles and basic skills of floating, gliding and propulsion through the water
- recreational and competitive stroke development through whole and part stroke practices, timed swims, distance swims and stroke medley swims
- experience of competition against personal targets and other pupils.

Reference to the above guidelines can be made when schools negotiate and develop the Swimming curriculum for their children.

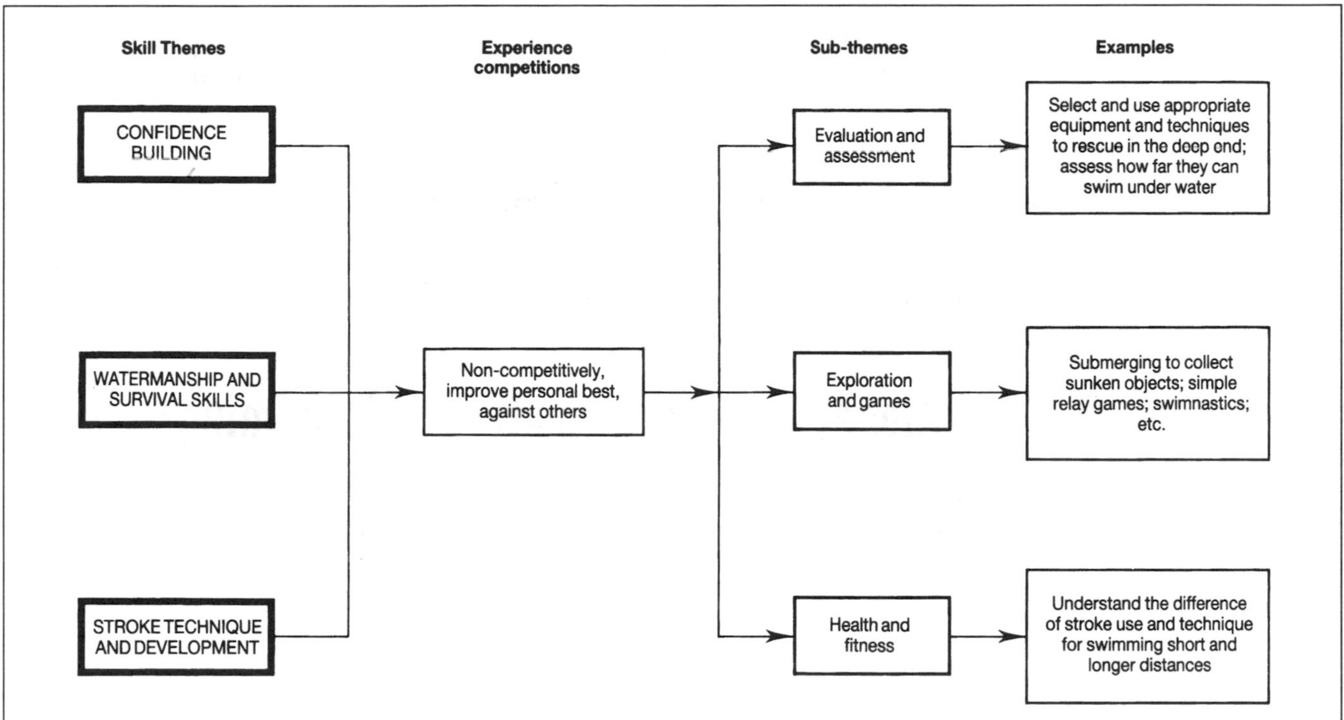

Figure 9.1 Swimming Skill Themes

9.5 Structure of lessons

A structure for a lesson of 30 minutes in the water is suggested below.

INTRODUCTORY ACTIVITY

This section should consist of vigorous, lively activity appropriate to their level of ability and age of the pupils. It should also create atmosphere and achieve warm-up. No new skill learning or teaching points should be necessary, only short explanations of essential organisational points. (With beginners this section should be positive but cautious, as successful initial entry to the water is so important.)

SKILL DEVELOPMENT

The main section should normally use about half the total water time. The children should be split into groups according to their ability, in the categories of 'beginners' and 'improvers'. Towards the end of Key Stage 2 a third group of 'proficient swimmers' may be organised to cater for a greater range in ability and the desired level of improvement in the pupils. The activities planned for these ability groups within the main section of the lesson will necessarily be different. The section for beginners should contain a large variety of exercises of short duration and should follow the multistroke approach. At improver and proficient level the whole–part–whole method of stroke teaching is effective, following a pattern where the whole stroke is attempted first, then it is broken down into sections (e.g. the leg kick, arm action), and practised as separate components, before finally the parts are put together and practised as a whole stroke again.

CONTRASTING ACTIVITY

This part of the lesson should provide a contrasting activity to the main part of the lesson in order to add variety and interest (e.g. playing with a ball with a partner).

CLOSING ACTIVITY

This should be short and can take the form of supervised free practice of any activity that has been taught during the main part of the lesson.

9.6 End-of-Key-Stage statements

The Swimming Scheme of Work will contribute towards the end-of-Key-Stage statements as set out on page 151.

9.7 National governing body for Swimming

The Amateur Swimming Association, Harold Fern House, Derby Square, Loughborough, Leicestershire, LE11 0AL. Telephone 0509 230431.

Record-keeping and assessment

10.1 Introduction

Without doubt, next to safety, assessment in Physical Education is the one area that causes anxiety among primary teachers. This chapter provides information and guidance about record-keeping and assessment in Physical Education. A model for assessment and the associated record-keeping is presented for schools and teachers to consider when planning their own practices and methods.

The following extracts from the Proposals of the Secretary of State, Physical Education 5–16 provide an insight into assessment.

> *'Assessment in Physical Education is concerned primarily with the observation and recording of achievement in the practical context. It should be a continuous activity, blended in as part of normal teaching. It can be used for several purposes:*
>
> - *to recognise pupil achievement and inform future teaching/learning strategies (formative assessment)*
> - *to identify learning difficulties to enable appropriate, specific strategies to be implemented (diagnostic assessment)*
> - *to document achievement to date for each child at given intervals (summative assessment)*
> - *to facilitate evaluation of aspects of the school's curriculum delivery.'*
>
> (DES 1991, page 41, paragraph 10.4)

The document goes on to indicate that in Physical Education:

> *'The statutory framework for the National Curriculum will entail assessment of each child's achievements at the end of each Key Stage in relation to the end-of-Key-Stage statements. Assessment at Key Stages 1–3 will fall to the teacher alone, that is to say there will be no nationally produced test materials.'*
>
> (DES 1991, page 41, paragraph 10.5)

Within these guidelines, it is down to individual schools and teachers to design their own documentation and practices for record-keeping and assessment.

10.2 Record-keeping

It is both necessary and good practice to ensure that a record is kept of curriculum planning and teaching content in Physical Education. Not only does it ensure that the requirements of the National Curriculum are met, but it also allows evaluation to take place, facilitates formative and diagnostic assessment and consequently informs future planning and teaching. It is strongly recommended that schools and teachers adopt the following record-keeping procedures:

- whole curriculum planning
- Schemes of Work with recommendations for future planning and content
- Forward Plans for each Unit of Work within the scheme, with a summary and recommendations for future teaching content in subsequent units
- records of lessons taught with reference to the content outline in the Forward Plan, including an evaluation of each lesson and recommendations for the next lesson.

One model designed to meet these recommendations is presented in Chapter 2, but schools may wish to adapt this model to suit their own whole curriculum planning needs. For example, if time constraints make it impossible to teach three 40-minute lessons of Physical Education per week, a model based on two lessons may be adopted. The six areas of activity will then need to be allocated accordingly. This is not ideal, since the time available to deliver the curriculum is greatly reduced, but it may be the only option available. A blank document for this purpose is contained in the Appendix (pages 169–183).

If the recording documents described above are used with reference to curriculum planning and delivery, assessment will become a continuous process as a natural extension of planning, recording and teaching. Without this, or a similar system, effective evaluation of the school's curriculum delivery, and accurate assessment of children's ability and progress, will be virtually impossible.

10.3 Assessment

There are two distinct aspects of effective assessment. The first requires teachers to make informed judgements about a child's level of achievement. The second involves designing and using a method of recording these judgements that is manageable and time efficient.

The Proposals of the Secretary of State, Physical Education 5–16 (DES 1991), state that the practical implication of assessment for teachers at Key Stages 1 and 2 is that *'the main means of gaining evidence of achievement is by direct observation'* (page 41, paragraph 10.8). The end-of-Key-Stage statements indicate, in general terms, what the children should have achieved by the end of the Key Stage. They do not, however, provide teachers with a specific indication of what they should observe as 'evidence of achievement'. In order for the statement to be useful, teachers must understand what this evidence is.

Achievement of skill and ability is evident if teachers can observe children:

PLANNING AND COMPOSING

- clear actions leading to successful outcome
- appropriate solutions to the task
- safe performance
- imaginative performance.

PARTICIPATING AND PERFORMING

- with accuracy, efficiency, consistency, adaptability
- able to do more than one thing at a time
- with good line/design
- with effective expression.

APPRECIATING AND EVALUATING

- selecting key features
- making appropriate comparisons with other and/or previous performances
- expressing pleasure in the performance
- using and devising both functional and aesthetic criteria in making judgements.

If the above characteristics can be observed, there is evidence of a satisfactory level of achievement. It is down to individual teachers to decide whether or not they have observed this evidence when assessing individual children based on their own knowledge and understanding. This knowledge and understanding will develop with practice and experience.

Assessment will be easier if a manageable and effective method of recording evidence and teacher's judgements of pupils' achievements in relation to the end-of-Key-Stage statements is developed. Schools and teachers are recommended to adopt the following procedures:

- ongoing observation and recording of class progress in relation to the aims and pupil targets of each of the Units of Work
- assessment and recording of individual pupil's progress with reference to end-of-Key-Stage statements, updated at the end of each Unit of Work (mainly formative and diagnostic)
- school summative records for individual pupils with reference to end-of-Key-Stage statements at the end of each year and at the end of each Key Stage.

Two documents that can be used in conjunction to record the above have been designed and are shown on the following pages. The first is a Sample Unit of Work Record of Pupil Progress document (pages 159–162). The example is based on Unit 10 in the Gymnastic Activities Scheme of Work in Chapter 5. The document allows information about the class and the aims of the unit to be recorded. Taking into account the unit aims and the teaching content, the teacher can select a number of pupil target outcomes which the children will work towards during the unit. Examples are shown in the document. Individual pupil's progress in relation to these targets and to the appropriate end-of-Key-Stage statements can then be recorded in the space provided on an ongoing basis throughout the unit. Teachers may devise their own key for comments or use those suggested in the example. Space is also provided to allow specific observations of individual pupil's progress to be made. (This can be done in pencil during the unit and final comments can then be entered in pen at the end of the unit.)

Once a Unit of Work has been completed, teachers will be able to transfer information about individual pupil progress to the record of achievement document shown on page 163. The document is based on the assumption that if sufficient observable characteristics (listed above) have been recorded across all the areas of activity, the child has achieved the corresponding end-of-Key-Stage statements. This should satisfy the statutory requirements and provide sufficient information for school summative records of individual pupil's achievement in the National Curriculum.

It is hoped that schools and teachers will be able to adapt the suggested models and documents or develop their own models for planning, record-keeping and assessment to meet the individual needs of their school and pupils within the requirements of the National Curriculum.

The following four pages (159–162) show a sample Unit of Work Record of Pupil Progress document. This example is based on Unit 10 in the Gymnastics Activities Scheme of Work in Chapter 5. A blank document for schools and teachers to use is included in the Appendix on pages 180–183.

Unit of Work Record of Pupil Progress

Area of Activity: Gymnastic Activities

Unit: 10 | **Title:** Consolidation of rolling

Spring 1st half term | 7 x 40 minute lessons | **Day:** Tuesday pm

Class: 5ER **Age:** 9/10 | **No. in class:** 14m, 18f | **Teacher:** E Robertson

Previous knowledge and experience

The children have been taught travelling, jumping and landing, balance and introduced to transference of weight. They have good locomotion and jumping and landing skills, with simple balance skills. The previous Unit of Work covered forward and backward rolls. Mats and large apparatus have been used previously, though organisation and handling skills need to be reinforced. They have used the group system, with the group/apparatus layout and work card. Well behaved class with good understanding of safety and discipline. Sub-themes of direction, levels, pathways, space have been grasped. Little group co-operation and poor quality of movement.

Aims of the Unit of Work

- to consolidate previously learned skills and understanding of Gymnastics
- to develop skills of weight transference, e.g. forward and backward rolls
- to improve the quality of skills/movement performance
- to introduce sequence building and develop this using apparatus
- to increase awareness of others in the group and safe co-operation on apparatus

Unit 10 Consolidation of Rolling

Key to comments for pupil targets and EKSS		
✓ = Present	**A** = Achieved	**CA** = Consistently achieved
O = Absent	**HD** = Has difficulty with	**NA** = Needs attention
WT = Working towards	**CT** = Contributed towards	

Name	Attendance register									Targets achieved				
									Total	1	2	3	4	5

Pupil target outcome

1. Demonstrate the ability to perform previously learned skills.
2. Develop skill in the side roll, salmon roll, forward roll and backward roll.
3. Perform the skills with good quality of movement performance.
4. Combine the skills together to form sequences on floor and using apparatus.
5. Show awareness of, and consideration for others in group and co-operate safely on the floor and while using apparatus.

Other comments	End of KS statements				
	1	2	3	4	5

Programme of Study requirements

Gymnastic Activities Programme of Study requirements

'Pupils should:

- *be enabled, both on the floor and using apparatus to find more ways of rolling, jumping, swinging, balancing and taking weight on hands, and to adapt, practise and refine these actions.*
- *be guided to perform in a controlled manner, and to understand that the ending of one action can become the beginning of the next.*
- *be given opportunities, both on the floor and using apparatus in response to set tasks, to explore, select, develop, practise and refine a longer series of actions, making increasingly complex movement sequences which they are able to repeat.*
- *be enabled to respond to a variety of tasks alone or with a partner, emphasising changing shape, speed and direction through gymnastic actions.'*

End-of-Key-Stage statements

'By the end of the key stage pupils should be able to:

- *plan, practise, improve and remember more complex sequences of movement.*
- *respond safely, alone and with others, to challenging tasks, taking account of levels of skill and understanding.*
- *evaluate how well they and others perform and behave against criteria suggested by the teacher, and suggest ways of improving performance.*
- *sustain energetic activity over appropriate periods of time in a range of physical activities and understand the effects of exercise on the body.'*

Physical Education Key Stage 2 Record of Achievement

Pupil's name ______________________ d.o.b. ________

Address ______________________ Year of entry to school ______

______________________ Year of exit from school ______

____

____

Observable characteristics	Areas of Activity in Physical Education						End of Key Stage statements
	Athletic Activities	Dance	Games	Gymnastic Activities	Outdoor and Adventurous Activities	Swimming	
clear action leading to successful outcome							plan, practise, improve, and remember more complex sequences of movements
appropriate solution to the task							
safe performance							perform effectively in activities requiring quick decision making
imaginative performance							
accuracy							respond safely, alone and with others, to challenging tasks, taking account of levels of skill and understanding
efficiency							
consistency							
adaptability							swim unaided at least 25 metres and demonstrate an understanding of water safety
ability to do more than one thing at a time							
good line/design							sustain energetic activity over appropriate periods of time in a range of physical activities and understand the effects on the body
effective expression							
selecting key features							evaluate how well they and others perform and behave against criteria suggested by the teacher, and suggest ways of improving performance
make appropriate comparisons							
expressing pleasure							
using and devising criteria							

Other issues in Physical Education

11.1 Introduction

This chapter is not intended to provide a comprehensive discussion of important issues in Physical Education, but attempts to give some guidance and advice to schools and teachers where this might be useful.

11.2 Cross-curricular matters

In this section, we deal with cross-curricular skills, cross-curricular themes and cross-curricular links. The cross-curricular dimensions of equal opportunities and special educational needs are dealt with in separate sections later.

The National Curriculum Council *Curriculum Guidance Series* Numbers 2 and 3 (NCC 1989), provide valid and clear guidance relating to cross-curricular matters and the whole curriculum, and the reader is referred to these publications for general information.

Cross-curricular skills

The identified cross-curricular skills of communication, numeracy, study, problem-solving, personal and social development and information technology are the shared responsibility of all teachers. The development of these skills should form an integral part of all subjects and the role of Physical Education in this should not be underestimated (as is sometimes the case). Planning an integrated range of teaching and learning styles will allow for cross-curricular skills to be developed and enhanced within the Physical Education curriculum. The appropriate use of language, careful presentation of tasks requiring problem-solving skills, integrated partner work, small group work and team work and the imaginative selection and use of resources will lead to the development of many of the cross-curricular skills.

Cross-curricular themes

Many opportunities exist within Physical Education to develop the defined cross-curricular themes. Probably the most obvious is the theme of Health Education, but Environmental Education and Education for Citizenship can be developed very naturally through a number of the areas of activity, and planning should occur with this in mind.

Cross-curricular links

A number of Local Education Authorities advocate a cross-curricular 'thematic' or 'topic' approach to planning the National Curriculum and many schools have adopted such an approach. Planning and teaching is centred around a chosen theme or topic, and links are made across subjects so that curriculum content is seen to be relevant by pupils. In many instances Physical Education is not seen as part of this integrated cross-curricular planning; consequently, appropriate and relevant links are not made, which in fact would have been highly advantageous in enhancing relevance and continuity. In other instances, Physical Education is integrated into this planning to a point where dubious and tenuous links are made which have little or no relevance to what should be taught in a balanced Physical Education curriculum. The most suitable approach to adopt is one where the teaching content of the Physical Education curriculum allows natural and unforced links to be made with teaching content in other subjects. An example of this could be using samples of creative writing from English as a stimulus in Dance. However, caution is advocated when making links, so that the curriculum content that should be taught in Physical Education is not abandoned for the sake of making the link.

Teachers are referred to the specific section in *Non-Statutory Guidance* (NCC 1992) relating to cross-curricular matters, as this may provide some additional advice.

11.3 Equal opportunities

The dimension of equal opportunities in Physical Education requires special consideration, but it has not been thought appropriate within the scope of this chapter to discuss in detail all the issues involved. It will, however, very briefly highlight aspects relevant to Physical Education which should be considered within a whole school policy on equal opportunities.

The Secretary of State's Proposals for Physical Education 5–16 (DES 1991) stated that:

> *'The NCC has identified equal opportunities as a cross-curricular dimension which should permeate all subjects. For Physical Education this means that all children should be allowed access to and given confidence in the different activities involved, regardless of their ability, sex, or cultural/ethnic background.'*
>
> (DES 1991, paragraph 6.2, page 15)

> *'Working towards equality of opportunity . . . requires an understanding and appreciation of the range of pupils' responses to femininity, masculinity and sexuality . . . range of ability and disability, to ethnic, social and cultural diversity and the ways in which these relate to Physical Education. This will require . . . a critical review of prevailing practice, rigorous and continuous appraisal and often willingness to question long held beliefs and prejudices.'*
>
> (DES 1991, paragraph 6.6, page 15)

The above extracts highlight issues which need to be addressed by schools to ensure that equal opportunity is provided in Physical Education. Teachers need to take account of the way in which the areas of activity are delivered to pupils. Are all pupils, regardless of their ability, gender, ethnic, cultural and socio-economic background, given the same opportunities in all areas of activity? Are mixed gender or single sex groups used in certain areas of activity, and if so, what is the justification for this? Are extra-curricular activities accessible to all pupils within the school? These are just some of the questions that schools should raise when considering the equal opportunities dimension.

The final extract below provides guiding principles towards the presentation of equal opportunities within the Physical Education curriculum. It is for individual schools to develop their own practices that meet these principles.

> *'The implications for teachers . . . sharing responsibility for equal opportunities are that decisions on the content, grouping and style of learning experiences must be based on:*
>
> - *awareness of the issues and the commitment to confront prevailing attitudes and to change practices where they conflict with the principles of equality of opportunity*
> - *the willingness to see physical activities as educational vehicles, rather than as ends in themselves*

- *clarification and understanding of the role and legal status of curricular Physical Education, extra-curricular activity and representative school sport*
- *a knowledge of the effect of different kinds of groupings on the learning experience of girls and boys from all ethnic groups, with varied educational needs.'*

(DES 1991, paragraph 52, pages 59–60)

All LEAs have a clear policy on equal opportunities and it may be useful for schools to make reference to this, to assist them with developing their own policy and practice in Physical Education.

11.4 Special educational needs provision

The NCC *Curriculum Guidance Series* Number 2 (NCC 1989) provides valid and clear guidance relating to teaching pupils with special educational needs in the whole curriculum. However, this document is now out of print and is gradually being superseded by subject–specific guidance. Because of the nature of Physical Education, the dimension of special educational needs requires special consideration, and it is hoped that *Teaching Physical Education to Pupils with Special Educational Needs* will be one of the titles within the Curriculum Guidance Series in the near future.

In mainstream schools it is necessary to draw a distinction between children with special educational needs, as defined by the 1981 Education Act, and children who have special educational needs in Physical Education. The latter group will include both children who have movement learning difficulties (for whatever reason), and children who are physically gifted. Children in these categories are unlikely to have formal statements of special educational needs in Physical Education, but they need to be recognised and catered for in the Physical Education curriculum.

The Secretary of State's Proposals for Physical Education 5–16 (DES 1991) make particular reference to the teaching of the Programmes of Study to children with special educational needs, and the reader is referred to that document for detailed advice and information.

In the above document (pages 56–60), the Working Party for Physical Education recommends a number of principles which are worthwhile including in a summarised form here.

- All children, including children with special educational needs, are entitled to the Physical Education programme of the National Curriculum. The nature of their impairments . . . may indicate that activities need modifying to make them accessible. However, that does not lessen the entitlement in any way.
- Planning for the delivery of the Programmes of Study . . . should be so stated that specific interpretation or modification of teaching content is required for as few children as possible.
- Clearly, some children will have greater difficulties than others, but it is important that this does not lead to their complete exclusion from an activity. Inclusion may be arranged in a variety of ways: by modifying an activity; by substituting one activity for another, or by letting all children experience the modified version of an activity.
- Mainstream schools need to take account of what is required to give pupils with special educational needs access to a broad and balanced curriculum.

- Children with disabilities should participate in National Curriculum Physical Education alongside their able-bodied peers, without alteration of the activity, wherever the nature of the activity proposed makes this a possibility. Where this is not possible, the alternative of modifying either rules or equipment, or both, should be explored to facilitate integrated participation.
- Only where complete integration with or without modification is not possible should the option of segregation or substitution be considered, and it is essential that the activity which results should have educational integrity.

Schools should give due consideration to these principles when planning their Physical Education programme. Teachers may identify individual in-service training possibilities to help them to deliver the curriculum more successfully to children with special educational needs. Developing links with local clubs and sports organisations may also assist in providing for children with disabilities or with particular gifts in Physical Education. These can provide specialist advice and assistance for teachers, and extra-curricular opportunities for individuals or groups of children.

The issue of assessment of children with special educational needs in Physical Education may be one which causes particular anxiety to teachers at Key Stage 2. In the Secretary of State's Proposals, the Working Party made the following suggestions for assessment, which are also useful to keep in mind when preparing teaching material.

> *'In some cases either or both the process of assessment and the context within which each key stage statement will be assessed may require modification and adaptation to ensure that all pupils can achieve it. No pupil need be excluded. Adaptations may include:*
>
> - *modification of movement and action responses. For example: jumping with support; swimming with aids; response to stimuli with minimal voluntary control*
> - *more stable conditions in terms of both the range of equipment used and the context of the task set*
> - *moving only part of the body as opposed to total body involvement*
> - *alternative contexts for assessment in relation to children with sensory impairment.'*

(DES 1991, paragraph 10.30, page 43)

Prior to the hoped-for publication of the Curriculum Guidance Series *Teaching Physical Education to Pupils with Special Educational Needs*, teachers are referred to the specific section in *Non-Statutory Guidance* (NCC 1992) relating to special educational needs provision.

11.5 Extra-curricular activities

Extra-curricular physical activities include any aspect of recreation, sport, dance or physical activity that is organised by the school (sometimes in partnership with other groups or organisations) but takes place outside school curriculum time. These activities can form an important part of a child's social and emotional development and schools are encouraged to provide extra-curricular opportunities where at all possible. Schools are also strongly recommended to adopt a whole school policy towards these activities and to develop clear guidelines for participation which are in keeping with the general ethos and philosophy of the school.

11.6 Useful organisations

Sports Council, 16 Upper Woburn Place, London, WC1H 0QP. Telephone 071 388 1277. (The Sports Council's Information Section is very helpful and will provide contacts, addresses and telephone numbers for a number of local, national and international organisations for a very nominal charge to cover costs. They will also provide excellent information and references on areas of the curriculum, sports and activities, or topics suggested by individuals or schools.)

British Sports Association for the Disabled, Solecast House, 13–27 Brunswick Place, London, N1 6DX.

National Coaching Foundation, 114 Cardigan Road, Leeds, LS6 3BJ.

National Council for School Sports, 4 Barston Lane, Solihull, West Midlands, B91 2SS.

Commission for Racial Equality, Elliot House, 10-12 Allington Street, London SW1E 5EH.

Equal Opportunities Commission, Overseas House, Quay Street, Manchester M3 3HN.

British Association of Advisers and Lecturers in Physical Education (BAALPE), Nelson House, 3/6 The Beacon, Exmouth, Devon, EX8 2AG.

British Council for Physical Education (BCPE), Liverpool Institute of H.E., P.O. Box 6, Woolton Road, Liverpool, L16 8ND.

Physical Education Association of Great Britain and Northern Ireland (PEA), Ling House, 5 Western Court, Bromley Street, Digbeth, Birmingham, B9 4AN.

Appendix

School Profile

BACKGROUND

FACILITIES

RESOURCES

CURRICULUM POLICY

SCHOOL ETHOS AND PHILOSOPHY

PHYSICAL EDUCATION POLICY

SUBJECT ALLOCATION

Whole Curriculum Planning

Year (age)	**Term**		**Lesson 1**	**Lesson 2**	**Lesson 3**
Y3	Autumn	1st half			
(7/8)		2nd half			
	Spring	1st half			
		2nd half			
	Summer	1st half			
		2nd half			
Y4	Autumn	1st half			
(8/9)		2nd half			
	Spring	1st half			
		2nd half			
	Summer	1st half			
		2nd half			
Y5	Autumn	1st half			
(9/10)		2nd half			
	Spring	1st half			
		2nd half			
	Summer	1st half			
		2nd half			
Y6	Autumn	1st half			
(10/11)		2nd half			
	Spring	1st half			
		2nd half			
	Summer	1st half			
		2nd half			

Note: the Autumn term is divided into half terms of seven and eight weeks, the Spring term into half terms of seven and six weeks, and the Summer term into two half terms of six weeks.

Scheme of Work

Key Stage: | **Area of activity:** | **Cohort:**

Units of Work (length of unit x length of lessons)

	Autumn	Spring	Summer
Year:			
Year:			
Year:			
Year:			

Process aims

The Scheme of Work will work towards enabling the pupils to carry out the following

PLANNING AND COMPOSING

PARTICIPATING AND PERFORMING

APPRECIATING AND EVALUATING

Programme of Study requirements

Teaching Content Outline

Year: **Unit:**

half term

Title:

x minute lessons

Outline:

Year: **Unit:**

half term

Title:

x minute lessons

Outline:

Year: **Unit:**

half term

Title:

x minute lessons

Outline:

Year: **Unit:**

half term

Title:

x minute lessons

Outline:

Organisational strategies

Staff, facilities and equipment required

Safety precautions

Special needs

Record-keeping and assessment procedures

Record-keeping with reference to teaching content will include:

Assessment procedures will include:

End-of-Key-Stage statements

Evaluation of scheme

Recommendations for future planning

Unit of Work Forward Plan

Area of Activity:		
Unit:	**Title:**	
half term	x minute lessons	**Day:**
Class: **Age:**	**No. in class:**	**Teacher:**

Previous knowledge and experience

Aims of the Unit of Work

CONTENT OUTLINE

LESSON

LESSON

LESSON

LESSON

LESSON

Organisational strategies

Facilities and equipment required

Safety precautions

Special needs provision

Equipment and group positions

Evaluation of lessons

LESSON 1

LESSON 2

LESSON 3

LESSON 4

LESSON 5

LESSON 6

LESSON 7

LESSON 8

Summary and recommendations for next unit

Lesson Plan

Key Stage:	Unit of Work:

Lesson number in unit:	Date:
Time:	Length of lesson:
Class: Age:	Teacher:
No. in class:	Venue:

Lesson objectives

Facilities and equipment

Lesson evaluation

Lesson Plan

Phase	Tasks/activities	Teaching points/Coaching feedback	Organisation of pupils and equipment

Programme of Study requirements

Programme of Study requirements

End-of-Key-stage statements

Unit of Work Record of Pupil Progress

Area of Activity:

Unit: Title:

half term x minute lessons Day:

Class: Age: No. in class: Teacher:

Previous knowledge and experience

Aims of the Unit of Work

Key to comments for pupil targets and EKSS		
✓ = Present	**A** = Achieved	**CA** = Consistently achieved
0 = Absent	**HD** = Has difficulty with	**NA** = Needs attention
WT = Working towards	**CT** = Contributed towards	

Name	**Attendance register**									**Targets achieved**				
									Total	1	2	3	4	5

Pupil target outcome

1. Demonstrate the ability to perform previously learned skills.
2. Develop skill in the side roll, salmon roll, forward roll and backward roll.
3. Perform the skills with good quality of movement performance.
4. Combine the skills together to form sequences on floor and using apparatus.
5. Show awareness of, and consideration for others in group and co-operate safely on the floor and while using apparatus.

Other comments	End of KS statements				
	1	2	3	4	5

Bibliography

Armstrong, N. (editor) (1992) *New Directions in Physical Education Volume 2. Towards a National Curriculum.* The Falmer Press, London.

Armstrong, N. and Sparkes, A. (1991) *Issues in Physical Education.* Cassell, London.

ASA (1989) *The Teaching of Swimming.* Amateur Swimming Association, in liaison with ASA Swimming Enterprises, Leicester.

BAALPE (1990) *Safe Practice in Physical Education.* BAALPE, Exmouth.

Burton, C. and Kent, G. (1993) *Bright Ideas – Inspirations for Physical Education.* Scholastic Publications, Leamington Spa.

Cooper, A. (1982) *The Development of Games Skills – a Scheme of Work for Teachers.* Basil Blackwell, Oxford.

Cregeen, A. and Noble, J. (1988) *Swimming Games and Activities.* A & C Black, London.

Cross, R. (editor) (1991) *Swimming, Teaching and Coaching Level 1.* Amateur Swimming Association, Loughborough.

DES (1989) *National Curriculum from Policy to Practice.* NCC, York.

DES (1989) *Safety in Outdoor Education.* HMSO, London.

DES (1990) *National Curriculum Physical Education Working Group Interim Report.* DES, London.

DES (1991) *Physical Education for Ages 5 to 16 – Proposals of the Secretary of State for Education and Science and the Secretary of State for Wales.* HMSO, London.

DES (1992) *Physical Education in the National Curriculum.* HMSO, London.

Dyson, M. and Shapland, J. (1992) *The Competent Swimmer: A step-by-step Teaching Manual.* A & C Black, London.

Evans, D. A. (1984) *Teaching Athletics 8–13, Guidelines for the Non-specialist.* Hodder & Stoughton, London.

Jackman, J. and Currier, B. (1992) *Gymnastics Skills and Games.* A & C Black, London.

Low, T. (1990) *Gymnastics – Floor, Vault, Beam and Bars.* The Crowded Press, Marlborough.

Mace, R. and Benn, B. (1982) *Gymnastic Skills – the Theory and Practice of Teaching and Coaching.* Batsford, London.

Manners, H.K. and Carroll, M.E. (1991) *Movement Education Leading to Gymnastics 7–11: A Session-by-Session Approach to Key Stage 2.* The Falmer Press, London.

Martland, J. and Walsh, S. (1993) *Developing Navigational Skills.* The National Coaching Foundation, Leeds.

McNeill, C. Martland, J. and Palmer, P. (1992) *Orienteering in the National Curriculum.* Harveys, Doune, Scotland.

NCC (1989) *Curriculum Guidance 2 – A Curriculum for All. Special Educational Needs in the National Curriculum.* NCC, York.

NCC (1992) *Physical Education Consultation Report.* NCC, York.

NCC (1992) *Physical Education Non-Statutory Guidance.* NCC, York.

NCC (1992) *Starting Out with the National Curriculum.* NCC, York.

Read, B. and Edwards, P. (compiled by) (1992) *Teaching Children to Play Games.* BCPE, The National Coaching Foundation and the Sports Council, Leeds.

Russell, J. (1986) *Creative Dance in the Primary School.* MacDonald & Evans, London.

Sabin, V. (1990) *Primary School Gymnastics – a Teaching Manual.* Education Department, Northampton County Council, Northampton.

Scottish Office Education Department (1992) *Curriculum and Assessment in Scotland – National Guidelines: Expressive Arts 5–14.* HMSO Scotland, Edinburgh.

Shreeves, R. (1991) *Children Dancing.* Ward Lock Educational, East Grinstead.

Sleap, M. (1981) *Mini Sport.* Heinemann Educational Books, London.

Sykes, R. (1986) *Games for Physical Education – A Teacher's Guide.* A & C Black, London.

Thomas, D.G. (1989) *Swimming: Steps to Success.* Human Kinetics Publishers, Leeds.

Williams, A. (editor) (1989) *Issues in Physical Education for the Primary Years.* The Falmer Press, London.

Williams, J. (1987) *Themes for Educational Gymnastics.* A & C Black, London.

Woodland, E.J.M. (1974) *Poems for Movements.* HarperCollins, London.